TOUCHED BY THE SAVIOR

Compelling Stories of Lives Changed by the Master's Hand

MIKE YORKEY

WORD PUBLISHING

NASHVILLE

A Thomas Nelson Company

Unless otherwise indicated, Scripture quotations used in this book are from the *Holy Bible, New International Version* (NIV). Copyright © 1973, 1978, 1984, International Bible Society. Used by permission of Zondervan Bible Publishers.

Other Scripture references are from the following sources:

The *Revised Standard Version* of the Bible (RSV). Copyright © 1946, 1952, 1971, 1973 by the Division of Christian Education of the National Council of the Churches of Christ in the USA. Used by permission.

The Living Bible (TLB), copyright © 1971 by Tyndale House Publishers, Wheaton, Ill. Used by permission.

Library of Congress Cataloging-in-Publication Data

Yorkey, Mike
    Touched by the Savior : compelling stories of lives changed by the Master's hand / by Mike Yorkey.
        p.   cm.
    ISBN 0-8499-1607-0
    1. Converts Biography. 2. Christian biography. I. Title
    BV4930.Y67 1999
    248.2'4'0922—dc21
    [B]   99-24194
                                                                        CIP

Printed in the United States of America.

9 0 1 2 3 4 QPV 9 8 7 6 5 4 3 2 1

DEDICATION

To my one and only brother Pry
(1955–88)

I haven't forgotten.

TABLE OF CONTENTS

\\\|///

Contents

ACKNOWLEDGMENTS

This book would not be possible without several key persons. I would like to thank my literary agent, Greg Johnson, for outlining to me the vision of *Touched by the Savior*. The idea for this book is his. Barbara Stephens did a magnificent job editing the manuscript, and I appreciate the thoughtful critiques from Bobbie McCasland and Bobbi Lucas. Janice Coy was instrumental in helping me with Kimberly Davis's story.

Finally, my heartfelt thanks to the wonderful people who participated in this book. May your stories inspire many others.

INTRODUCTION

Long before Leonardo DiCaprio held Kate Winslet's outstretched arms on the R.M.S. *Titanic*'s bow, I was a *Titanic* buff. I wasn't a rivet-counter, mind you, but as a young boy, I loved thumbing through picture books with color illustrations of the massive ship "that even God couldn't sink." Particularly compelling were the grainy black-and-white photos of her passengers—the men, women, and children who represented virtually every social and economic class, from first class to steerage.

The *Titanic*'s sinking also represented an incredible study of how humans react when faced with certain demise. Think about this: How many of us will ever know that our lives will be snuffed out in two hours? Virtually none. These days, sudden death strikes like a thunderbolt: car crashes and airplane disasters happen in just seconds. At the other end of the spectrum, people usually do not succumb quickly to disease; modern medicine can extend life for months or years.

So imagine, if you will, what it must have been like standing on the upper deck of the *Titanic* after the last lifeboat had been lowered to the water. Soon, very soon, you will die a horrible death. Knowing that you are standing on the precipice of eternity, would you have fallen to your knees and worshipped the Lord of the universe, or would you have looked to the heavens and cursed God out of anger and bitterness?

John Harper, a *Titanic* passenger traveling to Chicago to become the pastor of Moody Memorial Church, stayed with the ship until the very end. When she raised up and slid into the deep, icy waters, Harper jumped free. While thrashing about in the frigid water, Harper won his last convert just before drowning—a young Scotsman who was one of the few to survive the actual sinking.

The Scotsman said Harper clung to a floating spar and called out, "Are ye saved, mon?" and quoted Acts 16:31 ("Believe in the Lord Jesus, and you will be saved") before the frozen seas claimed him.

You didn't see that scene in James Cameron's billion-dollar-grossing *Titanic* movie, did you? Nor did you view another scene outside the White Star Line office in Liverpool in the days following the sinking. According to a newspaper account, a great crowd of the passengers' relatives gathered outside the Liverpool office. Two large boards were placed on each side of the entrance. Above each was printed in large letters: KNOWN TO BE SAVED and KNOWN TO BE LOST.

A newspaper account described it thusly: "Every now and then, a man would appear from the office bearing a large piece of cardboard on which was written the name of one of the passengers. As he held up the name, a deathly stillness swept over the crowd; it watched to see to which of the boards he would pin the name."

Was the *Titanic* passenger physically saved or lost? Asked from a spiritual perspective, had that person accepted the free gift of salvation through believing in Jesus Christ? Where was he or she spending eternity? In Scripture the "Roman Road" teaches us everyone has sinned (see Rom. 3:23), the penalty for our sin is death (see Rom. 6:23), Jesus Christ died for our sins (see Rom. 5:8), and to be forgiven for our sins, we must believe and confess that Jesus is Lord because salvation only comes through Jesus Christ (see Rom. 10:8–10).

This book is about people who traveled the Roman Road at some point in their lives. But I also want *Touched by the Savior* to serve as an encouragement to those who wonder if their loved ones and close relatives will *ever* come to know the Lord. I know that happened to me when my younger brother, Pry, experienced a grand mal seizure at age twenty-nine and learned a couple of years later that a cancerous brain tumor would soon take his life. My wife, Nicole, and I led Pry to Christ on his deathbed—at the eleventh hour—and it was one of the greatest experiences the Lord has given me. (You can read Pry's story in the epilogue to this book.)

God does know what He's doing. His timing is always perfect. Some family members, however, will refuse to accept the outstretched hand of Jesus Christ, and while it breaks our hearts, we must accept the sovereignty of God's control over all things. All He asks is for us to do our part: share the Good News. Like the parable of the Sower, some seed will take root, prosper, and grow. Other seed will not penetrate the "hard ground" of a person's heart. When that happens, we must remind ourselves that the heart's door is opened only from the inside.

In the following pages, you'll find first- and third-person accounts of how people's lives dramatically changed when they accepted Jesus Christ as Lord and Savior. It is my hope that *Touched by the Savior* will encourage you with the reminder that God can touch anyone at any time.

1

Kim Eastman:
HE TURNED TO ME
AND HEARD MY CRY

AGE:
forty-three
OCCUPATION:
homemaker
RESIDENCE:
Del Mar, California
FAMILY SITUATION:
married twenty-one years to Earl; mother of
Robby, seventeen; Lindsey, fifteen; and Natalie, eleven

The day before my high school graduation in Hollywood, Florida, my mother and stepfather walked into my bedroom. When I looked up, Mom and Dad had angry expressions on their faces, and I immediately sensed something was up.

"You tell her, Bill," said Mom.

"Okay," he sighed, as he searched for the right words. During the silence, I racked my brain to figure out what I had done wrong. All I knew was that Mom seemed to be incredibly angry with me—all the time. All through elementary school and my adolescent years, I never felt consistent love and acceptance from my mother. It had something to do with Mom's past; when I was a kindergartner, Mom told me that my father was not my real father and that she had been married before.

My young mind didn't comprehend what all this meant, but what I did understand was the torrent of verbal and physical abuse that often came my way. It usually began after dinner after Mom sipped her fifth cocktail of the evening; the alcohol produced incredible Jekyll-and-Hyde personality changes in her.

I learned to make myself scarce during those occasions by staying in my bedroom and doing my homework. But Mom would walk in and ask me an innocuous question, such as, "Did you drink the open Coke in the refrigerator?"

"No, Mom, why would I do that?"

"You @#$%^& spoiled brat!" she'd scream and curse, signaling the start of another tirade. "Yes, you did drink the Coke. That Coke belonged to your brother. I hope you end up in the gutter! That's where you deserve to be. That's what you're worth."

I was so hurt, and when that happened, I would wake up the next morning, hoping she would apologize to me.

"What's wrong with you?" she'd ask at the breakfast table. "Why do you have that look on your face?"

"Do you remember what you told me last night, that you wished I would end up in the gutter?"

"I never said any such thing to you. What are you talking about?"

It was useless to speak to her, but that wasn't the worst of it. At different times, she would send my father to my room. "Now, Bill, you hit her," she would instruct. "You hit her good. She deserves it."

My stepfather would pull the leather belt out of his pants and start hitting me, striking me over and over. I tried to block the blows with my arms, but he was too strong and powerful for me.

I can remember falling to my knees after they left, crying out to a God whom I didn't know. *Please help me! Are you there, God? I need help!*

My view of Christianity was fairly warped, but that's because I saw Christ through the lens of my parents. When I was in elementary school, we started attending a small denominational church, but Jesus was taught in a storybook way, so He never seemed real to me. Having a personal relationship with Christ and what that meant were never mentioned.

My parents hosted Saturday night parties, inviting their church friends. There was a lot of pinching of rear ends and too much drinking. After that, I figured Christianity was a hoax and a sham.

Another time, when I was in high school, Mom received a phone tip: her husband had stolen away to the Jo-Lin Motel with his file clerk. Mom had already gotten a head start on drinking that afternoon, and the news caused her to become unhinged and suicidal.

"I'm going to kill myself, just you wait," she slurred to me.

"Mom, you can't do that."

"Ya wanna bet? Well, I'm going to," she said, as she fumbled for her car keys.

"Well, if you are going to kill yourself, I'm going with you," I said.

We piled into our green Chevy Impala, and she started racing down Park Road. I slid over and sat close to her, thinking I might have to grab the wheel of the car. She was carrying on about what a lousy husband she had, and then she snuffed out her lighted cigarette on my leg. (I still have the scar today.)

I didn't feel angry. Actually, I was feeling responsible for keeping her alive. No matter what my mother did to me, I still loved her. She was my mom.

We drove into the parking lot of the Jo-Lin Motel, and sure enough, Dad was holed up in a room with the file clerk. Mom confronted him, and he begged for forgiveness. They nearly got divorced over that incident, but she eventually allowed him to return home.

Not long after that incident, my parents came into my room on the day before my high school graduation.

I looked up from my bed, wondering what I was going to be blamed for.

"You were never wanted," my stepfather announced, "and your mom has sacrificed everything for you. I can tell you this: if abortion had been legal, you would have been aborted."

Aborted? My mother wanted to kill me?

"Instead, she decided to keep and raise you, working very hard all these years, and that's something I don't think you've appreciated very much."

Before I could recover from my deep shock, Mom spoke up. "Kim, I'm through with you. If you want a college education, you're on your own. As far as I'm concerned, you are free to leave this house at any time. The sooner the better."

I heard the door close, and suddenly, the pieces of the puzzle came together for me. I laid on my bed, sobbing, *Oh, God, please help me!* I wished I were dead.

The phone rang. Silvia Rizikow, my best friend, was on the line.

"What's wrong, Kimmy?" she asked in her lilting accent. Silvia was a high school friend who came from an Argentinean Jewish family living in South Florida. I couldn't talk to her because I was sobbing so much. I hung up.

She called me back.

"Mom just told me I had to leave. I can't talk right now," I blurted out.

"Let me go talk to Mom. I'll call you right back," she said.

Silvia ran to her mother, told her the situation, and then dialed me back.

"My mom says you don't have to take this anymore, and we're coming to pick you up. You're going to live with us now."

Fifteen minutes later, Mrs. Rizikow pulled up in her station wagon, and Silvia rang the doorbell. I answered the door, with my mother not far behind me. She wanted to see what all the commotion was about.

"I'm leaving," I stated.

"Fine. You take what you came into this world with."

I wasn't about to leave the house stark naked, but with that statement ringing in my ears, I walked out with the clothes on my back, although I did manage to sneak into the house a few days later and grab some other clothes and personal belongings.

The Rizikows took me in like a stray puppy. Mr. Rizikow told me in his thick accent, "I love you, Kimmy, like one of my daughters, and where I come from in Argentina, we don't have the custom of sending our daughters away from home at age eighteen to college. No, our daughters stay home until they find a nice guy, and I want you to stay here until you find a nice fellow and get married."

The Rizikows never charged me room and board. "You can live here free of charge, as long as you pay for your personal expenses and college tuition," said Mr. Rizikow.

I started working in the toy department at Sears to earn some money, and that summer between high school and college a good friend, Betty Jo Ducanis, invited me to a week-long Christian camp at Florida Bible Church.

"But I don't have any money," I said.

"Kim, I know that, but they want to give you a scholarship," replied Betty Jo.

I was out of excuses. I had always thought Christianity was for weak people, a crutch to lean on. I was not a weak person. I couldn't be, or I would never survive.

Betty Jo, however, wasn't a weak person, either. She was captain of the cheerleading squad, a smart brunette with wholesome beauty. She drove a Mercedes and came from a nice family. I recalled the time when she invited me over to her birthday party, a Saturday morning breakfast at her house. Before we left, she asked her friends to listen.

"What would you do if you had the cure for cancer?" she asked. "Wouldn't you want to share that discovery with someone else?"

"Of course we would," said one girl.

"Then that's why I want to share what's on my heart today," said Betty Jo, and she proceeded to explain why she was a Christian with such intensity that she broke down and cried.

So when Betty Jo asked me to join her at the Christian camp, I knew she was for real. I said yes.

For a week, I was immersed in Scripture and God's people. They had a big push for everyone to accept Christ, and I was thinking about it. I got into a big circle with some other guys and gals on the final day to discuss what we had learned that week. Several guys said they were no longer going to smoke pot or drink because they had invited Jesus into their lives.

That was the common theme as we went around the circle, and I could feel the tension mounting as my turn neared. But I felt a hardness of heart. *I'm not on drugs, I'm not on alcohol, and I don't need a crutch,* I thought. *I've always pulled myself up by my own bootstraps, and I can help myself.*

So I passed, although looking back, I can state that seeds were planted at a crucial, pivotal time in my life.

I went to work at an upscale clothing store and enrolled in the University of Miami, where I pursued a business degree. My life was an around-the-clock attempt to cram in as much school, work, and study as I could.

During my junior year, I met another business major named Earl Eastman. He asked me to take a particular business class with him, so I changed my whole schedule because I thought he was cute.

On the first date, he invited me to the beach, and on the second date, he invited me to church. He was a stagnant Christian at the time, but he wanted to make our relationship right, and making it right meant going to church.

Earl escorted me to Key Biscayne Presbyterian Church, where

Steve Brown was in the pulpit. When he preached, Pastor Brown assumed that everyone in the congregation was a skeptic and an unbeliever, and every time I went to church, I felt he was speaking just to me. "Christianity is not a religion but a relationship with an infinite, personal God through Jesus Christ," he said, and I started nodding my head for the first time.

Since this was the midseventies Pastor Brown talked a lot about Josh McDowell's new book called *Evidence That Demands a Verdict*, which pointed out that the truth of the gospel rested upon the truth and power of the Resurrection. "If a dead man didn't get up and walk out of a grave, then we are to be pitied, but He did," said Pastor Brown. "God loved us enough that He interceded in time, space, and history in the person of Jesus Christ to show us what His love was like. As Blaise Pascal once wrote, 'Inside of every man, there is a God-shaped vacuum, and no one can fill that up but Christ Himself.'"

That made a lot of sense to me. Pastor Brown never issued an altar call, but he would say, "If you're sitting here today and you have come to a point where you want to accept Christ and ask Him to be Lord of your life, just pray with me right where you are sitting." One day, after being in his church for nearly a year, I prayed along with him.

I didn't tell Earl what I had done because I was still stubborn and mistrusting, and I didn't want to be seen as being vulnerable. Eventually, I did inform him because I came to see that Earl and his family were ready to love me unconditionally—a poor girl estranged from her family—just as Jesus accepted me right where I was.

After we were married, I was imbued with a great desire to know more about Christ, so we joined a Sunday school class, attended the Sunday and Wednesday night services, and participated in a couples' Bible study on Thursday nights. We started to become friends with other Christians, something I had never done before. I began to see that Christians were "normal" people, too. I had always thought that when I became a Christian that I couldn't look my best or wear makeup and jewelry, but then I met some female friends at church who dressed nicely and wore make-up and jewelry. As I became more mature in my faith, I saw that what was more important was the condition of their hearts.

My relationship with Christ has also allowed me to forgive my mother and my stepfather, realizing that since He forgave me my sins, He has called me to forgive others, including my parents. Christ has continued to bring healing to those relationships. Although I have never known the love of my natural father, I have known the love of my heavenly Father, and that is good enough for me.

Several years after I became a Christian, I discovered Psalm 40, and when I read verses 1–3 for the first time, I felt David wrote it just for me:

> I waited patiently for the Lord;
> he turned to me and heard my cry.
> He lifted me out of the slimy pit,
> out of the mud and mire;
> he set my feet on a rock
> and gave me a firm place to stand.
> He put a new song in my mouth,
> a hymn of praise to our God.
> Many will see and fear
> and put their trust in the Lord.

2

John Trent:
MEETING THE FATHER

AGE:
forty-five
OCCUPATION:
president of Encouraging Words, a
ministry committed to strengthening marriage and
family relationships; and author
RESIDENCE:
Phoenix, Arizona
FAMILY SITUATION:
married to Cindy for twenty-one years;
father of Kari, thirteen; and Laura, eight

I never had a picture of my father in my mind while growing up—literally. My father left my mother and us three boys when I was only two months old. He never made an attempt to see me, call me, or drop a card in the mail. Mom didn't keep out any of his photos, so I had no idea what he looked like.

Then one day while I was in elementary school, I happened to be rifling through mom's drawers, determined to find a board game. I shuffled through some papers and noticed a yellowed newspaper clipping. It showed a young soldier, dressed in combat fatigues, being pinned with a medal by one of the army's top brass.

"Mom, who's this?" I asked, as I handed over the clipping.

"It's your dad," she said with an air of resignation.

I studied the photo, trying to learn everything I could about the young soldier in the halftone five-by-seven. Mom, sensing my need for details, filled in some of the gaps.

"The photo was taken during the war following the Battle of Guadalcanal against the Japanese," she began. "He risked his life to save a wounded comrade. Under enemy fire, he picked up the soldier and carried him to safety."

My dad, a war hero, I thought.

His decision never to contact me left a huge hole in my life, so I turned to sports as an outlet for approval. I played traditional sports in high school—football and baseball—and would have gone out for basketball if I wasn't such a good wrestler. Perhaps I had inherited some of my father's fighting spirit. I was small, but what I lacked in size I made up with desire. In those days, coaches called athletes like me "scrappy" because we fought for every yard, every takedown, every pitch.

Then the phone call came that I had secretly been hoping for. A Phoenix newspaper had published a story on the gridiron prowess of my brother and me. "Jeff and John Trent: Twin Starters for the Mighty Titans" was the catchy headline.

My father read the paper that day, saw the picture, and, for the first time, picked up the phone to call us. He talked to Mom about coming to see our big game on Friday night against Westwood High, a crosstown rival led by Danny White, who would later become a Dallas Cowboys quarterback. It turned out that Dad lived not far from the stadium, and he said he would meet us after the game.

We were so excited! As a linebacker responsible for slowing down Danny White's passing game, I played with my heart on my sleeve because I knew my father was watching my every move from the stands. He had played college football before the war, so he knew all the sacrifices that went into being a football player. He would understand.

The contest seesawed for four quarters, but, late in the game, Danny White connected for two touchdown passes to clinch the victory. Neither Jeff nor I was crushed by the loss, however, because we knew we'd played our hearts out. Besides, in some way we felt we had already won. Something more special than a title was going to happen after the final gun—we would meet our father for the first time.

Mom, my older brother Joe, Jeff, and I walked over to the meeting place. We took off our helmets and waited for him to walk into our lives. I wondered what I would say, how I would greet him. I wondered if I should shake his hand or wrap my arms around his neck. I wondered how I should act.

The crowd thinned out, and the team bus left without us as we continued to wait. We stood our spot, hoping against hope. But when the stadium lights were shut off, we knew.

Our father was not going to show.

On the way home, I could have ripped the car door off its hinges, I was so angry. Not much was said on the drive home, as no one wanted to give voice to the deep hurt we were experiencing. What was I going to say at school? All my buddies had seen us standing there with our helmets on our hips, waiting to see our father for the first time.

As we traveled Phoenix's long boulevards home, I cursed the name of my father. I cursed God for passing it on to me. "Son of a Trent" came out as an expletive. I invented rotten names and pinned them on my father. I felt he was a gutless jerk who wasn't even man enough to come meet the children he brought into this world.

At the age of seventeen, a junior in high school, I was an angry young man. I had been wronged, and my only weapon was to stay angry. That was the only choice I felt I could make to deal with the pain of feeling neglected.

A MAN WITH A SMILE

His name was Doug Barram, and he was the Young Life leader at our school. He was fresh out of college, where he had played offensive tackle. At six-foot-four inches tall and 225 pounds, he looked like he could still suit up for any Division I college team.

Doug happened to be the warmest, gentlest, most loving man who ever took an interest in me. Whenever we would meet, he'd wrap one of his arms around me and give me a bright smile that told me he cared about me. "How ya doin'?" he'd ask, and then he would listen closely to my response.

I knew Doug cared for me because he had been hanging around our football practices since my freshman year. *No one* ever went to a freshman football practice, but Doug did. *No one* ever cared about fatherless boys, but Doug did. *No one* took an interest in others without expecting something else in return, but Doug did.

Doug stood on the sidelines of every game, yelling encouragement, telling us to "fire up" and play hard. After losing a real heartbreaker one evening, I jogged off the field with tears running down my face, too ashamed to take off my helmet. That's when I felt Doug's arms wrap around me, and when I looked up, I noticed the tears streaming down his face, too. Doug cared enough to hurt when I hurt.

Doug cared about a lot of people. He made friends with everyone at high school, from the quarterback and cheerleaders to the nerds and outcasts (we called them "geeks" in those days). His "How ya doin'?" rang through the halls, and he listened to everyone in the same friendly, interested way.

He invited anyone to drop by his house to hang out, and I took him up on that. Every Wednesday night, a bunch of the guys and I would choose sides and play "bull moose" football—a leadfooted, ponderous version in which all of us had to move in slow motion. We laughed until our sides hurt.

Then we'd repair to Doug's house, where he'd read through the

Bible with us. Doug had given me my first Bible—a J. B. Phillips version that was easy to read. I loved underlining verses that Doug pointed out. But he didn't tell us what to *think* about God's Word; instead, he preferred to ask us what we thought. And when the time was appropriate, he would make a salient point or gently underscore what we were learning from God's Word.

One evening, Doug invited me and a bunch of the guys over for dinner. He had been married for a few years, and, for the first time ever, I studied a man who kissed his wife upon coming home, told his wife that he loved her, and was polite around the dinner table. I watched a man who bounced an infant boy on one knee and let another son climb all over him. I watched him read bedtime stories, answer their questions, and lovingly fulfill the eighth request for something to drink.

At Doug's home, the custom before eating was for everyone to hold hands and pray a sentence or two of thanks. When Doug began, I knew in a few short seconds that it would be my turn to pray for the first time out loud in front of a group. To make matters worse, I was sitting with my peers. Somehow, I managed to croak out a few "thank-yous" and "bless everyones." Doug took it in stride and made me feel accepted even though I wasn't that sophisticated with prayer talk.

I loved hanging around Doug and his family. I even volunteered to mow his lawn every week. I would have done anything for him—including weeding his garden—just to watch him hug his kids and tell his wife how much he enjoyed her. Looking in from the outside of his home was a better view than the inside of my home.

THE RIGHT MOVE

In my junior year, Doug invited me and a bunch of guys on the football team to see a film at a local theater. If he had told us that it was a religious film, we never would have gone, but we didn't ask. I thought the movie was a boring waste of time, and when the house lights came on, I motioned to a buddy to get up and go.

Unfortunately, a speaker was on the edge of the stage asking us to stay, and my heart sank. I knew I wouldn't be getting out of there anytime soon. The man presented the gospel message, then gave us an opportunity to come forward and place our faith in Christ.

This is how I described the next few moments in my book *Choosing to Live the Blessing* (Waterbrook Press, 1998):

> I thought as I sat there, *I still have my senior year ahead of me. The parties. The good times. The cruisin' and boozin'. Nope. Wouldn't be me breaking ranks.* I wedged myself a little more snugly into my velvet-cushioned seat. And from that seat, I looked down the row at my brother Jeff. Then at my friends. Finally at Doug.
>
> Then suddenly, unexpectedly, something moved me. I stood up. Jeff stood up. One of our friends stood up, too. Filing out of our row and into the aisle, the three of us went forward. Doug trailed behind us, and when we reached the front of the theater, he talked with us and prayed with us, as one by one we gave our lives to Christ.
>
> Something moved me that night at the theater. What was it? What was it that touched my heart and turned my life around? It wasn't the film. It wasn't the appeal of the man in the front of the theater. What then?
>
> I think it was the cumulative effect of all the pictures Doug Barram had been leaving in my life. Pictures that said you matter, you have a place in my heart and at my table, what you think is important, why you hurt is important, who you are is important, to me, to my family, and to God.
>
> In an instant, the Holy Spirit brought those pictures together to form a composite. When I leaned forward and looked at Doug, the picture I saw was Jesus. It was Jesus I had heard in Doug's voice. Jesus I had seen in his smile. Jesus I had felt in his hugs, in his home, in his heart. All along it was Jesus he was showing me.
>
> I just never recognized him in a six-foot-four-inch frame.

3

Mickey Mantle:
TWO OUTS IN THE BOTTOM
OF THE NINTH

AGE:
lived from 1931–95
OCCUPATION:
New York Yankees center fielder, 1951–69
RESIDENCE:
Dallas, Texas
FAMILY SITUATION:
survived by his wife, Merlyn, three adult sons,
and three grandchildren

Editor's note: If you were a boy growing up in the fifties and sixties, either Mickey Mantle or Willie Mays was your idol. You couldn't fence-sit with these larger-than-life center fielders for the Yankees and Giants. You had to choose your allegiance.

I was a Willie Mays fan, as was my Little League coach, who ordered new uniforms one year that were numbered 20–32, not the standard 1–13. I got first dibs on magic number 24, and I never felt so proud as the day I stepped inside the lines with two-four on my back.

Mickey Mantle? He played for the hated New York Yankees, an arrogant bunch who found themselves in the World Series every year. That's what I thought of "the Mick" until I heard the following story:

Bobby Richardson knocked lightly on the hospital door, and then he was ushered inside. The wan-looking patient inside the private room in Dallas's Baylor University Medical Center was Mickey Mantle. Cancer cells were overwhelming his lungs, heart cavity, and other vital organs; the last-ditch chemotherapy treatment wasn't working. In the summer of 1995, sixty-three-year-old Mickey Mantle lay on death's door.

Bobby Richardson had been Mickey's teammate throughout the glory years of the Yankee dynasty, an era that began in the early fifties and lasted until 1964. Bobby, a sure-handed second baseman, had accepted Christ as a teenager, but Mickey hadn't.

Bobby surveyed the hospital room and noticed several gospel tracts on the nightstand. He also spied an audiocassette of "Pistol Pete" Maravich, the testimony of a basketball legend who experienced a miraculous conversion.

As Bobby walked to Mickey's bedside, he knew something was different about his longtime friend. Before he could open his mouth, however, Mickey stopped him. "Bobby, I want to tell you something. I have trusted Christ as my Savior."

Bobby suddenly felt a tremendous weight fall from his shoulders. For more than three decades, Bobby had been sharing the Good News of Jesus Christ with Mickey by witnessing to him, inviting him to church, and giving him books and Bibles. Bobby didn't know when Mickey had made that decision, but it had to have been in the last week or so. *What about those gospel tracts on the nightstand?* thought Bobby. *Did a hospital orderly slip them on Mickey's food tray?*

"That's great, Mickey," Bobby grinned, as he looked into the eyes of his longtime friend. "I love you, and I'm glad you will spend eternity with me in heaven."

Bobby knew that Mickey was standing deep in the batter's box against cancer and that Mickey was down to his last strike. Yet whatever pitch would be delivered in his final hours, Mickey would handle it because he was going to heaven.

The story of Mickey Mantle begins in tiny Commerce, Oklahoma, where Mickey's father, Mutt Mantle, labored as a lead and zinc miner. Following each eight-hour shift, Mutt returned home hacking from the dust and dampness that filled his lungs. Mutt descended into the dark mine shafts six days a week to keep food on the table during the Depression years of the thirties.

If Mutt couldn't escape the mines, he wanted to make sure that his son would. When Mickey was five years old, Mutt started tossing baseballs to the young boy, teaching him to switch-hit—that is, bat from his right and left sides. In high school, young Mantle excelled on the baseball diamond, where he caught the practiced eye of a Yankee scout. At the age of seventeen, Mickey was signed by the storied ball club and ballyhooed as the next Joe DiMaggio.

Mickey tore up minor league pitching and was promoted to the parent club for the 1951 season—the same year that another rookie, Willie Mays, was called up by the crosstown New York Giants. Mickey's manager, Casey Stengel, predicted nothing but greatness for his nineteen-year-old prospect. "Mickey should lead the league in everything," observed Ol' Casey during Mickey's rookie season. "He has a combination of speed and power that makes him a Triple Crown threat every year."

Mickey arrived in New York a country rube, a golden-haired teenager with lumberjack forearms and lightning speed. Baseball, in those early days of television, really was the national pastime—and looking for new heroes. Joe DiMaggio, the Yankee Clipper, was in his final season, and everyone knew the torch was being passed to the fresh-faced kid from Oklahoma's Indian territory.

With a fawning press in the country's media capital, Mickey Mantle quickly became a household name. He shared an apartment above the Stage Delicatessen with teammates Hank Bauer and Johnny Hopp. Downstairs, he feasted on generous helpings of corned beef, cheesecake, and matzo ball soup—and gained twenty-five pounds. But Mickey was also introduced by other teammates to a new kind of diet: alcohol. Mickey became a switch-hitting drinker who could pour it down with either hand.

After a successful rookie season, Mickey's father, Mutt, died of Hodgkin's disease at age forty. This continued a tragic end for males in the Mantle clan: Mickey's grandfather and two uncles had succumbed to the same disease before they turned forty. Assuming he was doomed to an early grave, Mickey adopted the fatalistic lifestyle of "eat, drink, and be merry, for tomorrow we die." He and teammate Billy Martin ribbed each other on whose liver would go first. But Mickey's alcoholism was no joke, and it would later cause great pain in the Mantle family.

Meanwhile, Casey Stengel was proven right: Mickey did bat his way to a rare Triple Crown in 1956, when he led the American League in batting average (.353), home runs (52), and runs-batted-in (130). The Triple Crown secured Mickey's place as an American icon, the possessor of a prodigious home-run stroke that smashed balls into second decks.

Although he was an MVP on the baseball diamond, Mickey was MIA on the home front. He had married Merlyn in 1952 and sired four sons: Mickey Jr., David, Billy, and Danny. Mickey was a wayward husband who was more interested in drinking with his buddies than being a good father and husband. He even left on a hunting trip with Billy Martin when Merlyn was about to give birth to Billy.

Mickey's drinking problems worsened after he left the game in 1969. He played celebrity golf tournaments in a tipsy state, and he could be surly and mean with an adoring public. When it became apparent that there was life after baseball and he wasn't going to die young, forty-six-year-old Mickey quipped, "If I knew I was going to live this long, I would have taken better care of myself."

But the dreaded Hodgkin's disease skipped a generation, and Billy Mantle was diagnosed with it in 1977 when he was only twenty years old. Then, in 1982, Merlyn discovered that her husband had been unfaithful in a series of affairs, which led to a seven-year separation.

Meanwhile, Mickey's life spiraled out of control. His days were spent attending big-bucks memorabilia shows where Mickey autographed anything thrust in front of him for twenty-five or fifty dollars each. Although simply signing his name was lucrative, Mickey usually retreated afterward to his hotel room—to binge on alcohol. When he became a partner in a Manhattan restaurant bearing his name, radio DJ Don Imus made sport of Mantle's drinking habits: "Drop by Mantle's restaurant about two any morning," quipped Imus, "and try to guess which table Mantle's under."

In 1994, Mickey reached the bottom. His hands shaking from tremors, his mind debilitated by years of drinking, Mickey sought out CBS sportscaster Pat Summerall, who had won his own battle with alcoholism. They met in Dallas, where they talked about Mickey's drinking problem. Summerall suggested that Mickey check himself into alcohol rehab at the Betty Ford Center in Palm Desert, California.

Mickey took that important first step. He called Summerall from Palm Desert and said, "If I ever take another drink, I want you to promise me that you'll kill me."

Mickey came out of the Betty Ford Clinic a changed man. He went public with his disease, even appearing on the cover of *Sports Illustrated* with the headline: "Don't Do As I Did."

Then Billy, who had been battling Hodgkin's disease for years, became addicted to the painkillers given to him as part of an experimental drug treatment. He went into drug rehab but then died when his heart gave out. "If I'd gone to Betty Ford sooner, Billy still might be here," said his guilt-wracked father.

Good to his word, Mickey never took another drink, but he still sensed there was something missing in his life. He just wasn't sure what it was. Forty years of drinking, however, had damaged his liver, and, in June 1995, doctors discovered that cancer had destroyed it. He was fortunate to receive an immediate liver transplant, and it looked like Mickey would see his grandchildren grow up.

After receiving his new liver, Mickey called Bobby Richardson and asked him to pray for him, which Bobby gladly did over the phone. Then Bobby's wife, Betsy, told Mickey, "I know how much you appreciate the organ donation and the opportunity to live longer, but I want you to think of this as God's gift to you, Mickey, because this is just a reprieve. God loves you, and He wants to spend eternity with you."

After a few days, however, Mickey was stricken with severe abdominal pain. Doctors at Baylor University Medical Center discovered that cancer had aggressively spread to his vital organs, and death was imminent. The Mantle family asked Bobby and Betsy to fly out from their South Carolina home to visit Mickey in the Dallas hospital. It was understood between Mickey and Bobby—from a request made eleven years earlier at the funeral of teammate Roger Maris—that Bobby would speak at Mickey's memorial service.

Many, many people wished to see Mickey before he died, but only seven people were on the approved list: Merlyn, their three surviving sons (and their families), the family attorney, and the Richardsons.

After Mickey told Bobby that he had trusted Jesus Christ as his Savior, Bobby asked him some questions—just to be sure. Bobby walked through the Four Spiritual Laws with Mickey.

"Did you acknowledge that Jesus Christ is the Son of God and that He came on this earth to die for our sins?"

"Yes, I did," replied Mickey.

"Did you acknowledge that you are a sinner?"

"Yes, I did."

"Did you ask for forgiveness of your sins?"

"Yes."

"And did you ask Jesus Christ into your heart so that you can spend eternity with Him?"

"Yes, I did, Bobby."

Faced with the crushing weight of his sins against a holy God and its dire consequence—eternal separation from God—Mickey had asked for and received the forgiveness he so desperately needed.

Before he became a Christian, Mickey liked to tell a funny story about his death and arrival at the Pearly Gates, where St. Peter somberly looked in his big book, and then shook his head no. Crestfallen, Mickey turned to leave.

"Oh, before you go," St. Peter said, "God wants to know if you'll sign these six dozen balls."

When Mickey Mantle arrived into the glory of God on August 13, 1995, there were no baseballs waiting for his autograph. Instead, the King of Kings greeted him with open arms to thunderous applause, like none Mickey had ever heard in Yankee Stadium.

4

Dr. James Dobson:
TOUCHED AT A
VERY YOUNG AGE

AGE:
sixty-three
OCCUPATION:
president and founder of
Focus on the Family and leader of
the profamily movement
RESIDENCE:
Colorado Springs, Colorado
FAMILY SITUATION:
married nearly forty years to Shirley;
father of two adult children: Danae and Ryan,
who is married to Cezanne

Editor's note: I was editor of Dr. Dobson's Focus on the
Family *magazine for more than eleven years, and while my contact with this remarkable man was limited, I saw enough to
understand that I was working with someone who sought the
Lord's guidance every day.*

W hen Christian historians one hundred years from now look back to the last quarter of the twentieth century, they will recognize Dr. James Dobson as the founder of Focus on the Family, a ministry that has touched and changed literally millions of families around the world.

A typical Dr. Dobson story comes from a fellow who was enjoying a fast-food meal with his family in North Carolina. Suddenly, someone who looked like James Dobson walked in and ordered a meal. The man wondered if he was really the famous radio host in the flesh. Out of the corner of his eye, he spied the visitor carrying his plastic tray to a small table in the back. Without looking right or left, the visitor bowed his head and thanked the Lord for the food and sustenance he was about to receive.

That's when the man knew the diner was James Dobson.

Another story concerns Andy and Becky Hammer, a childless couple in their early thirties. After hearing a "Focus on the Family" radio broadcast about foreign adoption, they called the ministry for more information.

The Hammers were given phone numbers of agencies to call, and they started the adoption process. It took nearly a year for the paperwork before they were told they could adopt Abigail from Pune, India.

Abigail, just eighteen months old, was put on a plane in Bombay with two adoption agency representatives. The plane was scheduled to fly her from Bombay to Denver with stops in Frankfurt and Washington, D.C.

Andy and Becky went to the Denver airport on September 15, 1995, never so excited in their lives. When the plane landed at Gate 42, one of the first persons to come out of the Jetway was Dr. Dobson! He had boarded the plane in Washington, where someone had told him that Abigail was in the back of the plane. Dr. Dobson walked over to the expectant couple and said, "I've seen your baby. She's tired, but she's beautiful." Then he gave them each a warm hug.

Dr. Dobson asked if he could stand by and watch Abigail come off the plane and into their arms. "Sure," Becky said, and when that incredible moment occurred, they were all wiping tears from their eyes.

As writer Tim Stafford noted in *Christianity Today* magazine, "Dr. Dobson is an extremely likable person. He is genuinely interested in other people. He can converse for hours without mentioning himself or his great successes. He does not drop names. When Dr. Dobson credits God for his accomplishments, he appears to mean what he says."

The Lord has accomplished much through James Dobson, ever since the first radio broadcast launched the ministry on March 26, 1977. Today, God is using Focus on the Family to reach, inspire, equip, and aid families. The "Focus on the Family" broadcast, heard Monday through Friday, has a regular listenership of nearly eight million per week. Eleven magazines, ranging from *Focus on the Family* to special-interest publications for children, teens, doctors, senior adults, teachers, and single parents, reach more than three million homes each month.

So, how did this wonderful man become a Christian?

Born in 1936, young James Dobson was raised by James Dobson Sr. and Myrtle Dobson. His father was an evangelist in the Nazarene denomination.

Now, imagine you are James Dobson at three years of age. You have seen your father on his knees so much that you know that the soles of his black shoes have holes in them. You know that your parents love Jesus Christ; He's all they talk about with friends and neighbors.

One Sunday, you're sitting in the back of the church with your mother. Your father is standing in the pulpit. You hear your father's voice, the voice you love so much. Your father's asking you—yes, you!—if you want to come forward and be saved by Jesus Christ.

The answer is yes, and without any prompting, without asking permission, you step into the aisle of that tiny church and start walking forward to meet your Creator. You don't notice the gasps of surprise or pay attention to the whispers. All you know is that you want to go forward and say yes to Jesus.

And that's how it happened for James Dobson in 1939 at the tender age of three. "I recall crying and asking Jesus to forgive my sins," Dr. Dobson says in his biography, *Turning Hearts Toward Home* (Word Publishing, 1992). "I know that sounds strange, but that's the way it occurred. It is overwhelming for me to think about that event today. Imagine the King of the universe, Creator of all heaven and earth, caring about an insignificant kid barely out of toddlerhood! It makes no sense, but I know it happened."

Innocent. Trusting. Without hesitation. And it's been a love for a lifetime.

5

Steve Largent:
A Great Catch
by the Savior

Age:
forty-five
Occupation:
U.S. Congressman from Oklahoma's First District
Residence:
splits time between Washington, D.C., and Tulsa, Oklahoma
Family Situation:
married to Terry for twenty-four years;
father of Kyle, twenty; Casie, nineteen; Kelly, fifteen;
and Kramer, thirteen

Sweat was forming on Steve Largent's upper lip. *I didn't plan that one right,* he thought. Steve and his Young Life buddies had just heard a clear presentation of the gospel at a Southern Baptist revival event, the organist was playing a dirge-like rendition of "Just As I Am," and God was calling him out of his seat. What should he do?

Steve slumped in the pew. To his left and to his right, he was flanked by five or six friends. If he responded to the pastor's invitation, he'd have to make a scene and say "excuse me" a half-dozen times. That would definitely cause his cool quotient to evaporate.

Steve was sixteen years old, a high school sophomore. His father deserted the family when he was six, and his parents divorced not long after that event. His mother remarried when he was nine, but his step-father was a boozer who abused the family. On more than one occasion, he and his brothers had to separate physically their warring parents after his stepfather had one beer too many.

Being around home was a drag, but sports was fun, so Steve stayed outside catching footballs, shooting baskets, or hitting base-balls. "The way I dealt with my environment was to escape it," he remembers. "Sports was a great avenue to stay away from home."

So were the Monday night Young Life meetings. Steve's family didn't attend church often, and hanging out with the guys at Young Life was goofy fun. When everyone said they were piling in the car and going downtown to a revival meeting, Steve tagged along. At least it got him out of the house.

The pastor wore an electric blue suit, waved a big Bible in his left hand, and swung a long P.A. cord in the other. "I want you to imagine a huge wall that divides this room," he said, sweeping his left arm from side to side. "On one side of the wall is where God lives, and on the other side of the wall is where you live. That wall, or barrier, is what the Bible refers to as sin. Romans 3:23 says, 'For all have sinned and fall short of the glory of God.' In other words, we were all brought into this world separated from God. In Romans, we are told that the wages of sin is separation from God and eternal death, but God loved us so much that He provided a way, a way at great expense. The door that He provided in the wall was His Son, Jesus Christ. All of us who were born separated from God by this barrier can now come to Christ and know Him in a personal way."

Steve had never been hit between the eyes with the gospel message before, and he knew God was speaking to him.

The pastor wasn't finished, however. "Jesus says in Revelation 3:20,

'Here I am! I stand at the door and knock. If anyone hears my voice and opens the door, I will come in and eat with him, and he with me.'"

Steve knew that God was knocking on the door of his heart, saying, *Follow Me, Steve. Come and follow Me.*

After the pastor invited those in the audience to come forward and pray to receive Christ, the organist struck up "Just As I Am." While the audience sang the song one, two, three, four, five, six times, the pastor continued to issue the invitation for folks to come forward.

Perspiration formed on Steve's upper lip. *Should I go?* Steve figured if he kept asking that question long enough, they would finish singing and he wouldn't have to answer the question. When "Just As I Am" finished and reprised for the tenth time, Steve was out of excuses. *Okay. If they sing one more time, I'm going down,* he thought.

Steve didn't know it, but he was experiencing peer pressure and spiritual warfare. Sure enough, when "Just As I Am" reprised for the eleventh time, Steve kept his promise to the Lord.

Steve stood up, stepped on a few of his friends' feet, excused himself, and walked forward, where a counselor led him to Christ. As he was praying on his knees, he heard the audience sing "Just As I Am" two more times.

Rats, he thought. *I could have waited!*

THE BIG THREE

Steve's sophomore year turned out to be a big one. He made three of the most important decisions of his life that year:

1. He met Christ.
2. He met his future wife, Terry, in Latin class, when she caught him peeking at her homework. She also went to Young Life with Steve.
3. His mom convinced him not to quit the football team.

Steve was a good athlete, and, after high school, he played football at Tulsa University, where he was an outstanding pass receiver. At five-foot-eleven and 190 pounds, however, he wasn't given much chance of catching on with the National Football League. But Seattle Seahawk wide-receiver coach Jerry Rhome saw talent in Steve—unbelievable hands and surefooted quickness. While he may not have been able to sprint the forty-yard dash in 4.3 seconds, he was able to run quick and precise pass routes. Once the ball was in the air, his hands were like Hoover vacuum attachments.

He played fourteen seasons with the Seahawks—three times the league average—and enjoyed a stellar career. When he retired in 1989, he had caught more passes than any other NFL receiver, set numerous other career records, and had been featured on the Wheaties cereal box.

Even at the height of his pro football career, when Steve couldn't eat in a Seattle restaurant without being interrupted by autograph seekers, he was known as someone who put his faith and family first.

In a society that exalts pro athletes who live life in the fast lane, Steve ran a refreshingly different route. He stayed home and baked chocolate chip cookies with the kids on Thursday nights instead of hamming it up at trendy sports bars. He jealously guarded his Friday evening "date nights" with Terry instead of hitting Seattle's hot spots with teammates.

He was—and remains—active in Pro Athletes Outreach, according to Norm Evans, the ministry's president. "Steve has taken to heart his commitments," said Evans. "The most important thing in his life is his relationship with Christ. And he realizes that if you're going to keep the rest of your life in order, you have to be committed to your wife before your fans and committed to your children before Christian ministry."

That commitment to family was tested on November 11, 1985, when their youngest son, Kramer, was born with spina bifida. When they learned the news that evening, Steve and Terry wept. When a baby is born with an exposed spinal cord, he can have severe handicaps, both mental and physical. These days Kramer has overcome many of his disabilities, but his value to the family has nothing to do with his accomplishments or physical characteristics. "We love him unconditionally," says Steve.

Following retirement from the NFL, reporters asked Steve what he planned to do with the rest of his life. "I've got a lot of opportunities; I don't know what I'm going to do," he replied. "But I can guarantee you two things that I will never be: a coach or politician."

The family moved back to Tulsa, where Steve launched a successful promotional firm and represented Focus on the Family when he spoke before audiences. He had spoken at a fund-raising event for Oklahoma Senator Don Nickles, and early in 1994, Nickles called Steve and posed the following question: "Why don't you run for Congress?"

Wait a minute. Steve remembered that he had said he would never enter politics, so the quick answer was that he was not interested. Several weeks passed, and Senator Nickles called again, urging him to toss his helmet into the ring.

Steve and Terry got on their knees for a ten-day period of prayer and fasting, as they sought the Lord's guidance on whether he should run for Congress. They emerged from their prayer vigil with an assurance that the Lord wanted him to run for the U.S. Congress. "Actually, God changed my heart," said Steve. "I did a 180-degree turn."

MR. LARGENT GOES TO WASHINGTON

Steve was part of the Republican "freshman class" that swept into Washington, D.C., in early 1995. Being a U.S. Congressman has been an education—and an eyeopener. Steve, who was afraid that a voter would ask him how a bill gets passed in Congress, purchased a copy of *Robert's Rules of Order* and mastered it quickly.

He and Terry decided not to move the family to Washington. Tulsa was their home, and the kids were enrolled in a great Christian school. Steve moved into a Capitol Hill townhome with two other

Christian Congressmen, Zach Wamp of Tennessee and fellow Oklahoman Tom Coburn. He flies home every Friday night to spend the weekend with his family.

During the week, however, Steve realized that without Terry and the family, he was vulnerable to sexual temptation and other vices, so he started a men's accountability group in his townhome with Wamp, Coburn, and several other Congressmen who had left family behind in their home districts. Every Tuesday night, the men eat takeout food, pray for each other, and then get personal. They have each other's permission to ask probing questions, such as

- "How is it *really* going with your wife?"
- "How are you spending your free time?"
- "Are you reading your Bible regularly?"
- "Are you working too much?"
- "How are you handling sexual temptation?"

When a wife asks those questions, a husband often thinks she's nagging. But when a male friend asks the same questions in Christian love, it shows he genuinely cares for you.

"Men have very few friends whom they feel they can reveal everything to," says Steve. "A lot of men don't have anybody—not even their wives—whom they feel comfortable to talk with. By having an accountability group in Washington, we can build a spiritual firewall between us and the dominant culture of Capitol Hill, which is lonely, workaholic, and full of temptations."

Steve's leadership in accountability groups has led to the formation of several others around Capitol Hill. At least two dozen Congressmen are gathering in different residences to pray and lovingly hold each other accountable. On other evenings, Steve is a one-man social director, inviting the guys to Baltimore Orioles games or first-run movies. "This can be the loneliest city in the world," he says, "and if I didn't force some guys to get out, a lot of them would stay in their offices answering their e-mail until one in the morning."

Other times, Steve and his Congressional colleagues stay in and watch a video. One of his favorites is *Braveheart,* the 1995 Academy Award–winning Best Picture starring Mel Gibson as William Wallace, the thirteenth-century Scottish rebel who prods the Scottish nobility to take a more aggressive stand against English oppression. In one memorable scene, Wallace explains to the nobles that winning more support from the Scottish commoners will require greater boldness.

"People don't follow titles," bellows Wallace. "They follow courage."

Steve, who has seen the movie at least ten times, says that is his favorite line. He has called upon courage and his Christian faith as a conservative "backbencher" who hasn't shied away from taking on his own party.

One time Steve and ten other House Republicans were called on the carpet by House Speaker Newt Gingrich for helping defeat an appropriations bill the Speaker wanted passed, but which contained funding for huge increases in Congress's own committee funds. The renegade House Republicans were herded into the basement of the Capitol, where Gingrich awaited them. Before the Speaker could start the meeting, Steve walked from the back of the room to the microphone. Looking the Speaker directly in the eye, Steve said, "I've been in smaller rooms with bigger people, and I can't be intimidated." The room was galvanized. Gingrich shifted from confrontation to conciliation, and an important victory was won.

How many political victories lie ahead? Will Steve enter national politics, as some Republicans are whispering he should do?

Whatever he does, Steve knows that people don't follow titles or presidents or Speakers of the House; they follow courage—a courage that has resided in Steve's heart ever since he walked forward and was touched by the Savior in his sophomore year of high school.

6

Rebecca St. James:
IT'S ALL ABOUT GOD

AGE:
twenty-one
OCCUPATION:
Christian singer and youth evangelist
RESIDENCE:
Nashville, Tennessee
FAMILY SITUATION:
single

I grew up outside Sydney, Australia, as the oldest of seven children. I was raised in a Christian family and attended Pacific Hills Christian School in the Sydney suburb of Dural.

When I was in grade three, I joined the Girls Brigade, as did some of my classmates. This after-school program would be the equivalent of a Christian Girl Scouts in the U.S. We wore cute cadet uniforms and participated in Christian service projects that earned us little patches.

One afternoon the Girls Brigade held a service at a Baptist church in Thornleigh, about forty-five minutes west of Sydney. At the service, the preacher presented the gospel and asked us girls if we would like to give our lives to Jesus.

Mum sat on one side of me, and a good friend of mine, Lucy Prior, sat on the other. The speaker's words really affected me. Lucy, who had been studying my face, said, "We should go up, Becca. Let's go up together."

I thought long and hard about it, and I really felt in my heart it was something God wanted me to do. Nodding to Lucy, we both stood up and walked to the front, where a nice lady talked to me about Jesus. At the end of our conversation, when she asked me if I wanted to become a Christian, I said yes, and we prayed together.

When I got home with Mum, I remember sitting on her bed and talking about what happened.

"That was so sweet, Rebecca," said Mum, as she stroked my hair. "Did you know that Jesus died for you on the cross because He loves you so much?"

That's when the enormity of my decision struck me, and I started crying my little eyes out.

Mum held me close as the tears flowed.

"It makes me cry when I realize how much Jesus loves me," I said, sniffling back tears.

I returned to Pacific Hills Christian School a changed person, at least as much as any eight-year-old girl could be. My grade three teacher, Mrs. Burne, must have seen the difference in me. She had recognized that I enjoyed singing and could keep a tune, but she also knew me as a bit of a shy child. One day, she approached me and asked me to do something no one else had ever been asked to do before.

"Rebecca, the class is going to be singing a song at a school assembly in two weeks," she said, "and I'd like you to sing the solo part."

"Uh, I don't know . . ."

"Rebecca, I really think you can do this, and I wouldn't ask you to do anything that I didn't think you were capable of," insisted Mrs. Burne. "I've noticed that you have developed a lot of confidence lately. Can you do it for me?"

"Yes, Mrs. Burne."

It was there at school, with the rest of my class singing in the background, that I gave my first solo, singing "Jesus Put This Song in My Heart." I remember so well standing up in front of the whole primary school, and what a joy to know that what I was singing was true.

That's how my singing ministry started. When I was fourteen, our family went through a huge crisis. My dad promoted Christian concerts throughout Australia, but that is a tough business because Australia doesn't have many Christians, so it is difficult to fill seats. The artist is paid a guaranteed sum, so when not enough tickets are sold, the promoter eats the loss.

In 1990, Dad was promoting a major Christian artist, but the tour didn't do as well as expected, so we lost our house and promotion company. At the time, Dad had eight mouths to feed, so to get back on his feet, he took a job managing a Christian artist. Just one catch: we all had to move to Nashville, Tennessee, the center of the Christian music universe. With six children in tow, our family landed in Los Angeles and boarded an Amtrak train for the long ride to Tennessee.

When we arrived in Nashville, things started to go haywire. Dad's job fell through, and then the house that we were going to rent was taken off the market. We moved into a hotel and lived off fast-food hamburgers.

We were in a small room, and the younger kids were jumping on the beds all day because we couldn't go outside. We were sick of hamburgers, so we prayed that God would provide a good meal for us. We decided to take a ride on a trolley, and the first place we came across was a family restaurant called Shoney's. It was a Wednesday night, and kids ate free, which was a major miracle for a family with so many kids.

We finally managed to rent a home, but Dad couldn't find a job. We used to have family devotions on the floor because we didn't have any furniture, just pillows. With Dad out of work, we prayed that God would provide. And He did! We received groceries on our doorstep, unexplained checks in the mail, truck loads of furniture, and even a brand-new van!

This all happened during the fall, and one day my brothers and I went outside and raked up the leaves. A lady drove by and said, "Wow, you're doing a really good job. Could you rake up the leaves at my place?" We started doing all the lawns in the neighborhood to earn some money. Even Dad came out and helped. Raking leaves had to be pretty humbling for him. Then, to make ends meet, Mum and I started cleaning houses while the boys mowed lawns.

I never thought twice about cleaning someone else's house—even the toilets. I actually enjoy helping people, and I love to clean! God taught us a lot through cleaning other people's homes—that there is real joy in serving others. I can actually say that that time was a great preparation for our ministry now.

As you may know, these days I sing with a band, but the entire family pitches in. We travel from venue to venue in a big motor home, which certainly makes for cramped quarters. Dad is the driver and our road manager who runs the soundboard. Mum often mans the Compassion International table and keeps everyone on track. Daniel, nineteen, programs and runs the computer-driven light system and also sings background vocals on a few songs. Ben, seventeen, operates the light show when Daniel's on stage and is also our video archivist. Joel, fourteen, sings with me on the stage but also organizes the stage setup. Luke, twelve, operates spotlight number one. Josh, nine, runs spotlight number two. My only sister, Libby, is six, and she does a very nice job of looking cute.

One thing that Mum brings on every trip is a scrapbook for each child. Mine is a bright pink book filled with notations and letters, and she's told me that she will give it to me on my wedding day.

On the first page, she wrote in nice calligraphy:

Rebecca: Born on the 26th day of July 1977. Rebecca means "one who is bound," and we dedicate this book to you with all our love, and we hope that it will help you remember the precious moments of your childhood. May God always bless you.

Not long ago, I found this notation:

11th of November 1985

Last night we went to church, just you, your brother Ben, and myself. It was a Girls Brigade parade service, and you needed to receive your membership card. The visiting preacher was skilled in children's ministry and presented a simple gospel message. He then prayed a prayer of commitment at the end. The girls all paraded out, but he asked any who wanted to speak to him to return after the service. Lucy Prior asked you to go back with her and speak to him about giving your life to Christ. At first you were hesitant, but then you decided to go with her. Mrs. Gow from church spoke to you both and prayed with you.

As we were walking out afterward, you started to cry, and I asked what was the matter. You said, "It makes me want to cry when I think how much Jesus loves me." We had a good talk as I explained about what had happened and what you had done that evening. You confirmed to me the reality of your experience, and so we then talked about communion and the significance of the step you had taken. We prayed together with both of us crying. Today you seemed to be still excited about what had taken place and said to a few friends at school that last night you had become a Christian. I noticed this evening that there was even a more lovely spirit in your actions and that you were even more sincere about your desire to please and do the right thing.

Over the years, I've heard a lot of people describe dramatic changes in their lives after coming to Christ, and I think, *Boy, I don't have much of a testimony.* But I once heard someone say that to live consistently for Christ is just as much a testimony to God's holding power as somebody who went from a life of drugs and alcohol to a life of serving Him. I was really encouraged by that.

I am so grateful to know God. The more I live this Christian life, the more I realize how much more there is I can learn about Him. I have been fortunate to travel to places such as Canada, England, the Netherlands, Ecuador, New Zealand, and India. When I see how much hurt and sorrow are in people's lives, I understand better that we are living in a world that needs Jesus. That's why I am so grateful to share Him with audiences.

Isn't it ironic? Now I'm privileged to help people make decisions for Christ. When I announce in concert, "If you give your life to Jesus tonight, I promise you it will be the best decision you will ever make," I know I am telling the truth.

I remember giving an invitation and singing a song called "Above All Things." From the stage, I looked down and saw a young girl walking to the front. She couldn't have been older than six years or so, and she held her father's hand in one hand and her mother's hand in the other. Watching her come forward—so innocent, so ready, so accepting—made me start crying.

I could barely finish the song because she was doing the same thing I had done at a young age, and I was reminded of how much my decision has changed my life.

7

Paul of Tarsus:
HIS ROAD TO DAMASCUS

AGE:
born a few years after Jesus Christ and
martyred in Rome in 67 A.D.
OCCUPATION:
tentmaker, evangelist
RESIDENCE:
Jerusalem; traveled extensively in later years
FAMILY SITUATION:
unknown

Very unusual, thought Cephias, as he scanned the small scroll once again.

The Temple messenger stood in the doorway. "Sir, I'm required to continue my rounds posthaste, so if Your Excellency is finished reading the scroll, I will be on my way."

"Very well," said Cephias. "Where do you go next?"

"I must deliver this message to six more members of the Sanhedrin before the ninth hour, or the high priest will have me scourged. I best be on my way, sir."

"Yes, carry on," said Cephias, as he bade the messenger goodbye.

Anna, Cephias's wife, looked up from the dough she was kneading on a wooden board. "Who was that, dear?"

"One of the Temple messengers, my love," replied Cephias.

"Anything important?"

"Indeed. The high priest has called an emergency meeting of the Sanhedrin for the twelfth hour. It seems a group of renegade Christians slipped through our grasp and escaped the city walls. The largest group, we hear, reached Damascus."

"So? Damascus is a week north of Jerusalem. What can Christians do from there?"

"Don't you understand, Anna? We thought we had Christianity extinguished after that Jesus character died a few months ago, but his followers keep popping up like springtime weeds. Jews are converting to this baseless religion in droves, especially in Damascus, which seems to be a hotbed for them. If we don't do something about the Christian problem soon, they will demand equal standing with the Romans. We can't allow that."

TO THE TEMPLE

Cephias never tired of the twenty-minute walk to the Temple. He rather enjoyed striding through the busy thoroughfares and marketplaces, where he could be seen wearing his brilliant red tunic and gold-braided tassels over his beige robe.

"Here comes a Temple priest!" he heard one merchant yell out as people turned to him and bowed.

At least these people know how to show proper respect to members of the Jewish Council, thought Cephias.

"What brings His Excellency to the Temple?" called out a shopkeeper.

"The high priest has called an emergency meeting to deal with the Christian problem," replied Cephias.

"What do you think the Sanhedrin will decide, sir?" asked the baker.

"We will exterminate the vermin," declared Cephias with a steely resolve that surprised even him. "I can assure you that the Law will be applied with a vengeance to these blasphemers."

When the Temple came into view, he noticed that hundreds were gathered outside the entrance. *Word of the meeting got around quickly,* he thought.

He made eye contact with several other Council members as they walked through the large entrance door and into a series of hallways. The meeting room was just off the main worship hall. Cephias nodded to the stoic Temple guards as he filed past.

When the last member of the Sanhedrin entered the meeting room, the high priest gestured for everyone to sit on pillows. A bearded fellow in his late twenties sat cross-legged at the high priest's right side. Cephias tried to remember where he had seen the young man before.

Oh, yes, at Gamaliel's house, recalled Cephias. *He's a young Pharisee called Saul. Gamaliel told me to keep an eye on this one. He's a talented tentmaker by trade, but Gamaliel said he's being groomed for Temple leadership.*

The high priest shook Cephias back to attention. "My distinguished colleagues," he began, "thank you for coming on such short notice. I regret to inform you that we have a crisis. Let me summarize where we now stand. During Passover, we managed to bring to justice Jesus of Nazareth, who was executed, and rightly so, for claiming he was the Son of God. Since then, however, we have reports of thousands of people becoming followers of Jesus. They are calling themselves Christians, and a man named Peter—a fisherman, no less—is the ringleader of this sect. He escaped our clutches, but he cannot remain a fugitive forever. You will note, however, that we have brought his aide-de-camp Stephen to justice."

Saul, the young man seated next to the high priest, recoiled slightly when he heard Stephen's name. He hoped none of the Council members had noticed the reflex. Just a few days earlier, Stephen had stood before this very group and presented his defense of Christianity. His command of history was spellbinding, as he recounted God's promise that a whole country would belong to Abraham and his descendants at a time when he was very old and childless! Stephen continued with the story of Exodus: Abraham's descendants lived in the foreign land of Egypt, where they were slaves for four hundred years before Moses delivered them miraculously. The nation of Israel was founded, and Solomon built a temple for the God of Abraham.

The Sanhedrin knew their Torah well, so they wondered why Stephen was recounting Jewish history. Then Stephen committed a fatal mistake. He infuriated the Sanhedrin by demanding that they name one prophet whom their ancestors didn't persecute! "You killed the prophets who predicted the coming of Jesus Christ, and you killed the Messiah during the last Passover," roared Stephen. "Shame on you for disobeying God's laws, which you received from the hands of angels!"

There was only one sentence the Council could confer on Stephen for his blasphemy: death by stoning. Saul, a trusted aide to the high priest, accompanied the executioners into the public square as overseer.

"Will you watch our coats?" the executioners asked, as they laid a half-dozen garments at Saul's feet. Then they took up fist-sized stones and began pummeling the defenseless Stephen.

"Lord Jesus, receive my spirit!" Stephen cried out, as he lay in a fetal position. "Lord, don't charge them with this sin!" One of the executioners picked up a large boulder, stepped up to a nearly unconscious Stephen, and dropped it on his head, crushing his skull. A pool of deep-red blood formed quickly.

Saul turned away, sickened by what he had witnessed, but moved at the same time by the man's faith in Jesus. After a couple of days, however, Saul's view changed. *Stephen was just another zealot,* he thought. *He got what he deserved.*

DIRECTION FROM THE HIGH COURT

"Are we then all in agreement with this course of action?" asked the high priest.

Murmurs of affirmation greeted the high priest.

"Good," he said, pleased that the Sanhedrin had voiced approval to his plan. "Let it be so ordered that Saul will lead a small company to Damascus, where he will capture the Christian leaders and bring them back to this Council for justice."

"Hear, hear!" Cephias cried out. It was the prudent approach, he noted. Saul was the firebrand type, well-suited for a mission such as this one.

All eyes turned to Saul, who stood up and began pacing behind the Council members.

"Your Excellency and members of the Sanhedrin, I thank you for your confidence in me," began Saul. "Let me assure you that I eagerly accept your assignment to capture those blasphemers. I must state at the outset how dangerous this Christian movement has become to our way of life and our way of worship. These Christians have dared to believe that a man—a simple Nazarene carpenter—is the Son of God, but they have compounded their error by converting our Jewish brethren to their false religion. Jesus claimed to be the Messiah, but he died like the rest of them, and he will soon be forgotten, if we do our jobs properly.

"If it would please the Court, I will need from the Sanhedrin a letter that I can take to the synagogues in Damascus, requiring their cooperation in finding all Christians. I can assure you that any Christians I capture will wish for a speedy death after I am through with them, but I will not kill them, based on your directive. Instead, I will drag them back in chains to Jerusalem, where they will be brought to swift and orderly justice by this court. I can assure you that I hate Christians, and I will do everything in my power to destroy them!"

Gamaliel trained Saul well in that school of his, thought Cephias.

ON THE ROAD

It took two days for Saul to gather an elite team and load the donkeys with provisions from the Temple commissary.

"How many sets of chains do we have?" Saul asked the head herdsman.

"Only threescore," he replied, "but I've ordered another twenty, which should arrive before we leave in the morning."

"Very well," said Saul. "We can use ropes if we run out of chains, and we will, if all goes according to plan. Our Jewish brethren in Damascus are reporting that the Christians are becoming more aggressive than ever. They are preaching on the streets and drawing large crowds, and they will not stop until everybody becomes a Christian. That can't happen!"

"It won't, sir."

The caravan left the city gates at daybreak for the seven-day journey. Saul was more worried about the summertime heat than bandits because Roman justice was swift and deadly for robbers. Saul was right about the bandits—the caravan didn't encounter any along the Via Maris trade route. As Saul neared Damascus, he relished the thought of making short work of the Christians.

Suddenly, a brilliant light knocked Saul off his horse. Dazed and disoriented, he shielded his eyes and looked toward the source of the light.

"Saul, Saul, why are you persecuting Me?" thundered a loud voice.

Where is the voice coming from? thought Saul.

"Who is speaking, sir?" Saul asked.

"It is Jesus, whom you are persecuting. Now get up and go into the city and await My further instructions."

Saul's men were terrified because they heard a voice in the air but saw no one. "Who is it, sir?" asked his foreman. "We can't see anybody."

Saul stumbled to his feet. "Wait a minute!" he screamed. "I can't see! What's happening?"

"Saul, I'm over here," said the foreman.

"I can hear you, but I can't see you."

The foreman grabbed Saul's hand. "I'm right here, sir."

"I'm blind! I'm blind!" cried out Saul, as he fell to his knees.

"Don't worry, sir. We'll get you to Damascus and find help."

Saul refused to be put on his horse, so one of his men led him by the hand all the way into Damascus. When the caravan arrived at Judas's house, his men carried Saul's sagging body to one of the bedrooms and placed him on a bed of straw.

For three days, Saul tossed and turned, refusing to eat or drink. He knew he had met Jesus. He knew his life was about to change. He slipped off his bed, knelt beside it, and began to pray: "Dear Jesus, You are my Lord. You really are the Messiah, just as You said you were. I repent for persecuting You and Your believers. Please help me regain my sight so I can serve You."

Saul climbed back into bed and fell asleep. In a dream, he saw a tall fellow with a shock of gray hair coming into his room and placing his hands on him to restore his sight. When Saul awoke, his tunic was drenched in sweat. "Was that dream from You, Lord?" he cried out.

Four blocks to the west, a Jewish Christian named Ananias couldn't sleep either. Suddenly, his bedroom was filled with light.

"Ananias!" said a voice.

"Who is it?" asked Ananias, and then he knew it was the Lord Jesus.

"Go over to Straight Street, find the house of a man named Judas, and ask for Saul of Tarsus. He is praying to Me right now, for I have shown him a vision of you coming and laying hands on him so that he can see again."

"But, Lord," exclaimed Ananias. "I have heard about the horrible things this man has done to the believers in Jerusalem! And we hear that he is carrying arrest warrants authorizing him to capture every believer in Damascus."

"Never mind what you have heard," said the Lord. "Go ahead and do what I say. For Saul is My chosen instrument to take My message to the people of the world and before kings, as well as to the people of Israel. And I will show him how much he must suffer for Me."

Although it was the middle of the night, Ananias put on his tunic and found Judas's home on Straight Street.

"I am here to see Saul," he announced to the gruff man at the door. "I have a message for him."

"Very well," said the guard, as he waved him to the back.

Ananias was led to Saul, who was fully awake.

"The Lord told me He would send you," said Saul with conviction.

"I welcome you as a fellow believer in Jesus Christ," said Ananias, "and I am here to deliver you from your blindness through the power of Jesus Christ."

Ananias laid his hands on Saul's head and said, "Brother Saul, the Lord Jesus, who appeared to you on the road, has sent me so that you may be filled with the Holy Spirit and receive back your sight."

Saul nearly jumped out of his bed when his vision returned. "I can see!" he screamed with joy. "Oh, thank You, Jesus!"

"Would you like to be baptized?" asked Ananias.

"Yes, let's do that immediately." Saul stood up and gingerly placed one foot in front of the other.

"I know a place that's deep enough on the Barada River," said Ananias. "It's only a ten-minute walk."

After Saul was baptized, they returned to Judas's home and shared a meal of warm bread, fresh honey, and dried figs.

SAUL STANDS UP

Tibris lifted the stone block and waited for his partner, Urbanas, to slather enough mortar on the second-story wall.

"How much longer until lunch?" asked Urbanas.

"Three more rows and we can take a break," said Tibris, as he stood back and studied his next move.

Tibris dipped his trowel into the tub of mortar and looked down to the street. Ananias, one of the leaders of the underground Christian church, was walking purposefully with several other men. One was wearing the golden tassels of the Temple in Jerusalem.

"Who's that with Ananias?" wondered Urbanas.

"I'm not sure, but it could be . . ."

"You're right, Tibby. Isn't that Saul of Tarsus, the one who was sent by the Sanhedrin to persecute us and bring us back to Jerusalem?"

"Yes, I'm sure that's him," replied the mason. "Something very strange is going on, and I don't like it. What do you say we find out what's happening?"

The two stoneworkers put down their tools and followed Saul and Ananias from a distance.

"They're going to the synagogue; I'm sure of it," said Tibris.

"Why would they go to the synagogue? Saul's not going to find any Christians there."

When they arrived at Damascus's largest synagogue, a sizable noontime crowd had already formed in front of the steps.

"I guess word got out," said Tibris.

"Yes, let's listen," said Urbanas.

"I stand before you," began Saul, "to share the Good News about Jesus Christ. He is indeed the Son of God!"

A wave of murmurs swept through the crowd.

"I can't believe my ears," said Urbanas. "Did he say what I thought he said?"

"I believe he did," replied his friend.

For the next half-hour, Saul told his story about Jesus blinding him on the way to Damascus and Ananias restoring his sight by laying hands on him. "When something like scales fell from my eyes, I could see physically, and I could also see that Jesus Christ is exactly who He said He was—the Messiah and Son of Man."

Out of the corner of his eye, Paul saw several Jewish leaders sneaking themselves through the crowd.

"Saul, this way," whispered Ananias, and the two men, shielded by the crowd, slipped away through a back alley. The two masons knew where Ananias was taking Saul.

They knocked on the door an hour later.

"Welcome, brother," said the man who answered. "Come in."

Saul was sitting on a pillow in the main living room.

"A pleasure to meet you, sir," said Urbanas.

"The pleasure is all mine, and please, call me Paul," said the man as he extended his arms in greeting.

"Paul? I thought your name was Saul."

"It was. But after what happened to me on the road to Damascus, I've decided to be called Paul, the Greek version of my name. What do you think?"

"Splendid, sir, uh, Paul, I mean."

Tibris asked for permission to speak.

"Sir, the Jewish leaders will be watching the city gates day and night, and I'm sure they will kill you if they can lay their hands on you. We know a city wall that is under repair, and if we can get there in time, we can lower you in a basket to safety."

"May the Lord bless you, my brothers," said Paul. "I suggest we leave tonight."

"Then it's agreed."

Paul had a final question. "Ananias, whom should I see when I return to Jerusalem?"

"Ask for Barnabas, and tell him everything that has happened. Tell him you met Jesus Christ on the road to Damascus. Tell him your life will never be the same."

"I will, my friend. I will."

8

Jackie Kendall:
A FUEL LINE HOOKED UP
TO THE SAVIOR

AGE:
forty-eight
OCCUPATION:
author and speaker, especially to professional athletes
RESIDENCE:
Royal Palm Beach, Florida
FAMILY SITUATION:
married to Ken for twenty-five years; mother of Ben, nineteen;
and Jessica, seventeen

You could have called me "Sally Sosh" in high school because I was such a social butterfly. I went to a huge high school with nearly eight hundred students in each grade, and I liked to hang out with different groups—as long as they were cool. For instance, on weekends, I scored surf contests and partied afterward with the surf dudes. I showed up at Santana concerts and danced with the druggies. I ate lunch with the cheerleaders and told funny stories.

But there was one group at high school that I should have

noticed: the ones who quietly ate lunch in the back corner of the schoolyard. They were the Christians, and little did I know that they had noticed *me.*

The Christian kids were attending a Youth for Christ Bible study on Wednesday nights, and the YFC leaders knew that teens respond best when an invitation comes from another teen, not an adult. Because I was targeted as a class leader, they felt that if I became a Christian, not only would I be saved, but I would be able to lead others to Christ. So they put me on their prayer hit list.

Since I liked people and was always looking for something to do, I readily accepted their invitation to drop by their Bible study. The group didn't feel threatening because they held their study in one of the kid's homes, not in a church.

I can still remember the early evening when I walked into the Gilson home, which was two streets over from my house. The date was Wednesday, April 15, 1967, and I was a junior in high school. In the living room, a dozen kids were seated in a huge circle, each holding open Bibles.

I'm in trouble now, I thought. *Wait a minute. I can handle this.* I decided to stay and see what was going on. In less than an hour, I was absolutely captivated by the way my peers talked so personally about Jesus Christ. At first their discussions sounded sacrilegious. I grew up in a denomination in which you bowed your head and listened to the priest recite the prayers. Only he could read the Bible and interpret it.

When the teens closed in prayer, I stood up to leave. Another student Larry Munoz did a full confrontation on me: "Jackie, if you died today, would you go to heaven?"

"You can't know that." I was a Catholic, and I knew that only the Pope held that knowledge under his miter.

"Would you let me show you how you can be sure that you're going to heaven?"

"Oh, come on."

"No, Jackie, it's in this booklet."

Without any commentary, Larry read from *Have You Heard of the Four Spiritual Laws?*, and when he came to this final question—"Is there any reason why you can't ask Jesus to take control of your life?"—I replied, "I can't think of one."

The room became silent, and everyone's eyes fell on me.

"There's a prayer I want you to pray," said Larry.

"What kind of prayer is that?" All my prayers had been memorized.

"I'm going to pray a couple of sentences, and I want you to repeat after me if this is what you really believe."

We proceeded slowly, taking our time as I accepted the free gift of eternal life through Christ Jesus. The prayer had no magic, just a feeling of blessed assurance.

The minute I finished, I turned to my good friend Bobbie. "Do you want to receive Jesus, too?" I asked.

"No, I have to get home," she said.

"Ah, come on, Bobbie. We have time."

"Later, Jackie."

Although Bobbie passed up her chance, it's interesting how I immediately wanted to share Christ with other people.

Larry handed me a copy of *Good News for Modern Man* (the Living Bible translation) and said, "Jackie, this is your food. You have to read it. If you have any questions, ask me tomorrow."

The first thing I did when I got home was phone my best friend.

"Judy Farr, I have to tell you what happened!" I began, as I launched into a minute-by-minute account. Then I shared the gospel with her.

"Stop, I've already asked Jesus into my life."

"No, you haven't."

"Yes, I did, at summer camp."

"Trust me, you did not get what I just got. If you had, you would have told me."

That's how I was. You couldn't shut me up about Jesus. On Friday, I was two days old in the Lord, and I was asked to speak at a YFC sleepover—what they call "lock-ins" today. Kids hang out all night long in the church gymnasium or fellowship hall, and they do a lot of goofy teen things before hearing the gospel. Christians are supposed to invite non-Christian friends to the event.

"But I don't know one scripture," I protested after being asked to speak.

"Don't worry about it," said the YFC leader. "Just get up and tell everyone what happened on Wednesday night."

That's what I did.

THE LURKING SHADOWS

As the oldest of seven children, our family didn't have the money to send me to college. After high school graduation, I met Robert L. Turner, a millionaire who owned U.S. Auto Parts. We struck up a conversation after I had led his granddaughter to the Lord.

"Jackie, why aren't you in college?"

"Mr. Turner, the college I want to go to is a private Christian university, and I don't have the money for that."

Mr. Turner offered to pay all my college expenses, which included not only tuition and room and board, but also plane fares, telephone bills, and a monthly spending allowance. I attended Tennessee Temple University, a Christian liberal arts school in Chattanooga with a strong emphasis on the Bible. I wanted to learn the Word of God, so I majored in Bible and Education.

Early in my freshman year, a little incident happened. I was chosen as a chaplain for the girls' dorm and became good friends with one of the college's staff members, a psychology teacher. She asked me to take the Taylor Johnson Temperament test, an exam frequently given to engaged or young married couples to determine who is aggressive or passive, objective or subjective, dominant or submissive, etc.

The results were not what I expected, and the professors were surprised, as well. I came out as a "highly hostile" personality—some-one with something burning deep within the psyche.

My friend retested me just to be sure and then asked me to meet with her and Mrs. Cravens, a school counselor.

"Jackie, as you know, you are a strong leader on campus and a good student," said my friend. "But after reviewing your test with others, your results tell us that you must be hiding something. In fact, whatever's bothering you is so deep that you probably need counseling."

"Can I talk to Mrs. Cravens alone?" I asked politely. She was a counselor who taught some classes and was known as a good sound-ing board. She always looked to God's Word for answers.

Slowly, hesitantly, I began to tell her about my father, who, when I was fourteen years old, began coming into my bedroom late at night and climbing on top of me. He never raped me, but he did sexually abuse me.

"Did you tell your mother?" asked Mrs. Cravens.

I told her about the following conversation I had with my mother:

"Mom, he's always touching me," I had complained.

"Oh, he's just adjusting your sheets at night. It gets cold."

"No, Mom, it's more than that," I had insisted.

"All right, I'll tell your dad not to come into your room."

We put a lock on the door, but he broke the lock. Another time he climbed through my window. The man would not be denied his sex-ual pleasure.

When I became a Christian, he continued to sneak into my room from time to time, but I became more aggressive in yelling at him, hoping to wake up a younger sister with whom I shared the bed-room. He turned his attention from me and began abusing my other sisters.

As Mrs. Craven listened to my story, she started to weep. Her tears provoked such shame in me. Although she meant well, I began to shut down and wondered why I was telling my horrible story.

WEDDING BELLS

A year later, in 1974, I married a wonderful young Christian man named Ken Kendall. I thought a new life and a new name would make all that bad stuff go away. After college, we moved to Grand Rapids, Michigan, and began working with youth. Poor Ken: he was saved at eleven years old and loved my passion for God, but he had no idea about my past.

It didn't take long for Ken to catch the brunt of my deep-seated hostilities. I overreacted to just about everything, and my mindset was that if I couldn't hurt my dad, then I could hurt my husband. Ken would have to pay.

When our children were born in 1979 and 1982, we switched from youth to singles ministry. Suddenly I encountered young women confiding in me about being sexually abused by their fathers or family members.

Oh no, here we go again.

The problem was that I had never effectively dealt with my *own* sexual abuse. I remember speaking at a Miami conference when Lottie and Robin, two female counselors trained by author and counselor Larry Crabb, asked me to join them at T.G.I. Friday's.

Lottie looked over her Cobb salad and asked, "Can you tell us your story?"

"You mean my testimony?"

"No, we want to hear what fuels your passion."

"My passion is Jesus."

"But your passion is inordinate. You're holding something under."

I began bawling my head off in this public setting, terrified that what I was hiding was so obvious to the outside world. These two precious counselors volunteered to see me at their offices, which were about an hour's drive from my home in Royal Palm Beach.

In the counseling sessions, they drew memories out. I recalled how I would *never* forget the time that my father, who was a jeweler by trade, went into the garage, ostensibly to work on his jewelry. In the garage, my father took my high school senior picture, cut out my face, and pasted it on top of the face of Miss May from the *Playboy* centerfold. What a sick form of gratification.

I lived in a house of pornography. Dad had pictures of naked women on the back of his bathroom door (we lived in a two-bathroom house shared by nine people), and it was terrible when any of us had to use *that* bathroom.

One of my worst memories was when my dad was at home molesting one of my sisters while my mother was at the hospital with our dying grandmother. One of my other brothers has a vivid memory of her screams of resistance, screams that my mother never heard. My brother had tried to get our dad to stop, but he wasn't successful. How low could one go in perversion?

Through my counseling, I began to realize that Dad had started with me, the oldest child, and had progressed in his perversion as he moved through the lives of my sisters and brothers. His assaults on them resulted in incredibly destructive choices in their lives.

I had siblings who had babies out of wedlock, abortions, addictions to drugs and alcohol—so many poor choices. In 1984, I learned that there was a correlation between self-destructive choices and a background of verbal, physical, and sexual abuse—which were all part of our home life.

I remember Dad slamming Mom's head against a cabinet in front of all us kids for something one of us had done. Talk about incredible guilt. Another time, he beat one of my brothers brutally in the bathroom while all of us kids were screaming and trying to bash down the door, but we never succeeded. With all the trauma I experienced, I learned to swallow my pain. Tucked away in my heart was a question for a loving God: *Why did You place me in such a dysfunctional family?*

One time, I was invited to bring my husband and children for a weekend with my two counselors. At that time, I was confronted with the harsh reality of my total denial. I was still in a close relationship with my father: he and my mother had actually moved across the street from us in Florida. I felt my relationship with Dad had such a noble purpose: I wanted to win him to Jesus, even if that meant subjecting myself to his perverted verbal abuse. The counselors that weekend showed me how blind I was and how toxic my relationship with my dad had become.

My counselors drew strong boundaries: no contact with my father unless my husband was with me, and no unsupervised contact with our kids. At the time, I thought they were being overly cautious. *Dad wouldn't hurt my kids,* I thought, but that was my own denial. Yes, he could hurt them, and all I had to do was look at the human wreckage around me. I had one brother in our home for thirteen months during his rehab from cocaine. My sister Bobbie lived with us after undergoing alcohol rehab, which I helped pay for. In fact, she went through rehab a dozen times until a spring day in 1990, when she took an overdose of Quaaludes and died.

At the exact moment Bobbie was dying, I was onstage at a Christian youth event in a North Carolina field, warning teens about the dangerous effects of drugs. Bobbie's suicide devastated our family. I experienced pain from which I thought I would never recover.

After her suicide, I returned to Christian counseling, where I heard this advice: "You must ask God to show you how to forgive your dad because if you don't forgive him, you will be his slave for the rest of your life."

I studied Scripture on forgiveness and read many books on the subject. I wanted to be Jesus' slave, not my father's. After searching the Scriptures, I began the journey of forgiving my father. Unfortunately, not long after I started that journey, he died without Jesus. At his memorial service, one of my brothers was so distraught that when he stood up, he fell into the arms of several men and cried hysterically. A Christian counselor who witnessed my brother's disconsolate grief and knew of our family dynamics came to have a word with me. "If your brother doesn't deal with his hurt," he warned calmly, "he will be next." When I asked him why, the counselor explained that an abusive parent can still influence a son or daughter from the grave.

"What can be done to prevent that from happening?" I asked.

"By having the offended child begin the journey of forgiving the offender," he replied. "If one does not forgive the offender, his hand can come through the dirt and keep a finger on the adult child."

I confronted my brother John about his need to talk to a counselor about his painful relationship with our father. "That's the past," he responded. "It has nothing to do with the present."

Yet the past has everything to do with the present when it has been covered up and never dealt with. Three years after my father died and four years after my sister's suicide, my brother checked into a motel and blew out his brains.

REACHING OUT

Several years ago someone had heard me speak and invited me to address a conference for professional athletes and their wives. I was asked to talk about dealing with an abusive past and not being held hostage to it. Because I've read that three out of five women report being abused during their lifetimes, I was not surprised to learn how many wives grew up in abusive homes. Being married to a famous athlete can be wonderful, but it certainly is not an effective cover-up for past hurts.

I know all about the cover-up. I tell the young women that their only hope is being touched by the Savior. After all that I've been through, I'm living proof of His touch.

9

John Croyle:
THE LINE IN THE SAND

AGE:
forty-seven
OCCUPATION:
founder of the Big Oak Ranch,
a Christian home for children needing a chance
RESIDENCE:
Gadsden, Alabama
FAMILY SITUATION:
married to Teresa for twenty-four years;
father of Reagan, twenty; and Brodie, sixteen

Do you know where the expression "drawing a line in the sand" comes from? It dates back to the Alamo in San Antonio, Texas, during the Texas Revolution in 1836. The Alamo, founded as a mission by the Spaniards, was captured by Texas revolutionaries and put under siege by the Mexican Army, led by General Santa Anna.

Several thousand Mexican troops surrounded the garrison,

defended by 180 Texas revolutionaries. With the Mexicans closing in, General Sam Houston assembled his men in the middle of the fort and drew a line in the sand with his saber.

"Men, if you step over this line and stay to fight, you're probably going to die. You can choose to stay, or you can choose to leave. The decision is yours."

All but one of those 180 men stepped over that line, including David Crockett, Jim Bowie, and a wounded soldier named Travis, who asked that his cot be lifted over the line. Within days, they were all killed by Santa Anna's forces, prompting the famous cry, "Remember the Alamo!"

Similarly, there comes a time in every person's life when he has to draw a line in the sand and say, "That's it. I'm committed to this." It may be your marriage, your children, your business, or your decision to follow Christ.

I know that's the way it happened in my relationship with Jesus Christ. I had made nearly every mistake you can make as a man, a husband, and a father, but there came a time in my life when I drew a line in the sand and said, "No more," as you'll soon see.

THE EARLY YEARS

Growing up in Alabama, it was a given that you were going to go to church on Sunday morning. That's what everyone did, and our family was no different. My mom and dad took us every Sunday morning, and we returned for the Sunday night service. I went to church by rote, and it certainly didn't mean much to me.

When I was a high school junior, Campus Crusade for Christ held a meeting in town. I went out of curiosity—and to hang out with some of my friends. I listened to a speaker talk about how to become a Christian, and while his presentation made sense, I wasn't ready to make any sort of commitment to Christ.

As I was leaving, an old man started a conversation with me.

"If you were to die tonight, where would you stay for eternity?" he asked.

"Mister, I don't know, and I don't care," I retorted. "You just better get the heck out of here. Leave me alone."

I turned on my heels and walked away. "Jesus Christ can give you peace," he said, but I didn't acknowledge that I heard him.

Later that night, however, my conscience was bothering me. I mulled over what that old man had said. Maybe he was right. Maybe Jesus Christ could give me the peace I needed, a peace that "passes all understanding."

I knelt beside my bed and prayed: "God, Jesus, whoever, if You are who You claim to be, come in and change my life. If You do, I'll tell everybody that what You say about Yourself is true."

The next morning I got out of bed and stubbed my toe on the way to the bathroom. I said some unpleasant things, used a curse word or two, and for the first time in my life, I disappointed somebody—the Lord.

That was the beginning of my Christian life. Not much, but a start. Regretfully, I've disappointed Him a lot since then, but He's kept up His end of the bargain—always loving, always forgiving, and always disciplining when necessary.

I became a good football player in high school, and it was a dream come true for this Alabama kid to play for Coach Paul "Bear" Bryant at the University of 'Bama in the early seventies. I played defensive end, and during my senior year, National Football League scouts took an interest in me. They felt I was ready for the pros.

But something happened during the summer that I spent as a counselor at King's Arrow Ranch, a Christian summer camp in Mississippi. I met a twelve-year-old boy from New Orleans; his mom was a prostitute. Talk about helping out at home: the boy was the banker and the timekeeper while his mom "serviced" the clientele.

I sensed the boy's deep hunger to be loved. When I befriended him, the boy blossomed and accepted Christ after hearing me present the gospel. That's when it slowly dawned on me that I had been given a gift, a gift that helped a boy who felt worthless to feel loved. At that moment I knew my calling in life was to help kids like that boy from New Orleans.

Upon graduation from the University of Alabama, I asked for a meeting with Coach Bryant to discuss my plans to play pro ball and start a boys' home, figuring I could plow my NFL paychecks into the new ministry.

Coach Bryant looked off into the distance and then swung his chair toward me. "Here's my advice to you, John: Don't play professional football unless you're willing to marry it."

I wasn't willing to eat, sleep, and breathe NFL football.

A friend of mine John Hannah, an All-Pro center for the New England Patriots, heard about my desire to start a boys' home, and he made the down payment on a 120-acre ranch in Gadsden, Alabama. Five boys and I moved into a dilapidated farmhouse, and the journey began. I loved, disciplined, fed, clothed, hugged, bathed, and stayed up late with kids who had been literally abandoned by their parents. It wasn't unusual for a parent to pull into the driveway and announce that he or she was leaving the child with me—just like that and without any prior arrangements.

Reading this story, you're probably thinking that I had it all together, that I was Super Joe Christian. But I wasn't fooling anyone.

About fifteen years ago, a visitor dropped by the Big Oak Ranch. The man identified himself as a pastor from Birmingham and said God had sent him to see me.

Yeah, right, I thought. *If you only knew how many times I've heard that line . . .*

I recoiled because whenever I heard someone say God had sent him to see me, he usually wanted something. But this man was different. He didn't want anything. He only wanted to give.

We started to walk the grounds of the ranch. The pastor explained that he had been talking to a mutual friend of ours about the ranch, and he felt the Lord impress upon his heart to come see me. So he obeyed.

"Would you agree to meet with me for four Wednesdays in a row?" he asked.

"Sure," I replied, but inside I still didn't trust him.

After the fourth week, he said, "Let me share with you what the Lord has shared with me."

He looked me directly in the eye.

"You're dipping out of an empty bucket. You're not living as God designed you to live."

In other words, I couldn't give water to others when my bucket had no water in it. I was telling all these children how to live, but I wasn't anywhere close to it. Now was the time to grow up and show myself as a man. I had been trying to be a great person, a great husband, a great father, and a great provider, but in juggling all four balls, I wasn't juggling any of them well.

I learned to cherish my wife, Tee. I did that by paying more attention to her, picking up my clothes, vacuuming around the house, and helping with the kitchen duties. I had never done those things before. I learned to lead my children. I learned how to love God wholeheartedly.

Looking back, my life has been like a football game. You see, there comes a point in nearly every game when the momentum shifts and you know you're going to win. It may be the middle of the third quarter or the next-to-last play, but every game has a discernible shift in momentum when you know you are going to win.

That shift in momentum came for me when I stepped over the line in the sand.

10

Chuck Colson:
FROM THE WHITE HOUSE
TO THE JAILHOUSE

AGE:
sixty-eight
OCCUPATION:
chairman and founder of Prison Fellowship Ministries,
an evangelistic outreach that takes the gospel of Jesus Christ
to prison inmates and their families
RESIDENCE:
Washington, D.C.
FAMILY SITUATION:
married to Patricia for thirty-five years;
three children from a previous marriage

*Editor's note: If you're less than forty years old, you're proba-
bly too young to recall Chuck Colson's conversion experience. It
was as dramatic as it was astonishing because it occurred in a cultural milieu dominated by one of the most gut-wrenching times
in American political history: Watergate. As you'll see, when*

people learned that Chuck Colson had become a Christian, the news prompted two visceral reactions: disbelief and derision.

Chuck Colson, born to working-class parents in Winthrop, Massachusetts, spent his boyhood years growing up during World War II. His father kept books for a meat-packing plant, working long hours for modest pay, and his mother was a spendaholic who on occasion sold furniture and family possessions to pay the rent. To better the family's lot in life, Chuck's father attended law school at night and became a lawyer. No one on either side of Chuck's family had ever gone on to college.

The family's fortunes improved, at least enough to enroll Chuck in Browne and Nichols, a prestigious preparatory school in Cambridge. The next rung on the academic ladder was admission to an elite Ivy League school, Brown University. Chuck accepted a naval ROTC scholarship, which paid his tuition and gave him fifty dollars a month to live on.

Throughout his childhood and young adult years, Chuck was a class cutup and practical joker. He joined a fraternity house at Brown University and reveled in the all-night "bull sessions" and hijinks that were part of college life in the fifties.

One evening, Chuck slipped out at 2:00 A.M. and walked across the street to a phone booth. He dialed his fraternity house.

"Hello, this is Officer O'Connor at the forty-sixth precinct," he barked into the phone, adopting an Irish brogue. "We've picked up one of your fraternity brothers for drunk and disorderly conduct. His name is Chuck Colson, and unless you can come down to the station and pay his three-hundred-dollar fine, he will spend the night in jail."

"Three hundred dollars!" yelped his friend Jack. "That's a lot of money."

"Well, if you haven't got it," Chuck growled, "then he'll rot in jail. Makes no difference to us."

"No, no, don't do that," Jack insisted. "Let me see what I can do."

"Well, hurry up!" said Chuck, staying in character while managing not to burst out laughing. "You've got thirty minutes." *Click.*

From his vantage point, Chuck watched lights switch on as Jack raced down the dorm hall, passing a hat to bail out a frat brother in trouble. He thoroughly enjoyed the turmoil his ruse created.

Just before his fraternity brothers left the house, Chuck sauntered across the street, hands in his pocket, in the nick of time to save his buddies from a trip to the precinct house.

Upon graduating with academic honors, Chuck was commissioned in the marines and relished the discipline of this elite corps. After serving a two-year stint, he took a job in Washington, D.C., in the office of the Assistant Secretary of the Navy. There he met Senator Leverett Saltonstall from his home state of Massachusetts, and the senator hired the dynamic twenty-four-year-old on the spot. During this time, Chuck was earning a law degree at nights as his father had done.

With Senator Saltonstall, Chuck became the go-to guy, the person behind the candidate who made the campaign organization hum. He oversaw the "boiler room" operations: feeding reporters disinformation, sending out mailings that distorted the opponent's record, and squashing rumors—or planting them. When his last-minute mailer to Irish Democrats in the 1960 Massachusetts senatorial race made it sound as if Democrats were endorsing John Kennedy (a Democrat running for U.S. president) and Leverett Saltonstall (a Republican running for reelection to the Senate), Republican operatives took notice. This kid had a future in the bare-knuckle side of politics.

Chuck demurred instead, returning to private life and his budding law career. He continued, however, to keep a hand in politics throughout the early sixties. Chuck was introduced to Richard Nixon, and he entered into a close relationship with the man who would be president. When Nixon was elected in 1968, Chuck was offered several different posts by Cabinet members, but he turned them down to become Special Counsel to the President of the United States, a heady spot for lawyers who do the president's bidding. By working directly with the president, Chuck had direct access to the most powerful man in the world. Not bad for a Massachusetts boy from a working-class family.

WORKING FOR THE PRESIDENT

Chuck enjoyed sitting in on Cabinet meetings, communicating with congressmen on the president's behalf, and snuffing out political fires before they ignited into full-blown conflagrations. Nixon probably saw a little bit of himself in Chuck Colson and his can-do attitude. When Nixon needed someone to ferret out press leakers during "peace feelers" with the Vietnamese, Russians, and Chinese, Chuck got the call. When Daniel Ellsberg attempted to publish a purloined copy of the Pentagon Papers, Chuck was asked to head it off. His behind-the-scenes work caught the eye of the mainstream press: a *Wall Street Journal* headline in the fall of 1971 blared "Nixon's Hatchet Man: Chuck Colson Handles President's Dirty Work." The story line was buttressed by the following quote from Chuck: "I would do anything that Richard Nixon asks me to do—anything."

That became the template through which all Chuck Colson stories would pass. The Washington press corps, who loved tacking the phrase "the President's hatchet man" onto subsequent stories about him, didn't stop there. They decided the Special Counsel was abrasive, partisan, pompous, and obsessive—the man who said he would be willing to walk over his grandmother for President Nixon (a colorful quote, but one he didn't make). He certainly fit the media's stereotype of a Nixon hatchet man: horn-rimmed glasses, close-cropped hair, brusque ways, and unfettered devotion to his boss.

Actually, Chuck grew to like the "hatchet man" moniker, viewing it as shorthand for his do-anything-at-any-cost style. When the press began harping on a little break-in of Democratic Party offices during the 1972 presidential election cycle, Chuck didn't give it much thought until he received a phone call from the president's chief domestic policy aide, John Ehrlichman.

"Chuck, have you heard from your friend Howard Hunt lately?" asked Ehrlichman.

"I think Hunt is on the Reelection Committee for the president. Why?"

Then Ehrlichman told Colson about a robbery at Democratic Headquarters. "One of the burglars had something with Hunt's name on it in his pocket. I'll get back to you if anything else happens."

When Colson put down the phone, a horrible feeling filled his gut. He remembered months earlier when Howard Hunt had dropped by his office talking about some sort of intelligence plan. He couldn't remember the details, but he hoped this robbery wasn't part of that plan.

Within several weeks, the media linked Chuck to the break-in at the Watergate building since Howard Hunt had once worked for him. Before he knew it, the newspapers were talking as if Nixon's Hatchet Man had orchestrated the break-in.

However, the Watergate scandal failed to catch on with voters, who returned Nixon to the White House in a 1972 landslide. Chuck had already informed the president before the election that no matter who won, he planned to leave the White House and return to his lucrative private law practice. He followed through on that promise.

A Ray of Hope

Upon his return to private life, Chuck noticed that the edge had come off his zeal and competitive drive. Sometimes he felt he was just going through the motions of work.

One day Chuck traveled to Boston to handle some legal matters for an old client, the Raytheon Company, a large electronics company. Tom Phillips, the company president, had asked for the meeting.

Just before he stepped into Phillips's office, an executive cautioned Chuck, "You should know that Tom has changed," he whispered. "He's had a religious experience." Colson was surprised because Phillips had always been an aggressive businessman.

When he walked into his office, Colson noticed a peace about Tom, a peace he wished he had for himself. The Watergate imbroglio was tearing him apart.

After small talk, Chuck made the following observation: "Tom, you've changed. What happened to you?"

"Chuck, I accepted Jesus Christ and committed my life to Him," Tom stated. Chuck took a firm grip on the bottom of his chair. He had never heard anyone talk that way. For Chuck, Jesus Christ was a historical figure, but this executive said that he had accepted Christ as though He were here today. With a nervous feeling, Chuck quickly changed the subject.

Phillips would not be deterred. "Let's get together someday and talk about it more," he offered.

The news about the Watergate break-in continued to dominate the newspapers and television. One day an aide testified in a Senate hearing that all of the president's Oval Office meetings had been secretly taped since 1971.

Suddenly, Chuck was scared. What was on those tapes?

Chuck considered trying to see Tom Phillips. His memory of that meeting with Tom brought such peace to him. When Chuck thought about his Watergate troubles, he felt fear, worry, and pain.

On August 12, 1973, Chuck met with Tom Phillips to find out more about Tom's religious experience. What made him so different?

On a quiet street outside Boston, Chuck pulled into the long driveway of the Phillipses' house. A large, white home stood at the end of the driveway.

Tom led Chuck through the house to a porch with large screened windows. The unusually hot and humid weather helped Tom persuade Chuck to take off his suit coat and finally his necktie.

"Are you okay, Chuck?" Tom asked. The same question had started their conversation earlier in March.

"I'm getting a bit worn down from this Watergate business," Chuck confided. "But I'd prefer to talk about you, Tom. I saw you several years ago, and now you are different. I want to know about it."

That was all the opening Tom needed. He told Chuck how he had worked hard to get ahead. The added workload and success brought him many things: a big home, fancy cars, and corporate power. But he would wake up in the night and wonder how to find a personal relationship with God.

One day while in New York, Tom attended a Billy Graham Crusade and sat in the upper part of the stadium. He heard Dr. Graham say that Jesus was more than a historical figure—He was the living God. At the invitation, Tom Phillips came forward with hundreds of others and gave his life to Christ.

"Since then, there's a book that has meant so much to me," said Tom. "It's called *Mere Christianity* by C. S. Lewis, a university professor in England. I'd like to read a chapter to you, Chuck."

Tom proceeded to read from the chapter entitled, "The Great Sin, Pride." The words struck Colson like a thunderclap. Pride, Chuck realized, was the driving force behind his desire to work in the top echelons of the United States government and with the president of the United States.

"The Lord can change your life, Chuck," Tom said. "Will you pray with me?"

Chuck wasn't sure how to answer the question. He had never prayed with anyone except when someone said grace at mealtimes. Chuck didn't feel like he could pray in someone's living room. *Too much out in the open.*

So Chuck said, "No, but I'll listen as you pray."

Tom's prayers were something Chuck had never experienced. He simply talked with God and skipped the formalities. His prayer sounded like a conversation with a best friend. After a long period of silence, Tom finished with, "Amen."

The men walked back through the house to the kitchen door and said goodbye. Tears welled up in Chuck's eyes as he thought about Tom's relationship with Jesus Christ.

Before he pulled out of the driveway, the words sank in. Suddenly Chuck found that he couldn't get his keys into the ignition. Tears streamed down his cheeks, and he called out to God with the first honest prayer of his life. Over and over, Chuck prayed, "Lord, take me as I am."

The tough guy from the White House, the ex-marine captain and White House Hatchet Man, had found a personal relationship with Jesus Christ.

INSIDE THE BELTWAY

Chuck's decision to follow Christ was private at first. Not even some of his best friends or family knew about his new relationship with Christ, though Tom had arranged for a few Christians to befriend Chuck and help disciple him. But why should anyone else care?

Chuck was invited to a White House Bible study that met twice a month in the basement. One morning, Dan Rather of CBS News posed a question at the daily press briefing.

"Why is the president continuing to see Charles Colson?" Rather asked.

"I don't think he is," replied assistant press secretary Jerry Warren.

"Well, why was Colson at the White House today?" Rather followed.

"He was attending a prayer breakfast that the staff has every other week."

Prayer breakfast. Laughter roared through the press room. No one believed that the president's Hatchet Man would be remotely interested in prayer. When Warren insisted the story was true, panic broke out among the White House press corps. The reporters had a fresh Watergate story on their hands. Many reporters called Chuck at his Washington law office and asked about his decision to follow Christ. In simple and clear statements, Chuck explained his new-found faith.

In the weeks and months to follow, however, Chuck was scorned by the media. They wondered out loud how such an unrepentant defender of Richard Nixon could become a repentant Christian. One cartoonist lampooned Chuck by drawing him in a monk's habit, standing in front of the White House and painting "Repent" on a wall. Few in the political scene of Washington believed that a tough guy like Chuck Colson could change.

Yet his heart had changed. Although he knew he was innocent of planning the break-in, Chuck decided to plead guilty to something that was true: the spreading of false information about Daniel Ellsberg of Pentagon Papers fame.

His lawyer said he would end up in jail and lose his license to practice law.

"Calm down," replied Chuck. "Just tell the prosecutors that I want to tell the truth."

In less than ten minutes, the judge recorded and accepted Chuck Colson's guilty plea. As he lifted his gavel, the judge intoned, "The court will impose a sentence of one to three years and a fine of five thousand dollars." *Whack.*

The gavel sounded, and Chuck felt numb. Prison. That day as Chuck left the courtroom, he was surrounded by a row of micro-phones, cameras, and reporters.

"What happened today is the Lord's will," Chuck said. "I can work for Christ in prison or outside it."

PRISON CHANGES HIM

Jail was no church picnic. Everything that Chuck held important was stripped away from him. His law career. His schooling. His car. His home. His family. But even prison could not strip away his newfound relationship with Jesus Christ.

With a few other prisoners, Chuck began to attend a small Bible study and prayer meeting each evening. They would read the Bible and then pray on their knees. For Chuck, it was like going through spiritual boot camp.

One day a beefy prisoner stopped by his bunk. "Hey, Colson," Archie said. "You'll be out of here before too long. What are you going to do for us?"

"I'll never forget this stinking place or you guys," Chuck promised. "I'll help you in some way."

"Bull!" Archie exclaimed. "Everyone promises, but no one does anything. You'll forget us like the rest. Nobody cares. Nobody."

"Not me, Archie," Chuck said. "I'll remember."

Archie's face flushed with anger. "You'll forget, Colson."

When Chuck was released early after serving seven months, he couldn't put that conversation with Archie out of his mind. Colson knew he had to keep his word. He couldn't forget the men who were left behind.

Chuck decided he would return to prison to teach prisoners about Jesus Christ and how to live a Christian life "on the outside." Yes, he was being called to go back *into* the prisons. Chuck chose to start a ministry to some of the least powerful people in the world—people forgotten by the world, but not by him. Prison Fellowship Ministries would be its name. During the first year after his release, he and a cadre of volunteers began holding seminars and Bible studies in Washington-area prisons.

Those events happened nearly twenty-five years ago, and since then, the ministry has spread to eighty-five countries and virtually every prison in America. In addition, Angel Tree volunteers bring gifts and share Christ with five hundred thousand children of inmates each Christmas. But the impact of Prison Fellowship can hardly be measured in human terms. How many shattered lives have been turned around after hearing a Prison Fellowship chaplain share the gospel? How many prisoners' families have been changed after seeing the visible changes in their loved ones behind bars? How much has society benefited from ex-convicts whose lives were touched by the Savior?

The cliché is that Chuck Colson went from the penthouse to the outhouse, from the corridors of presidential power to three hots and a cot. But that's not the whole story. When the world thought he was history, God was just starting to use Chuck Colson. Since that August day when he asked the Lord to take him as he was, Chuck has founded a global ministry to prisoners and their families, written more than fifteen best-selling books, hosted a daily radio broadcast heard on one thousand stations, become a statesman of the Christian faith, and spoken out as a modern-day Elijah to a post-Christian America.

Assisting in this chapter was W. Terry Whalin of Colorado Springs, Colorado, author of Chuck Colson *(Zondervan Publishing House, 1994).*

11

Paul Stankowski:
AS IRON SHARPENS IRON

AGE:
twenty-nine
OCCUPATION:
golf professional on the PGA Tour
RESIDENCE:
Flower Mound, Texas
FAMILY SITUATION:
married six years to Regina

When I attended the University of Texas at El Paso, I majored in golf and minored in partying. Or maybe I majored in partying and minored in golf. It really depended upon the season, but how I became a Christian is more than birdies, bogeys, and booze, because it was buddies—Christian buddies—who helped me find Christ.

My story begins in the California seaside community of Oxnard, midway between Los Angeles and Santa Barbara. I took up golf when I was eight years old, playing my first round on Easter Sunday (after church, of course) and shooting a 147. I soon got better.

I broke eighty when I was twelve years old and fired my first sub-seventy round when I was fourteen. I loved the game so much that I set my sights on college golf and the University of Texas at El Paso.

I got my wish. In El Paso, I lived in adjoining townhomes with nine guys from the golf team, and life was *party hardy, dude.* I always knew there was a God, but that was as far as it went. I wanted to live life to the fullest, which meant sitting around drinking beer and hitting the bars.

As for college golf, our priorities were to rip the ball a long way, rag on each other, and party. We had no discipline, and it showed on the golf course.

OPEN TO THE GREEN

At the end of my freshman year, I attended a College Golf Fellowship dinner during the NCAA championships. Scott Simpson, who had won the U.S. Open the previous summer, was the guest speaker. For the first time, I heard someone present the gospel in a personal way, but I didn't care. Scott had beaten Tom Watson, my boyhood idol, to win the Open, so I didn't like Scott.

Still, a seed was planted. I filled out a card and checked a box saying I wanted to know more. In the mail, I received a Bible, which I opened a few times but never for long. I kept one spiked shoe in each world: I continued to attend College Golf Fellowship dinners and hear the gospel, but I couldn't stay away from the nineteenth hole—the bar scene.

My brother Tom would share Christ with me, and I can remember telling him, "I'm not ready, Tom. I'm in college, and I'm having a good time. I don't want to give it up. Besides, when I get out of college, I'll settle down."

A Christian buddy John Sosa gave me some Christian music by Michael W. Smith, Rich Mullins, and Geoff Moore & the Distance, urging me to listen. Mullins's "Awesome God" sent shivers down my spine, and one day, while reading the Bible that I had received from

College Golf Fellowship, I turned to the back and saw a section on how to receive Christ.

I followed the steps and prayed to receive Christ. It was March 9, 1990, and I wrote down in my Bible that I had asked Christ into my heart and had become a Christian. I thought this was really cool.

But don't forget: I was still living with nine guys who weren't Christians. In a week or two, I shut the Bible and returned to the care-free life.

On March 9, 1991, one year to the day that I had prayed to receive Christ, my brother Tom was getting married. I couldn't wait to go to the wedding because I knew I'd see some Christian friends who could help straighten me out. I spent all weekend hanging out with Tom and his buddies, but it was a different kind of fun than I had had with my golf buddies. This was *clean* fun, and I could see the joy in their lives.

Just before the wedding ceremony started, we formed a circle around Tom to pray for him. I was the last to pray, and when it came to my turn, I was so overwhelmed that all I could say was "Thank You, Lord, for my brother."

Tom was weeping, I was weeping, and it was one of those moments when I felt God's love. God took one part of my life—the partying—and wiped it out. I became an on-fire baby Christian, joined Fellowship of Christian Athletes, and hooked up with First Baptist Church in El Paso. I made some good Christian friends and began to understand what Proverbs 27:17 means: "As iron sharpens iron, so one man sharpens another."

At a dress rehearsal of a youth group musical, I saw a young singer named Regina. Instantly smitten, I asked her out. Our first date was church and Chili's, and we were married eighteen months later.

HITTING IN REGULATION

These days I'm one of many young players trying to make an impact on the PGA Tour. There are a lot of hot twenty-something players out there—David Duval, Phil Mickelson, Justin Leonard, Ernie Els, and some guy named Tiger. But let me tell you, it's a tough profession.

I first earned my PGA Tour card in 1993 at Q School, the PGA Tour qualifying tournament held during six days of intense competition. More than twelve hundred golfers compete for thirty-five spots on the PGA Tour.

As a rookie, I kept missing cuts by one or two strokes. Of course, when you miss cuts, you don't earn any money, and I needed to be in the top 125 on the money list to keep my card. I took a week off, and our church had a youth group program called "Disciple Now" in which Regina and I volunteered our time. We took a dozen sixth graders, played football with them, taught them the Word, and spent a long weekend with them. Then I got a phone call saying I could play the Bob Hope Classic in Palm Springs, but I hadn't been practicing at all. I hopped on a plane and amazingly finished sixth. That's when I realized I could play with the big boys.

Back at my home outside of Dallas, a commemorative glass from the 1996 Masters sits in a trophy case in my study. It's the sort of souvenir that spectators in the Masters gallery take home to impress their neighbors. I purchased the memento because I thought I would never return to the fabled grounds of the Augusta National Country Club after I played the event. I scooped a glassful of sand from one of Augusta's bunkers and placed on top of the sand the tee and ball that I used to birdie the final hole.

The commemorative glass serves as a reminder: At one time, I used to hoist a different kind of glass . . . one filled with beer. I don't need to do that anymore, not since I joined another gallery—the one following Jesus Christ.

12

Kimberly Davis:
FINDING THE LORD
OF THE DANCE

AGE:
forty-three
OCCUPATION:
homemaker
RESIDENCE:
Solana Beach, California

When I was a young girl, my mother impressed the following statements on me: "There will be no knight in shining armor in your life. Get everything you can for yourself—career, travel, and money— *before* you have children. Otherwise, it will be too late."

Pessimism reigned in our agnostic home. My parents, who were nonpracticing Jews, told me that religion caused more wars and more suffering than anything else on the planet. "When you're old enough, you can figure out for yourself if there is any God," said my mother.

I showed no interest in figuring that out. I decided at age four— after being mesmerized by Gene Kelly's dance steps in *Two on the*

Town—that I would become a dancer and let my little feet take me around the world.

I asked my mom to enroll me in dance lessons, where I poured myself into the joy of the music and the sheer delight of physical exertion. By the time I hit puberty, however, I was swaybacked, knock-kneed, pigeon-toed, and developing—while my dancing friends were flat-chested and trim. I overheard the head of the Los Angeles Ballet Company tell my mother, "She's a cute kid, but she'll never become a dancer!"

My parents divorced when I was twelve. We were forced to sell our family home, and my mother started selling real estate to make a living. We moved from apartment to apartment while she sat on model homes at various real estate tracts. While she worked long hours and weekends, I hid out at the ballet studio.

Meanwhile, school was easy for me; I tested out at sixteen years of age as a high school junior. I enrolled at UCLA on dance and academic scholarships and began winning disco-dance contests in the Los Angeles club scene. Disco dancing was hot in the mid- to late-seventies, and while I may not have been a great technical dancer, I was a great performer who knew how to sell myself.

I always had work—modeling, TV commercials, and background dancing in movies. I even choreographed late-night dance shows like *Wolfman Jack's Midnight Special* and *Hot City*. To keep a check on my weight, I turned to speed and cocaine. I was on a roller coaster, but a gilded one: I would dance three shows a night, join my friends, hit the discos until 4:00 or 5:00 A.M., and fall into bed and sleep until noon. Then I would wake up, swim, attend a ballet class, and start the first of my three shows. I was making entirely too much money for someone in her twenties with no parental supervision, but, by the world's standards, I had it all—success, wealth, youth, beauty, and thrills!

Inside, however, I was hollow and slowly dying.

My little feet did indeed take me all over the world, and in 1983, I began performing at the Sun City resort in Bophuthatswana, South

Africa. On my day off, Bernard, one of the maitre d's at the resort, talked me into riding a dirt bike in the bush. I was speeding along when I lost control and crashed, sliding under a Volkswagen bus. The dirt bike's gear shift impaled my left foot, and nearly every bone on the left side of my body was broken.

I endured three surgeries and traction for several months in South Africa. When I asked my doctors if I would ever dance again, they told me to worry about walking first. My body had failed me, and I was left without my chosen god—dancing.

The company I danced for tried to have me deported for breaking my contract. Homeless and unable to travel, I moved in with Bernard, the young Parisian who had befriended me. Swooning under his charming French accent and his sincere efforts to mend me back to health, Bernard became my new god. He asked me to make a baby with him, and I quickly agreed. When we left South Africa and moved to San Diego in 1985, I was visibly pregnant.

We were married, much to the dismay of my friends and the warnings of my mother. They could see that Bernard was a *charmeur,* but I couldn't. It was clear he wasn't the happiest or nicest man in the world, but he was my hero. Couldn't I change him with enough love? Wouldn't things be different with a baby?

The answers to both questions were no. Just after our daughter, Nathalie, was born, the verbal and emotional abuse began—finally escalating to physical abuse. Bernard was no longer my beloved; he was a monster driven by hatred and evil. He once admitted that he had sold his soul to the devil and said he couldn't sleep until he had made somebody miserable every day. That somebody usually turned out to be me.

The abuse never stopped. Eventually, he started applying emotional abuse to our daughter and our unplanned little baby boy, Nico. He favored Nathalie—who was his idea—and often doted on her. I let him get away with it, making excuses for him, not telling anyone. I wanted to have a picture-perfect family and to honor my marriage vows.

Meanwhile, my self-image was slipping away. I believed Bernard when he called me stupid and ugly. I believed him when he called me a lousy mother and terrible wife. When I threatened to leave him, he promised to kill me and the children. On other occasions, he talked about kidnapping our daughter and fleeing to a place where I could never find them. He assured me that if I ever tried to run away with the children, he would torture and kill my mother. In fact, his eyes lit up with delight when he described how he would take a knife to my mother and cut her up into pieces.

I was terrified of Bernard. He was brilliant and cunning beyond his years, and although I was financially supporting him (he had no green card yet) through a mail-order business I took over from my mother, all I could see was this horrible, clouded self-image.

On the evening of August 30, 1990, Bernard and I went out to dinner at a nearby Italian restaurant. We were leaving the parking lot when he asked me for the parking ticket. Realizing I had failed to have it validated, he went off on another one of his abusive jags. "You're fat, ugly, worthless, and incompetent!" he spat out. "You're stupid, so stupid!"

I threw the ticket into his lap. "Why don't you handle this yourself like any other man would?"

Silence filled the car. That was the *first* time I had ever talked back to him.

I was dead meat.

When we arrived home, Bernard attacked the furniture before he turned on me. He threw chairs, punched walls, kicked toys, broke dishes, and threw a knife at me, striking a copper pot hanging on a wall.

Then he turned on me, grabbing my neck with one hand and pinning me against our bedroom wall. He tried to suffocate me, and I gasped for air.

"I'm sick of you, I'm sick of this stupid country, and I'm going to bury you in that garden of yours that you care so much about," he screamed. "You and that son of yours."

He stomped out of the house and was gone all night. The next day, Nathalie went to spend the night with Grandma, and Nico and I gardened all day. After dinner, I kissed Nico goodnight and put him to sleep in his bedroom on the other side of the house.

Meanwhile, I waited for Bernard to come home from his work at an upscale restaurant. I lay in bed, wondering what he was going to do with me when he got home and very terrified about what could happen. Shortly after 1:00 A.M., he arrived and began pacing and swearing out loud in French.

Rage was building in him like an inferno. He was seething, and his eyes were practically glowing in the dark. I had never seen this much anger in a human being.

He started in again about how much he hated me and this country and how he was sick of me. "I'm going to bury you—dead or alive—in that garden you love so much!" he screamed.

He came to the edge of the bed, grabbed my throat, and started choking me again. I knew I was in a fight for my life, but I also knew that I was in a fight for my son's life. Suddenly, he let go and laughed at me. Satisfied that he had terrified me within an inch of my life, he lay down on the bed to sleep.

I decided I couldn't take it anymore. He had pushed me beyond my limit, and I knew it was a matter of time before he made good on his threats and didn't stop choking me. I reached under the bed and found a fishing knife that Bernard insisted I keep there to protect our daughter. I thrust the knife deep into his right lung. He jumped up, and we had a life-and-death struggle for the knife. During the fight I stabbed him four or five more times before he collapsed and died.

But I didn't know he was dead. I thought he would get up and come after me again. At dawn, when he hadn't moved for a couple of hours, I dragged his body to the garden and buried him so my son wouldn't see him. I didn't call the police for two days because I knew I would be going to prison for the rest of my life, and I wasn't ready to say goodbye to my babies.

Before I called 911, I phoned my brother in northern California and asked him to come take care of our mother. Then I called my mother and asked her to come take care of my children because I had just killed Bernard and was going to jail.

When the police arrived at the crime scene, they escorted me to jail and booked me on five counts of murder: first degree, second degree, voluntary and involuntary manslaughter, and assault with a deadly weapon. Each carried a sentence of thirty-five years to life in prison with no chance of parole.

After I spent two weeks in jail telling my story to the district attorney, I was released on bail. The trial date was set for June 1991.

Being home again with my children was such a relief. Then I started having recurring dreams in which I would hear a voice say, *Kimberly, go back to your roots . . . back to your roots.*

What were my roots? All I could think of was ballet. I enrolled in a class for broken-down, worn-out ballerinas, and even though my body couldn't respond the way it used to, it felt great to hear the music again!

After a month of class, on the second Friday in November, I was standing in the middle of the dance floor. We were starting the adagio section, which I loved and dreaded at the same time. As the strains of music pervaded the airy room, it filled with a bright, blinding light until I couldn't see myself in the mirror. I couldn't see my hand in front of my face. All I could see was light. Every hair on my body stood straight up, every pore was at attention, but why? I couldn't move!

I heard a voice, like no other, speak clearly to me. *Don't be afraid. I am with you, and I love you. You are going to be okay. I am going to protect you with My right hand. It is I, your God. Don't be afraid. I want you to go to My house and learn about My Son, Jesus Christ.*

The light faded, and I looked around the room to see if anybody else had heard or seen anything, but they were all dancing as if nothing had happened. I felt elated, yet calm, as I experienced God's presence. For one fleeting moment, I began to dance with a youthfulness that I hadn't experienced in a long time.

When I stopped, I turned to my instructor, and her mouth was wide open in amazement. Others had seen me dance, as well. "Where did that come from?" one asked.

Overwhelmed with emotion and fear, I ran from the dance studio and jumped into my car, crying.

I've lost my mind, I thought as I struggled to regain my composure. I was so frightened. Recently, I had lost my grandmother and father to cancer, killed my husband, was soon to lose my children, and now I was losing my mind!

I had to be mad. I started driving, and while stopped at a light, I noticed a community church at the intersection. I had passed that church a thousand times but had never been drawn to it before that day. I turned into the parking lot.

I walked into the chapel and caught my breath. Tears came, but I forced myself to stay under control. I slid into a pew and reached for a Bible. The book fell open to the first chapter of Proverbs. I began to read verse 7: "The fear of the LORD is the beginning of knowledge, but fools despise wisdom and discipline."

Hmmm, that's interesting, I thought. Then I read verses 27–33:

> . . . . when calamity overtakes you like a storm, when disaster sweeps over you like a whirlwind, when distress and trouble overwhelm you. Then they will call to me but I will not answer; they will look for me but will not find me. Since they hated knowledge and did not choose to fear the LORD, since they would not accept my advice and spurned my rebuke, they will eat the fruit of their ways and be filled with the fruit of their schemes. For the waywardness of the simple will kill them, and the complacency of fools will destroy them; but whoever listens to me will live in safety and be at ease, without fear of harm.

That's my life, I thought. *My life has been a calamity—just like my stage name, Calamity—for many years. Everywhere I go, trouble follows. I've always said people who believe in God are idiots, freaks who need some fairy-tale crutch. I don't even know if there is a God, except that He has just talked to me. Unless I am crazy!*

I went to the church office and asked the secretary if I could talk to someone immediately. God, in His great compassion, sent me a woman pastor. I told her the whole story in almost one breath. She asked if I had a Bible, and I replied no. I remembered the man who had slipped a Bible under my door in the prison cell, but I had kicked it back into the hallway. *I don't want that thing cluttering up my life,* I had thought. *What rubbish.*

"Kimberly, I'd like to read something to you," said Mary, the pastor. She opened a Bible to Isaiah 41:10, 13 and asked me to read with her: "So do not fear, for I am with you; do not be dismayed, for I am your God. I will strengthen you and help you; I will uphold you with my righteous right hand. . . . For I am the LORD, your God, who takes hold of your right hand and says to you, Do not fear; I will help you."

"That's exactly what He said to me earlier today!" I cried out in amazement. She told me that these same words were spoken to a man named Isaiah nearly three thousand years ago. I could hardly contain myself. I knew in that instant that everything in the Bible was true. I knew that God was real and that Jesus was His Son. I knew I wasn't crazy.

Later that day, I picked up my five-year-old daughter, Nathalie, from kindergarten. The first words out of her mouth were, "Mom, do you believe in God?"

I looked at her in shock. "If you had asked me that question a week or even a day ago, I would have said that I wasn't sure. But today, I can wholeheartedly tell you, yes!"

"Me, too, Mommy! Today, on the playground, God talked to me and told me He loved me."

Our next stop was to pick up her three-year-old brother from the preschool at the Presbyterian church. (My neighbor had enrolled Nico there while I was in jail. Was that a coincidence?) As we walked to the classroom to pick him up, he ran out to greet us.

"Mom, guess what?"

"What is it, Nico?" I already knew.

"We had our chapel visit today, and Baby Jesus spoke to me and told me He loved me."

I stood up with tears rolling down my cheeks. God had spoken to all three of us at the same time. I wasn't crazy or imagining every-thing.

Lord Jesus, I believe in You, I prayed silently.

When I got home, I called the church secretary and asked her, "Well, how do you go to church? Do I have to sign up?"

"All you have to do is come," she replied kindly.

"Is there any cost?"

"No, the church is free and open to all who want to come," she chuckled.

Thus started my long walk of faith, based on a burning desire to know about an omnipresent God who was alive, who was real, and who loved me and my children.

But I still had to face a murder trial for killing my husband. I knew I would be convicted and spend the rest of my life in prison. My time was limited, so I joined a women's Bible study and learned all I could about Jesus, whose love for me was so great that He died for me—a killer.

All sorts of supernatural things happened during my trial, includ-ing the beautiful, golden-haired journalist who passed me a piece of paper that contained a thirteenth-century prayer for winning in court, complete with detailed instructions and scripture. Later, when I turned to point her out to my attorney, she was gone. At the break, I asked the gentleman who had been sitting next to her where she had gone.

"What woman?" he asked, looking at me curiously. "That chair has been vacant all morning."

On June 26, 1991, the verdict came in. During the entire trial, I had prayed, "Lord, when the bailiff walks over here to put me in handcuffs to take me away, let me go with dignity and not kicking and screaming!"

But the Lord never does what you expect—or gives you what you deserve. Zechariah 4:6 says, "'Not by might [the attorneys] nor by power [the courts], but by my Spirit,' says the LORD Almighty."

On the charge of murder in the first degree, we find the defendant not guilty. On the charge of murder in the second degree, we find the defendant not guilty. . . .

Jesus took my guilt with Him to a cross, and He died so that I might have eternal life.

After the trial, I sold my mail-order business and began leading a women's Bible study. A couple of years after the acquittal, the Lord provided a wonderful husband when I met and fell in love with David Davis. We are currently rearing three children together: Danielle, Nathalie, and Nico.

13

Dr. Bill Bright:
A FIFTY-YEAR CRUSADE

AGE:
seventy-eight
OCCUPATION:
founder and president of
Campus Crusade for Christ International
RESIDENCE:
Orlando, Florida
FAMILY SITUATION:
married to Vonette for fifty-one years;
father of two adult children and grandfather of four grandchildren

Editor's note: Dr. Bill Bright and the organization he founded, Campus Crusade for Christ, have led millions to salvation through Jesus Christ. He literally wrote the book on modern-day evangelism. In 1957, Dr. Bright authored Have You Heard of the Four Spiritual Laws, *and that life-saving tract has been reproduced approximately two billion times and translated into two hundred languages.*

Time has passed so quickly, and it seems impossible to comprehend that my spiritual journey began fifty-five years ago. I had the good fortune to be reared in a wonderful home on an Oklahoma ranch by a nonbelieving father and a saintly mother who prayed for me every day of my life. I was vaguely aware of this, but I wrongly assumed that all mothers were equally devout. But Mom also gave me a high standard of ethics and integrity.

For all practical purposes, however, I was an atheist. The idea of God, the Bible, or a Savior had little place in my life. I was more interested in accomplishing the materialistic goals I had set for myself and becoming the captain of my universe.

As part of my grand quest, I moved to Hollywood, California. I was in my midtwenties, ready to make my fortune in the confectionery business through hard work and long hours. I started Bright's California Confections, selling brandied fruits, candies, jams, jellies, and special epicurean delights to big department stores such as Neiman Marcus, J. W. Robinson's, and Bullock's Wilshire.

Then one day, I remember distinctly, I first sensed in a powerful way an unseen presence in my life. I can only describe it as a sovereign visit from God. An elderly couple asked me to join them at First Presbyterian Church of Hollywood. It was there, for the first time, that I heard about the great Creator God of the universe, who, according to the Bible, spoke and created what astronomers describe as one hundred billion or more galaxies, and that Earth was like a grain of sand in all the vastness of His creation.

This started a journey of inquiry for me. Who was behind this creation? What I discovered was absolutely astonishing. To my surprise, three hundred details of Jesus' life had been predicted by ancient Hebrew scholars and prophets hundreds of years before He was born. Micah predicted He would be born in Bethlehem; Moses said He would be from the tribe of Judah and from the seed of Abraham, Isaac, and Jacob; Daniel predicted the actual time of His coming; Isaiah said that He would be born of a virgin, a conception necessary for the God-man; and David told of His resurrection and ascension into heaven.

Philosophers, I learned, said that Jesus uttered the greatest words ever spoken. He cleansed the lepers, healed the sick, cast out devils, raised the dead, and performed miracles such as no other person has ever performed. He claimed to be God in the flesh. He claimed that He was the only way to the Father and that He came to show us the way to eternal life. He predicted His own death and resurrection. After His resurrection, He was seen by the disciples on several occasions and by more than five hundred people at one time.

I was attending classes led by Dr. Henrietta Mears, Hollywood Presbyterian's Director of Christian Education. One day, after outlining the story of Paul's conversion experience on the way to Damascus, she challenged us to receive Christ. I went home that night and, in the privacy of my home, got down on my knees and asked Jesus Christ to be my Savior and Lord of my life.

In 1946, I enrolled in Princeton Theological Seminary while running my Hollywood business long-distance. Fuller Theological Seminary opened its doors in 1947 in Pasadena, California, so I enrolled in the first class. I attended classes in the mornings while operating my confectionery business in the afternoons and evenings.

The same year I enrolled in Princeton, I became engaged to a lovely young woman named Vonette Zachary, whom I had known since she was a little girl. However, there was only one problem: Vonette had been active in the Methodist Church since she was a child, but after our engagement, I discovered that she wasn't a Christian! Since we were in love, I feared that Vonette would say yes to Christ just to please me. I asked Dr. Mears to explain the gospel to her, and I can't tell you how great I felt when Vonette gave her heart to the Lord. Soon after, we were married on December 30, 1948.

Although we had both been very materialistic and ambitious, three years after our marriage Vonette and I came to the same conclusion: knowing and serving Jesus were more important than all the wealth and the power in the world. On a Sunday afternoon in the spring of 1951, Vonette and I, in our Hollywood Hills home, got on our knees and prayed, "Lord, we surrender our lives to do Your will. We will go where You want us to go and do what You want us to do, whatever the cost. We want to be Yours completely, irrevocably."

Then we backed up our words. We wrote out and actually signed a contract with the Lord, surrendering our whole lives to Him. Vonette and I made a decision to relinquish all of our rights, all of our possessions, everything we would ever own, and give them to our Master and Lord. Since then, we have experienced a most incredible, rich, fulfilling, and rewarding adventure.

What It Means to Really Live

Vonette and I were deeply inspired by the Lord's challenge recorded in Mark 8: "If any of you wants to be my follower . . . you must put aside your own pleasures and shoulder your cross, and follow me closely. If you insist on saving your life, you will lose it. Only those who throw away their lives for my sake and for the sake of the Good News will ever know what it means to really live" (vv. 34–35, TLB).

To really live! Vonette and I had known an exciting life already in our young marriage, but here was a promise that exceeded everything we had experienced. We were further encouraged by that wonderful passage in Mark 10, where Peter approached Jesus and said, "We've given up everything to follow you." In effect, Peter was asking, "What are Your plans for our future? What is going to happen to us?"

Jesus replied, "Let me assure you that no one has ever given up anything—home, brothers, sisters, mother, father, children, or property—for love of me and to tell others the Good News, who won't be given back, a hundred times over, homes, brothers, sisters, mothers, children, and land—with persecutions! All these will be his here on earth, and in the world to come he shall have eternal life" (vv. 29–30, TLB).

As a businessman, that sounded like a good investment to me.

Whatever I invested in the kingdom of God, Jesus said it would be returned one hundredfold! How could anyone turn down such a remarkable offer from our Lord Himself? I must say, however, that my real motive in living for and serving Jesus was because of who He is and for all that He had done for me.

As I wondered what I should do next, I recalled the days of my youth growing up on a ranch in Oklahoma. My father and mother, with five sons and two daughters, grew grain for livestock. I remember one summer was unseasonably rainy, and a big flooding storm came at harvest time. There was a particular area near a small river where the soil was very rich and the grain was magnificent.

Quickly, all that harvest grain was covered with rain. When the water receded, my father made an important decision: we could save the grain if we went all out. So all of us, including neighbors, went into the muddy field with heavy equipment and managed to salvage the grain with great difficulty. My father's view was that other things around the farm would have to wait until we saved our choicest grain.

God has a similar principle. There are many important things in life, but there is nothing more important in God's economy than salvaging the immediate harvest—the harvest of souls that will otherwise be lost.

This was an early lesson for me. God has called me to help bring in the harvest by working with others to complete the Great Commission given by our Lord Jesus Christ shortly before His ascension. By God's grace and with His help, I founded Campus Crusade for Christ in 1951. Now, forty-eight years later, we have almost twenty thousand full-time staff members and more than three hundred thousand trained associates and volunteers in 172 countries.

As of June 1, 1998, we have had the privilege of taking the gospel to more than three billion people. Tens of millions, if not hundreds of millions, have indicated salvation decisions. In the midseventies, we produced the *Jesus* film, a full-length movie on the life of Christ. The film has now been viewed by more than 1.5 billion people in 475 languages in 222 countries. Billions more are just waiting for someone to tell them the truth about our Lord Jesus Christ.

Some years ago, I encountered one such person. I was speaking on a large university campus when a young radical confronted me. I discovered later that he was the head of the Communist Party on this big campus. He stood up before all the students and railed at me. He didn't like the idea that I was encouraging students to follow Christ as their Lord and Savior. He had other plans for these students, namely, training them to be communists. Rather than argue, I invited him to come to our home for dinner, and he accepted.

I found him to be a brilliant man, articulate and winsome. We talked about a wide range of subjects throughout dinner, and he proved to be a delightful guest. Finally, after the dessert plates had been taken away, I picked up my Bible and said, "I want to read something to you from the Bible."

"I have read the Bible from cover to cover," he reacted with obvious irritation. "It's a ridiculous book. It's filled with contradictions, lies, and myths. I don't want to hear anything from the Bible."

"If you don't mind, I would like to read anyway." I started reading from the Gospel of John:

> Before anything else existed, there was Christ, with God. He has always been alive and is himself God. He created everything there is—nothing exists that he didn't make. Eternal life is in him, and this life gives light to all mankind. His life is the light that shines through the darkness—and the darkness can never extinguish it. . . . And Christ became a human being and lived here on earth among us and was full of loving forgiveness and truth. And some of us have seen his glory—the glory of the only Son of the heavenly Father! (1:1–5, 14, TLB)

Remember, he had told me that he had read the Bible from cover to cover. When I finished that passage, however, he said, "Let me read that. I don't remember seeing that." He read it thoughtfully and handed the Bible back to me without comment. Then I turned to a passage in Colossians and read it out loud:

> For he has rescued us out of the darkness and gloom of Satan's kingdom and brought us into the kingdom of his dear Son, who bought our freedom with his blood and forgave us all our sins. Christ is the exact likeness of the unseen God. He existed before God made anything at all, and, in fact, Christ himself is the Creator who made everything in heaven and earth, the things we can see and the things we can't; the spirit world with its kings and kingdoms, its rulers and authorities; all were made by Christ for his own use and glory. He was before all else began and it is his power that holds everything together. . . .
>
> This is what I have asked God for you: that you will be encouraged and knit together by strong ties of love, and that you will have the rich experience of knowing Christ with real certainty and clear understanding. *For God's secret plan, now at last made known, is Christ himself.* In him lie hidden all the mighty, untapped treasures of wisdom and knowledge. (1:13–17; 2:2–3, TLB)

Again the young student said, "I have never seen that before. May I read it?" I handed the Bible to him again. When he was finished, he soberly handed it back to me without comment. I turned to the Book of Hebrews:

> Long ago God spoke in many different ways to our fathers through the prophets [in visions, dreams, and even face to face], telling them little by little about his plans. But now in these days he has spoken to us through his Son to whom he has given everything, and through whom he made the world and everything there is. (1:1–2, TLB)

By this time, the young man was obviously moved. His entire attitude and countenance had changed. We chatted for some time, and when he stood to leave, I asked if he would write in our guest book. He penned his name and address, after which he wrote these words: "The night of decision," a decision to receive and follow Jesus.

THE LEAST OF THESE

Needless to say, I have had many moving experiences in the past fifty years of helping people find God—thereby finding meaning and purpose in their lives. I remember the time I was invited by a warden to speak to the inmates at the notorious Federal Penitentiary in Atlanta. Before I spoke, I heard several prisoners talk about how they had been forgiven by God through faith in Christ. One man spoke of how he had murdered five people; another mentioned three. Others had committed similarly horrible crimes.

Tears streamed down my face as I listened to these testimonies of God's forgiveness, grace, goodness, and love. Again and again, each prisoner said, "I'm glad I'm here. If I had not been sent here, I would not know Christ, and I would probably be dead because of my life of crime."

I contrasted the prisoners to the guests at a Hollywood dinner that I had attended two nights previously. It was a gala event in which famous movie stars, producers, directors, and entertainers were gathered to honor one of their own.

I sat next to the wife of a famous actor. I had hardly taken my seat when the woman began to tell me how miserable she was and how she was thinking about committing suicide. She said she had nothing to live for, although she lived in a palatial mansion and had a great fortune at her disposal.

When I happily shared the joyful news of Christ's love for her, I saw a dramatic change in her countenance. She seemed overwhelmed to learn that God loved her and had a wonderful plan for her life. She asked if she could keep the evangelistic *Four Spiritual Laws* booklet that I had shared with her. She found its contents were so wonderful that she wanted to read it over and over again.

The contrast was overwhelming. I thought of the people in Hollywood with wealth, fame, power, and their own egocentric and materialistic desires and pursuits. They thought they were free, but they were actually in prison, a self-imposed prison. Sadly this is true for most people throughout the world today.

Then I thought of the prisoners in the Atlanta federal penitentiary. They were free, even though they were serving life sentences and would never see the light of day outside those gray, bleak walls. They were still free, rejoicing and giving thanks to their Savior. Oh, what a contrast! God's pardon, peace, purpose, and power are available to everyone—from prisoners to Hollywood actors and actresses.

Dear friends, the driving force of my life is to help complete the Great Commission given by our Lord, and we don't have much time. It is obvious that, because of our disobedience, America and much of the world are coming under God's judgment. Violence is widespread, nuclear and biological weapons are available to terrorists, and new strains of disease are epidemic. The interdependent world economy is a house of cards built on debt, electronic money transfers, and computer entries. This economy could collapse with one major disaster.

I am greatly concerned about the spiritual condition and future of my own country. God has blessed America with prosperity and power above all nations in history. With only 6 percent of the world's population, America owns more than 50 percent of the world's wealth.

But there is no doubt that America is losing God's former blessings and is now under His discipline. This has resulted from almost four decades of anti-God sentiment in our government and society.

To give us a better understanding of what awaits us if we do not turn back to the God of creation, we need only to look at modern-day Russia. Russia had more than nine hundred years of Christianity and was rich in culture, art, literature, music, poetry, and mineral resources (oil and precious metals). But after seventy-two years of atheistic communism, when God was outlawed from every segment of society, the country today is a pathetic wasteland—morally, spiritually, economically, and politically. The great and wonderful people of Russia are victims of a cruel, godless system of tyrannical leaders who rejected the truth of what Jesus taught and led the nation astray.

By contrast, South Korea was a devastated nation at the end of the Korean War in 1953. Starvation was a serious problem. North Korea was a belligerent neighbor and constantly threatened to invade. Because of their desperate plight, the South Koreans were forced to pray, fast, and cry out for God's help. And now, miracle of miracles, South Korea has become a model for the Christians of the world. In less than twenty-five years, that desperate country has become one of the most dynamic spiritual countries of the world. The followers of Christ grew from one million in the fifties to eleven million in the nineties. South Korea is now sending missionaries to many countries around the globe, including the United States!

That's why God's promise to Solomon for ancient Israel, recorded in 2 Chronicles 7:14, can be claimed by believers of all nations: "If my people, who are called by my name, will humble themselves and pray and seek my face and turn from their wicked ways, then will I hear from heaven and will forgive their sin and will heal their land."

In the lengthening shadows of my life, I am preparing to pass the torch to you and to others. Will you accept that torch and join with me and millions of others who are already committed to following Christ, proclaiming "the most joyful news ever announced," to help populate the kingdom of heaven, and to help build a better world here on planet Earth?

More than half the people who have ever been alive are alive today. Those who do not know God desperately need to meet our great Creator and heavenly Father who "so loved the world that he gave his one and only Son, that whoever believes in him shall not perish but have eternal life" (John 3:16).

14

Mary Gaites:
TOUCHED BY HER SISTERS

AGE:
forty-two
OCCUPATION:
homemaker
RESIDENCE:
Flowery Branch, Georgia
FAMILY SITUATION:
married to Trent Gaites for twenty years;
mother of Travis, fifteen; and Taylor, eleven

I grew up in Battle Creek, Michigan, the sixth of seven children. My parents were hard-working, salt-of-the-earth people, and I remember a wonderful childhood with always someone to play with. My story begins with the religion I was raised in. My mom was brought up in the Christian Science church and my dad was a Methodist, but for whatever reason, Christian Science was the church of choice in our home.

In case you do not know much about Christian Science, the religion was founded in 1879 by Mary Baker Eddy, who ordained herself as pastor of the "Mother Church." Christian Scientists do not believe that you must accept Jesus Christ as Lord for salvation. In fact, it is a religion that says everyone is going to heaven—more or less—because there is no such thing as hell. There is also no such thing as disease, sin, the judgment of God, or the need for repentance. Christian Science prides itself on being a "mind-over-matter" religion, and the only thing I remember hearing about Christ in the Christian Science church was that Jesus was a good man.

Our family moved to the Atlanta area when I was ten years old. In my seventh-grade year during Thanksgiving break, my family drove to Daytona Beach, Florida, for a few days. Naturally, everyone spent most of the day at the beach, but since the weather was overcast most of the time, sunscreen did not seem necessary. When everyone got sunburned, no one thought much about it.

My sister Wendy suffered the worst burn, which caused her legs, ankles, and feet to swell up. At the time, we thought it was a bad case of sun poisoning. A few days later, however, Wendy went into convulsions and experienced a seizure. She was rushed to the hospital, where doctors conducted a series of tests. They determined that she was suffering from the most severe form of lupus called systemic lupus erythematosus (SLE), which attacks the internal organs as well as the skin. Symptoms were fever, painful and swollen joints, facial rashes, loss of hair, and sores on the body, mouth, and nose. Wendy was displaying severe symptoms of SLE.

The doctors told us the disease involved a breakdown of the body's immune system. Did her sunburn cause it? They didn't want to say, but it seems too coincidental to rule out. Not much was known about SLE in 1970, especially how to treat it. Wendy's doctors told my parents they were only aware of three other cases similar to Wendy's SLE.

Her damaged kidneys were not able to process the fluids inside her body. She swelled up with forty pounds of extra water, which settled mainly from her waist down. Sores appeared constantly on her face, and they oozed with a horrible odor. Doctors prescribed strong doses of prednisone and cortisone. Wendy tried to stay out of the sun as much as possible, but her condition remained the same.

On several occasions, her body went into seizures because of too much water, which caused her to be hospitalized for two to three weeks in order to drain off the excess fluid. I can't begin to imagine what must have been going through her mind. Wendy was an eighteen-year-old senior in high school, an outgoing young woman who played on the volleyball, basketball, and fencing teams. She was engaged to a prince of a guy who thought she still looked beautiful.

Seeing doctors was against the tenets of the Christian Science church, which believes in Christian Science practitioners and not conventional medicine. The practitioners are little more than faith healers who "pray" over the disease or wounded area and urge adherents to use mind over matter to heal themselves.

Wendy steadily lost hope that she would ever get better. Remember, we were still attending a Christian Science church, and Wendy felt that she was a hypocrite for not consulting a Christian Science practitioner. Since she wasn't getting better by following doctor's orders, Wendy decided to place her faith in a Christian Science practitioner. Her regular doctors never made it clear to my parents that Wendy would die if she stopped taking her medicine. Since my parents could see Wendy was not getting any better, they were willing and desperate to do anything at this point, including seeing a Christian Science practitioner.

"I need you to support me," Wendy pleaded to the family near the end of her senior year, and we did.

As a seventh grader I didn't understand that she was making a life-or-death decision—and she probably didn't, either. As she received "treatment" from a practitioner, her condition steadily worsened. I remember watching her struggle to walk across the stage to receive her high school diploma. With each passing week, her condition noticeably worsened, but Wendy had put her total faith in Christian Science and the practitioner trying to heal her.

I was beginning to wonder where God was and why He was not healing her. Suddenly, after a session with her practitioner, Wendy returned home looking remarkably better. Her facial rash had virtually disappeared. Our family was shocked. I fell to my knees and said, *God, You really are going to heal her. Thank You!* I didn't have to worry anymore. God was taking care of her.

HANGING ON

A couple of days later, I spent the night with a girlfriend. The next morning, my mother called me.

"Wendy's in the hospital," Mom informed me. "We were sitting around the kitchen table last night, and Wendy said, 'Mom, take me to the hospital. I don't think I'm going to make it through the night.'"

She did make it through that night, but the following morning at 3:00 A.M., her kidneys and her heart couldn't handle the stress and extra fluid, and they stopped functioning. She died a few weeks before her nineteenth birthday.

I remember experiencing great shock and wondering, *Why, God? Why this apparent healing and then three days later she is dead?* The grief that my family experienced cannot adequately be conveyed. Mom and Dad blamed themselves and each other for her death.

"If only we had made her go to the doctor, she would still be with us," my mother said hundreds of times during the next few months. But Wendy had more faith and courage than anyone I had ever known; I don't believe she could have been persuaded to see a regular doctor.

Interestingly, only one person from the Christian Science church attended her funeral. After Wendy was buried, we were viewed by the Christian Science church as pariahs—laggards who hadn't prayed hard enough. We were the ones who had failed, not God.

We were not welcome anymore in the Christian Science church.

My mom was unable to function socially for a year: she cried for hours on end, could not leave the house, and barely left her bedroom.

During the next school year, I became very interested in God. Wendy's death had not caused me to lose my faith. At my high school, an organization called Campus Life, part of Campus Crusade for Christ, sponsored a campuswide program in which everyone was welcome.

It was at one of these meetings that I heard for the first time things about Jesus Christ that I had never heard before. I naturally resisted what I was hearing; in fact, I fought the gospel because I did not want to admit that I had not been taught the truth. The thought of needing to surrender my life to this person named Jesus was very difficult to embrace.

I was curious about how Christianity lined up with my Christian Science theology. I asked the Campus Life leaders such questions as

- "If God is the God of love, how could He send people to hell?"

- "Why did God allow Wendy to die?"

- "Why did Wendy look like she was going to be healed and then die three days later? Why all this heartache in my family? Aren't we good people?"

In my sophomore year, I attended a Campus Life retreat at Covenant College in Chattanooga, Tennessee. There I realized everything I had heard for the last couple of years was the truth. As I asked more questions, I could tell my Campus Life leaders were patiently loving me, and, for the first time, the Holy Spirit drew me close to Him. I remember listening to the speakers talk about what it meant to be a Christian, and everything they said rang true. When a group called Truth sang "Amazing Grace," I realized that I needed the Lord.

When the evening came to a close, the leaders asked us to go outside and talk to God. Sitting beneath a huge tree under an ink-black sky, I surrendered my life to Him, something I had never thought necessary.

"Jesus, I'm ready to believe in You and ask You into my heart," I said as I looked to the heavens.

ANOTHER SISTER

Little did I realize how my faith in Christ would be tested in the years to come. Another sister of mine, Sally Mills, lived in Loveland, Colorado. She was a forty-year-old divorced mother of two boys, Chris and Jason, ages fourteen and eleven. After her marital breakup, she returned to college to earn a teaching degree. She had promised her boys a trip to Disneyland after she graduated as a thank-you for all the sacrifices they made while she was in college.

After receiving her degree in the fall of 1988, Sally worked as a kindergarten aide at the local elementary school. She also took a part-time waitressing job at the River House restaurant, one of Loveland's nicer steakhouses, to earn some extra money for their Disneyland vacation during the Christmas break.

Sally and I had several conversations over the years about God and eternal life. I remember her telling me, "I believe we have to work out our own salvation." For several holiday seasons, I tucked a gospel tract into her Christmas card. When we spoke on the phone a few days before Christmas, I told her how much we would miss seeing her and the family in Georgia, but I told her that Disneyland would be a great time for her and the boys.

I thought about asking Sally if she read the tract, but I let the thought pass. When she and the boys returned from Disneyland just before New Year's, she decided to work a few more weeks at her part-time job. On Tuesday, January 3, 1989, Sally was not scheduled to wait tables, but a friend asked her to cover her shift. Sally agreed to work.

Meanwhile, not far from the River House restaurant, a Vietnam veteran named Wayne Strozzi was arguing violently with his estranged wife, who had moved out.

"What do you mean you don't want to live with me any longer?" he screamed.

"Because I don't want you around me!" she yelled back.

"How dare you say that to me! I'm going to get a gun and come back and kill you and the girls!"

Strozzi slammed the front door, jumped in his pickup truck, and spun gravel as he fishtailed the vehicle onto the country road.

Bobbi Strozzi called 911 and frantically reported that her husband had threatened to kill her and their two daughters. She fully believed he was capable of carrying out his threat. Strozzi had a long history of domestic violence and abusive, terrorizing behavior. In fact, he was in violation of parole and should have been in prison, where he had previously served time.

A sheriff deputy took the call, but before he drove to Strozzi's house, he stopped a quarter-mile from the home and called for backup from the Loveland Police Department. After a Loveland patrol officer arrived, Strozzi suddenly ambushed the deputy and police officer, firing into their patrol cars and wounding the deputy.

The wounded deputy returned fire and shot out a couple of tires. Strozzi then drove east toward Loveland on his flat tires with officers in pursuit. After about a mile's drive, he turned the disabled truck into the parking lot of the River House restaurant.

Armed with one Colt 9-mm semiautomatic pistol, Strozzi ran into the restaurant and took hostages. Sally was working in the restaurant's basement dining room, where the Loveland Lions Club was honoring several businessmen, including a local optometrist who donated eye care and glasses to needy kids in the community.

Most of the patrons were able to escape, but my sister and around thirty others were taken hostage. During the next ninety minutes, what happened inside that restaurant was pure terror. More than a dozen deputies and the Loveland SWAT team surrounded the restaurant and tried to negotiate with Strozzi by bullhorn and by telephone.

Strozzi demanded one million dollars in cash, a helicopter, and a pilot to fly him to Libya. As he and the police negotiated, Strozzi became more hostile and erratic. He tied up several hostages with duct tape, poured liquor on them, lighted a match, and tried unsuccessfully to set them on fire. He lined up three or four people in a row and placed the cold nozzle of his 9-mm pistol on the temple of the first hostage. He threatened to shoot and let the single bullet pass through each of their heads. Strozzi then led the hostages in the Lord's Prayer, telling them he was going to set a record for the number of hostages killed at one time. He also sent one of the hostages to his truck to fetch his cowboy boots, saying he wanted to "die with my boots on."

Strozzi forced hostages to stand in front of the windows and anytime he walked around the restaurant, he held a hostage close to him. Wayne Strozzi was not taking any chances.

Sally, for some reason, became his favorite human shield. He kept her with him at all times. With huge terrified eyes, she pleaded with Strozzi for her life.

The SWAT team continued to negotiate via the bullhorn after Strozzi tore out the telephone. Several hostages who had escaped told the SWAT team that Strozzi said he was going to start killing hostages at 9:00 P.M. At 8:45, the Loveland police chief gave the green light for the SWAT team sniper to shoot Strozzi. At seven minutes before nine o'clock, Strozzi approached the glass front door of the restaurant to yell at police. He was holding Sally close to him as his shield. When he turned sideways, the sniper triggered one round at Strozzi's upper chest region, but the glass door deflected the bullet, causing it to strike Strozzi in the lower side.

The nonfatal wounding enraged the madman. Knocked to the ground, he pointed his gun at Sally and fired a round into her back, then he triggered two more rounds into her legs. Then Strozzi turned the gun on himself.

When the shooting started, several hostages who were hiding in the restaurant's bathrooms feared that Strozzi's threatened massacre had begun. One of the hostages, the Lions Club president, dove through a bathroom window headfirst and began running toward a SWAT team member. The officer saw that he matched the description of the suspect and ordered him to freeze. The Lions Club president, who was legally intoxicated, ignored the warning and continued running toward the officer. In the darkness, the Loveland SWAT team sergeant had to make a split-second, life-or-death decision. Was the man Wayne Strozzi? When the Lions Club president still kept running, the sergeant shot him. The Lions Club president rose and ran again at the officer, who shot him a second time, fatally wounding him.

When the SWAT team rushed to the scene, Strozzi was dead, and Sally was mortally wounded. She never regained consciousness, and she died at the hospital.

I happened to be watching the 11:00 P.M. news in Georgia, and I heard the reporter discuss a hostage situation in Loveland, Colorado, that had ended in tragedy. Not for a moment did I think my sister could have been involved. I turned off the lights and went to sleep, but when the phone rang at 3:00 A.M., a terrible feeling swept over me.

"Aunt Mary, my mom is dead," Sally's oldest son, Chris, wailed over the phone.

Sally's boyfriend, John, then got on the line to give me more details.

My immediate thought was that my sister was not in heaven, which caused me to grieve very deeply. All I could think about was that missed opportunity to talk about Christ just ten days earlier. I had failed my sister, and that realization caused me the greatest sorrow I have ever known. *I have to know, Lord,* I thought. *Please let me know somehow whether she is in heaven or hell.*

The next day I flew with my parents to Denver. My mom and dad were in shock and total disbelief. John picked us up at Stapleton

Airport, and I thought if anybody knew if she was saved, he would be the one. They had been dating a couple of years and had talked about marriage.

As we walked to get his car, I asked, "John, do you know if Sally had ever asked Jesus into her heart?"

He turned to me with a puzzled look. "I guess so . . . I think so," he muttered.

His halting response didn't satisfy me.

In Sally's home, I looked for anything that might answer my nagging question. I found my Christmas card, but the tract was missing. Later that afternoon, Jim Adams, the minister who was going to perform the memorial service, came over to talk with the family.

At first, I was excited to meet the pastor because I didn't even know she had been attending a church. I thought he could give me an indication of what kind of house of worship she had been attending. Maybe it wasn't a church where "everyone has to work out their own salvation."

Not once during that visit, however, do I remember the pastor mentioning Jesus Christ or giving words of comfort. He only asked for stories from Sally's childhood and her life that he could incorporate into his homily.

Lord, please let me know.

I had an opportunity to be alone with my dad. I did not want to let another opportunity go by without asking him about Jesus. My folks had been attending a Methodist church for the past several years, but we never talked about that most important question.

"Dad, have you ever asked Jesus Christ to be your Lord and Savior?"

We were sitting at Sally's kitchen table. Dad was staring out the window at the bleak January landscape.

"Mary, I took care of that a long time ago, and there's something else I know: I never want to bury another one of my children."

I took my father's hand, and we wept.

The next evening, the police department and local counselors held a town meeting regarding the terrible shootings. Many questions were being asked in the aftermath of the carnage, including why the police shot a hostage to death and why they weren't able to keep my sister from being killed.

At the community meeting, a teenage girl, probably no more than sixteen years of age, stood up and said, "I just want to know what happened because my daddy is dead and he would have never killed anybody."

My sister Sue and I glanced at each other and realized we were looking at the daughter of the man who killed our sister. My heart went out to her. I knew she was grieving as much as we were. The young girl was another victim in this senseless tragedy. When the event was over, I walked up to her and introduced myself. I could tell she was uneasy in the way she crossed her arms.

"I'm so sorry," I said. "You know, sometimes it's not so good to be so strong. If you ever need to talk to somebody, call me anytime." I gave her my phone number, which she accepted. Then I said, "I don't understand what's going on either, but I don't hate your father, and I forgive him."

I gave her a hug, but she never called me.

WHERE IS SHE?

When I left the high school auditorium that chilly evening, I continued to cry out, *Lord, where is she? Where is Sally spending eternity? Please let me know.*

Back at Sally's house, I sat down at the kitchen table. I started sorting through her mail and other papers that piled up when something caught my eye: a bulletin from her church.

Lord, will this tell me the answer to my questions? I started reading the church bulletin, and from cover to cover, the message of the gospel was plainly presented. For the first time in two days, I had hope that my sister had heard the gospel of Jesus Christ in the church she was attending.

The next morning was the memorial service. Sally's church was packed with four hundred people, including the other hostages and their families. Before the service began, my family waited in a back room with Jim Adams, the pastor. I knew now was the time to ask him if he knew the answer to my question.

I pulled him aside and said, "Pastor, I'm going to ask you something, and I don't want you to tell me what you think I want to hear. I want you to tell me the truth. Do you know if Sally had ever accepted Jesus as her Savior?"

Pastor Adams looked at me with a reassuring smile. "Mary, about two months ago Sally accepted Christ as her Savior. She is in heaven."

The tears came again in another flood. I thanked God for His faithfulness to answer my prayer. The memorial service was now bearable. I had joy, hope, and comfort knowing that she was with the Lord right at that moment and forevermore. I don't know why Sally never discussed her decision for Christ with me, but I was thankful I had finally learned the truth.

John, the young man to whom she was about to be engaged, delivered a beautiful testimony. "This tragic event has driven me to examine my faith, and I am here to tell you that Sally was a believer in Jesus Christ!" he exclaimed from the pulpit.

LOOKING BACK

I know this: if Wendy had not died, I probably would not be a Christian today. I believe Wendy's apparent healing was done by Satan, the Great Deceiver who tried to make that healing look as if it came from the hand of God. Knowing that Christian Science is a cult, I believe God could not allow Satan to receive the glory. If Wendy would have been allowed to be healed, I probably would have stayed in Christian Science and not learned the truth.

Did Wendy know Christ as Savior? I don't know that answer. Only God knows what was in her heart, and I will have to wait to learn the answer to that question and many others when I arrive on the other side.

Many times during my life, I've asked, "Why, God?" Admittedly, most of my spiritual frustrations have not ended with an enlightened, "Oh, now I see what You were doing, Lord." I've decided that I just have to file this question under the "Things I Do Not Understand" heading and leave it there.

Scripture has been a great comfort to me. Isaiah 55:8–9 teaches: "'For my thoughts are not your thoughts, neither are your ways my ways,' declares the LORD. 'As the heavens are higher than the earth, so are my ways higher than your ways and my thoughts than your thoughts.'"

Over the years, since that fateful evening in Tennessee, my faith has grown stronger and deeper in the Lord. And what is faith? It is "being sure of what we hope for and certain of what we do not see" (Heb. 11:1).

If we truly understand the majesty of the Lord and the depth of His love for us, we would certainly accept those times when He defies human logic and sensibility. Confusing experiences will occur along the way, but they are opportunities for our faith to grow.

The death of my two sisters has touched me profoundly. Wendy's death brought me to faith in the Savior, and Sally's murder tested it by fire. Above all, I learned to hold fast to my faith because Scripture says "without faith it is impossible to please God" (Heb. 11:6).

15

Zig Ziglar: NOW HE'S SPOKEN FOR

AGE:
seventy-three
OCCUPATION:
speaker, author, and chairman of
Ziglar Training Systems in Carrolton, Texas
RESIDENCE:
Plano, Texas
FAMILY SITUATION:
married to Jean for fifty-two years; father of Suzan Witmeyer,
who went home to be with the Lord in 1995 at age forty-six;
Cindy Ann Oates, forty-six; Julie Ann Norman, forty-four;
and John Thomas Ziglar, thirty-four.
The Ziglars have four granddaughters.

Mary LoVerde, a Dallas mother, likes to pop a Zig Ziglar tape into the family's audiocassette player while caring for her three small children. There's something soothing about Zig's distinctive baritone that helps Mary's day go more smoothly.

One afternoon, Mary's five-year-old son Nicholas arrived home from kindergarten and proudly handed her a drawing.

"We studied the letter *Z* today, and I drew pictures," he announced.

Mary stooped down and looked at the large piece of construction paper with several primitive drawings. The first "picture" appeared to be several animals behind a fence.

"Is this a zoo?" she asked.

"Yes, Mommy!"

The next picture looked roughly like a four-legged animal with black-and-white stripes.

"I bet this one is a zebra," said Mary.

Nicholas's face beamed.

The next picture was a stick man. Mary wasn't sure what to say. "Gee, honey, this is a lovely picture of a man. But 'man' starts with an *M,* not a *Z.*"

"That's not a man," he retorted. "That's Zig Ziglar!"

Mary laughed. She knew Zig was famous, but famous enough to become a household name in kindergarten?

Why not? Zig Ziglar is probably the most popular motivational speaker on the planet today. Now in his early seventies, his speaking career has rocketed into another orbit. Zig is best-known as the speaker who knocks 'em "alive" at the hugely successful Peter Lowe Success seminars: daylong "yes-fests" that feature live appearances from notables such as George and Barbara Bush, Margaret Thatcher, Colin Powell, Larry King, Joe Montana, and Bill Cosby. The Lowe seminars are held two dozen times a year in cities around the country.

Zig is generally given the 8:45 A.M. slot following a national or local hero, and he never fails to deliver a stirring message to a second-cup-of-coffee crowd filling the sixteen-thousand-seat arenas. If you've never heard Zig Ziglar speak, then you aren't aware that he sounds like a warm-hearted Southern preacher sittin' for a spell while he enjoys a second slice of pecan pie. His folksy demeanor and message of hope resonate with any audience, young or old, down-and-out or well-to-do.

But for all his oratorical brilliance, even Zig Ziglar will tell you he was broke and going nowhere until he was touched by the Savior.

BACK TO THE BEGINNING

Born in the Alabama countryside in 1926, Zig stopped breathing when he was ten days old. The country doctor told his parents, "He's dead," so they took him and laid the tiny infant on the bed. Zig's grandmother picked him up and started talking to him—and to God, asking Him to spare a life that had barely begun. When all hope was lost, God chose to breathe life back into Zig.

The family struggled mightily during the Depression years, especially since Zig's father died when the boy was five years old. The family, which had been living in the country near Yazoo City, Mississippi, moved into "town" for better work opportunities.

In first grade, Zig contracted many of the childhood diseases— mumps, measles, and whooping cough—and missed about four months of school. Mrs. Dement Warren, his teacher, stopped by his house twice a week and tutored the lad. Without the extra help, Zig probably would have failed first grade. If he had failed first grade, he would have been drafted out of high school into World War II—and probably never gone on to college. Young Zig didn't have much time to study since he delivered the *Yazoo City Herald* newspaper every afternoon after school from the time he was in the fifth grade until he finished high school. That's what you had to do in a single-parent home in those days.

When America entered World War II, Zig set his sights on the Naval Air Corps, so in 1943 Zig attended summer school at Hinds Junior College to earn extra credits in math and science. His buddies thought Zig was wasting his time since he wasn't partial to studying. It turns out they were wrong. In January 1944, Zig was accepted into the Naval Air Corps, which accepted only five of every one hundred applicants. That gave a hefty confidence boost to the 120-pound seventeen-year-old who, up until then, walked through life with an "inferiority complex," as they called low self-esteem in those days.

When Zig departed for school, he packed with him a set of values from his mother, a godly woman of incredible faith. She constantly taught the children sentence sermonettes, which were filled with such values as

- "Tell the truth and tell it ever, costeth what it will. For he who hides the wrong he does, does the wrong thing still."

- "When a task is once begun, you leave it not until it's done."

- "Be a matter great or small, do it well or not at all."

His mother was one who literally milked the cows and cooked breakfast before daylight and quilted long after the kids had gone to bed. "She was an incredible example," remembers Zig. "And yet she always had time for us, always nurtured us. There was never any question about her love for us. But there was also never any question that she wanted things done right. She was, from a character-building point of view, superb."

Mama Ziglar also made sure the kids were in church, so Zig was raised in a Christian home. She constantly reminded the children that God created everyone equal in His eyes—a philosophy not readily accepted in Mississippi, one of the most racist states in the country.

"In my neighborhood, there was no such thing as a black lady," recalls Zig. "No, she was a black woman. There was no such thing as a black gentleman. No, he was a black man. And I saw some kids calling a sixty-five-year-old black man 'boy.' That was the mindset. That was the racial prejudice at that time. My mother always told us, 'One of these days you will stand in front of a color-blind Lord. Until then, you will treat your black brothers and sisters with respect and with dignity.'"

At age twenty, Zig married Jean Abernathy, whom he affectionately calls "The Redhead," and embarked on a sales career in South

Carolina. Heavy-duty waterless cookware was his product, but his young family lived on a financial roller coaster—lights turned off, telephone disconnected, car repossessed—until his sales career caught fire, finishing number two out of more than seven thousand salesmen in his company. He was on his way.

Telling others how he succeeded sounded like fun, so Zig accepted a position with a Dale Carnegie franchise on Long Island outside of New York City. The year was 1955, but the problem was he would leave home early in the morning when the girls were asleep, and when he came home at night, they would already be in bed. It took Zig only three months to realize that he didn't want to raise his little girls that way. The Ziglars pulled up stakes and moved back to South Carolina, where Zig became the supersalesman again.

Life became a series of making money and losing it, however. One day he had some, and the next day he didn't. In 1968, the dream of being a speaker, which he had nurtured on a part-time basis for fifteen years, led him to enter that field on a full-time basis. He continued to experience a bumpy flight, however, as he made a less than spectacular entrance into his new career.

Where was God in all this? Zig didn't know. "I had been in church probably two thousand times from the time I was a child," he said, "but I always went to church because it was the thing to do. An old expression sums up where I was: 'Going to church doesn't make you a Christian any more than going into a garage makes you an automobile.' I labored under the illusion that I was a Christian because I thought that going to church, coming from a good family, doing good things, never hurting anybody, and loving everybody made me a Christian. There's not a word of truth to that, however."

In 1972, at the age of forty-five, Zig's life changed forever.

"The Redhead and I met a woman everyone called Sister Jessie, an elderly African-American lady," said Zig. "A friend said we just *had* to meet this remarkable woman, so we invited her and her friend Ann Anderson to come to our Dallas home over the Fourth of July weekend."

Zig couldn't help but notice that all weekend long Sister Jessie talked about Christ. He could tell she loved the Lord.

During one discussion, Sister Jessie turned to Zig and said, "God has been waiting for you a long time."

The statement stunned Zig. The other thing she said was, "You drink a little, don't you?"

"Yes, I do," he replied.

"With the mind that God gave you?"

Zig felt like he had been hit in the head with a poleax. When he saw what she had—a close relationship with Christ—he wanted the same thing. "I *knew* who Christ was, but I never had any kind of relationship with Him," said Zig. "However, as I learned of God's love and grace, I decided that since I had done very little with my life outside of some sales and family success, I needed resources that exceeded anything I personally had myself. The promise of Christ seemed to fit my every need. With considerable excitement, I committed my life to Him that Fourth of July weekend, and I've never looked back."

Today, Zig believes God honored his mother when He permitted this African-American lady to bring him into the kingdom. After that event, it was almost as if God was saying to Zig, *I've let you waste forty-five years. Now I've got some things I want you to do. So I'm going to reveal myself and what I can do so that there will never be any doubt in your mind that I am God.* That's what happened, and his life took a total 180-degree turn for the good.

A CHILD SHALL LEAD THEM

The changes in Zig's life were major. The morning after he was saved, he opened a kitchen cabinet containing 250 one-ounce bottles of Cutty Sark and Jack Daniels that he collected when he flew first-class on the airlines. Zig wasn't a big drinker, but he did like to imbibe three or four times a month. Also inside the cabinet were several magnums of champagne. Zig pulled all the bottles off the shelf and dumped every ounce of alcohol down the kitchen sink. He also vowed never to take another drink.

That vow lasted nearly five months. The Redhead and Zig went out for their anniversary dinner to a German restaurant, where they were offered wine. "Don't misunderstand. You don't go to hell because you drink wine, but I had decided not to drink anymore," said Zig. "Proverbs says the prince does not drink wine, and I'm just one step above that since I'm a child of the King Himself. And this child of the King just doesn't drink booze. Every time you do, it kills some cells. Doctors can argue all they want to, but the facts are that alcohol—one drink a day—will not extend your life. It just won't. That's beside the point, however. I took the drink after I said I wouldn't."

When he got home that night, his seven-year-old son, Tom, asked, "Dad, did you drink anything tonight?"

Zig admitted to his son that he'd had a glass of wine. Little Tom looked his father in the eye and said, "Dad, I can't begin to tell you how disappointed I am in you."

That's the Holy Spirit talking to me, thought Zig. "As I'm fond of telling people, 'I've got a smart boy, but he isn't that smart.' I looked at my boy and I said, 'Son, I'll tell you what. If you'll forgive me this time, you'll never have to forgive me for that again.' And since that day, I've not knowingly had an ounce of alcohol."

Reading this chapter, or having heard Zig speak, you may have the impression that Zig has his Christian life together. So, is Zig Ziglar just about perfect these days?

"If I've given anyone that impression, then I'm doing a lousy job of communicating," responded Zig. "Many people have said some nice things about me, but the word *perfect* was noticeably absent from their comments. As I've often said, God is no respecter of persons, and I understand why because I know I'm human, and I know I still have a sin nature. But I've been saved by the blood of the Lamb—in the middle years of my life—and for that, I am eternally thankful."

16

David Berkowitz:
THE SON OF SAM
BECOMES THE SON OF HOPE

AGE:
forty-six
OCCUPATION:
Prisoner #78–A–1976, serving a 365-year
term for multiple murders
RESIDENCE:
Sullivan Correctional Facility in Fallsburg, New York
FAMILY SITUATION:
single

Editor's note: David Berkowitz doesn't like talking about his past, and for good reason. For eighteen panic-filled months in 1976–77, David Berkowitz terrorized New York City with a string of shootings that killed six people and seriously injured seven. Women changed hair color or cut their hair because they thought the killer preferred a certain hairstyle.

The carnage paralyzed the Big Apple because of Berkowitz's M.O.: he randomly approached male and female victims as they

sat on their brownstone stoops or in their parked cars, pointed a
.44 caliber pistol, and fired at point-blank range.

The New York tabloids whipped the populace into a frenzy,
and beat reporters dubbed the serial murderer the "Son of Sam"
after police discovered a note that Berkowitz had left behind at
one of his killing fields. "I am a monster. I am the Son of Sam,"
Berkowitz had scribbled. After his arrest, Berkowitz explained
that his neighbor's name was Sam and that Sam's dog had told
David to commit the murders.

Here is David Berkowitz's story:

I grew up as an only child in a small tenement in the Bronx, and I
had all kinds of emotional and childhood problems. I hated everybody. By the time I entered elementary school, I began suffering
seizures. I would rampage through the house, knocking over furniture
and rolling on the floor. My dad had to pin me down until the seizures
stopped because I had this powerful urge to break things and fight
with people.

I was always in trouble at my public school. I fought in the schoolyard. I stood up in the middle of class and started screaming at the
teacher. I was sent many times to the counselor, who summoned my
parents.

"Listen, Mr. and Mrs. Berkowitz," began one counselor. "We can't
control your child. If you want him to stay in school, you need to put
your son into some kind of therapy program."

Mom and I began taking the subway to see a child psychologist in
Manhattan every week, but all we did was talk in circles. "What are we
going to do with you?" asked Mom.

My parents were Jewish, but they never taught me anything about
God. Despite my horrible behavior, my parents showed me love, especially Mom, who tried to help as best she could. She was a heavy
smoker, however, and she died of lung cancer when I was fourteen.

When Mom passed away, I gave up on life. I became even more angry and self-destructive.

I started vandalizing buildings. I felt a powerful urge to damage and destroy things. I experimented with alcohol and drugs, especially the psychedelic LSD. I was intensely drawn to all forms of occult-related, satanic, and horror movies. Somehow I managed to graduate from high school, and I enlisted in the U.S. Army for a three-year stint. When I was discharged in 1974, I came back to the Bronx and discovered that my friends had moved away from the neighborhood. I was lonely, and then one day I was invited to a party.

We were standing around this guy's apartment not doing much, when one of them said, "Hey, we got some friends who meet in a park nearby. Whaddya say we go check it out?"

We went over to Pelham Bay Park in the Bronx and walked deep into the woods, where we found a couple dozen people drinking around a small fire.

Some were singing, and then they started chanting.

"What's this all about?" I asked someone dressed in black.

"Didn't anyone tell you we're pagans and witches?"

"No, they didn't," I replied.

They began asking me questions, checking me out, and then they invited me to return. They introduced me to Satanism and their rituals. We drew pentagrams in the dirt and called upon the demonic powers. I felt this surge of energy come upon me, and I liked that feeling.

I purchased a satanic bible, and just holding that black book gave me paranormal powers. I developed psychic abilities, which freaked out my friends. I remember walking up to a busy intersection, and I just knew there was going to be a car accident at the corner. So I waited, and sure enough, a minute or two later two cars piled into each other. It was so uncanny, and I visualized the whole incident in advance.

I dabbled more and more in Satanism until the day I was asked to join the group. Just one hitch: a satanic priest took me aside and said he needed a family photo.

"Why's that?"

"Listen, we want you to join, but we have a policy," said the priest. "You must provide a photo of some of your family members. We do this to protect ourselves, because if you ever leave and go tell anybody about us, we will know who your family is and we will hurt them."

I believed the priest's words. For months, I had witnessed animal sacrifices to appease the powers of darkness, but now we were being told that we were ready for the quantum leap: human sacrifices. At least that's what Samhain—one of the highest-ranking demons—told us. We were soldiers of Samhain, which became abbreviated to Sam. That's really how I became known as the "Son of Sam," and I made a complete surrender to these powers of darkness.

Some type of evil entity entered my body. I believed I was a soldier in Satan's army, and we were determined to bring New York City to its knees through a reign of terror. We began with vandalism and arson. Our group deliberately set around two thousand fires. I passed the threshold from casual participant to actual devil worshipper. Once I willingly gave the devil my body and my mind, the next step seemed logical: I became a killing machine and shed innocent blood. I can't explain why I did what I did, but I now know that those actions caused much grief in many families.

A PRISONER FOR LIFE

After a long manhunt, New York City policemen finally surrounded me on a hot, muggy night—August 10, 1977—their guns pointed at my head. One wrong move, and they would have blown me away.

I was found guilty and sentenced to 365 years in prison without the possibility of parole—effectively a life sentence. When I first entered prison, I was placed in an isolation cell; then I was sent to a psychiatric hospital because I was declared criminally insane. Prison authorities eventually released me to the general inmate population, and when that happened, I nearly died and would have been lost in hell for all eternity.

Here's what happened: I was in New York's Attica Correctional Facility in 1979 when another inmate—for some reason—took a razor and slashed me across the neck. This type of violence happens all the time in prisons.

Bleeding profusely, I was taken to the infirmary to be stitched up. The doctor peered at my wound and whistled. "Berkowitz, I don't know how you made it," he commented. "For some reason, this guy just missed your jugular vein. You're one lucky guy."

For years I lived by the prison code. I minded my own business and kept my eyes straight ahead. If somebody messed with me, however, I was ready to mess right back. The code was an eye for an eye, a tooth for a tooth. You take a punch at me; I'll take a punch at you. That was my attitude.

In 1987, I had been in prison for ten years. On one cold winter night, I was walking in circles around the exercise yard. Another inmate walked up to me and asked, "David, can I talk to you for a few minutes? I want to tell you something."

"Yeah, what's that?" I said, still maintaining my tough-guy exterior to the Hispanic inmate.

"Listen, I want you to know something: Jesus Christ loves you very much."

"What?"

"Just what I said. Jesus Christ loves you very much. God has a plan for your life. He told me to tell you that He has a plan and a purpose for your life."

"Listen, God ain't interested in me. I mean, I appreciate what you've just said, but God is not for me. I don't believe God loves me. I'm not a good person. I've never done anything good. Why would God love me?"

"Well, you don't understand," he replied. "If you'll let me, I'd like to be your friend. I'd like to talk to you about the Lord when we are working out in the gym."

"You can work out with me," I said, "but I tell you, you're wasting your time if you think you can talk to me about Jesus Christ because I know that God hates me and has no use for me. I'm a failure, man, and I blew it. You know that. I'm doing life in prison, and there's no hope for me at all."

LISTENING AND LEARNING

I got to know my newfound friend better in the weight room. We'd take a break from pumping iron, and he'd say, "Hey, David, let me read you something from the Bible. You don't mind, do you?"

"Nah, go right ahead."

Then he would read different portions of Scripture and talk about what God was doing in his life after being sentenced to prison for robbery. "Dave, I used to be into cocaine, but now I'm into Christ, and He's changed my life."

I listened politely, but I never thought God would ever do anything for me. I had done too much evil.

"Hey, David, listen to this: 'For God so loved the world that he gave his one and only Son, that whoever believes in him shall not perish but have eternal life.' Isn't that great? Do you want to hear the next verse?"

"Fine, read the next verse."

"John 3:17 says, 'For God did not send his Son into the world to condemn the world, but to save the world through him.' Isn't that great, Dave?"

"It sounds good, but what's that gotta do with me?"

"These verses are for you, Dave. God is reaching out to you. God is trying to touch your life, Dave."

I stewed on that one for a while.

Several weeks later, my newfound friend presented me with a Gideon pocket Bible. "Have you ever read the Bible, Dave?"

"No, I haven't," I replied. "Where do I start?"

"I'd start with the Psalms," he said, as he tucked the Bible into my prison-issue shirt.

Back in my cell I was shocked to read some of the most beautiful words imaginable. Psalm 18:1–3 touched my hardened heart: "I love you, O LORD, my strength. The LORD is my rock, my fortress and my deliverer; my God is my rock, in whom I take refuge. He is my shield and the horn of my salvation, my stronghold. I call to the LORD, who is worthy of praise, and I am saved from my enemies."

Enemies? I had enemies. When I wasn't watching over my shoulder, I was defending myself. One time, I fought with another inmate, and the guards had to jump me and drag me into the "box," where I stayed for ninety days in solitary confinement.

I was continually drawn to my pocket Bible and to the Psalms. I related to King David because he had my name, he was also Jewish like I was, and, like me, he had experienced all sorts of pain and suffering—and had made his share of wrong choices. When David wrote in Psalm 51:10, "Create in me a pure heart, O God, and renew a steadfast spirit within me," I took notice.

Over the span of several weeks, something began to happen inside me. My heart—a heart that hadn't felt anything for many years—began to thaw, little by little. When I became a soldier for Satan, I committed my life to evil, which hardened my heart. Yet when I read and reread the Psalms, I felt something stir deep inside.

I read the Bible in secret because I didn't want anybody to see me holding a Bible. There were times when I read the Psalms late at night that I would begin to cry. Yet as my heart warmed to Jesus and I learned about God's love and compassion, I felt so unworthy, so dirty. After all, hadn't I been such a bad person? Hadn't I shed innocent blood?

One evening, long after bed check, God touched me in that prison cell. He said in a quiet, still voice: *David, I love you. David, I love you. I'm willing to give you another chance. I know you know that you did wrong. I know that you are sorry for it, but I'm willing to give you another chance.*

I knelt down beside my bed and cupped my head in my hands. I prayed for the first time and poured out all my sins, all the heinous evil, all the dreck of my life. "Lord, You know I'm a guilty man. I've done so much evil. I've done so much wrong. I don't see how You could forgive me, but I plead with You to do that." I begged Him for forgiveness while warm tears streamed down my face. I hadn't cried like that ever in my life.

When I was finished talking to God, I stood up. My mind seemed to flood with a sense of peace. I knew in that moment that Jesus Christ had heard me. I sensed in my heart that I was forgiven and that I was now free from condemnation, just as Scripture told me I was. The demons that had tormented me for many years were banished.

That event happened more than a decade ago. Today I teach Bible studies in prison, as well as give words of encouragement during our chapel services. In addition, prison authorities allow me to work with men who have been labeled "mentally disturbed" or "low functioning." I have been able to counsel these people and help them with some of their spiritual needs.

The Lord has allowed me to establish a small missionary outreach to Africa, Russia, and Romania. We send Bibles and Christian literature to needy churches in those countries. Serving God is my greatest joy.

Not long ago, the *New York Daily News* published my letter to the editor on the twentieth anniversary of my arrest. I wrote, "The police and the news media used to call me the 'Son of Sam,' but God has given me a new name: the 'Son of Hope.' Now my life is about hope. I am no longer the son of the devil."

17

Steve Green:
THE COMEBACK KID

AGE:
forty-three
OCCUPATION:
Christian singer
RESIDENCE:
Franklin, Tennessee
FAMILY SITUATION:
married twenty-one years to Marijean;
father of Summer, eighteen; and Josiah, fourteen

If you ask Steve Green what the downside is of being a successful Christian singer, he'll tell you that a *lot* of people know *very little* about him.

Sure, some are aware that Steve can sing in English or Spanish with equal fluency, since he was born and raised in Argentina as a missionary kid. Some figure he's a great family man because they've seen the warm, fuzzy pictures of him and his wife, Marijean, with their two handsome children, Summer and Josiah.

Let's face it: Steve Green is one guy who appears to have it all together. His voice can belt out "Mighty Fortress" or cause the hankies to come out during "The Letter." His concerts, more than one hundred dates each year, appeal to everyone from three to ninety-three. He's performed at a half-dozen Promise Keeper weekends since 1993, and he and Larnell Harris collaborated on a song about racial reconciliation, "Teach Me to Love."

But behind his amazing voice and engaging stage presence, there's something Steve Green wants everyone to know about him. When you hear this story, you'll understand why he needed to be touched by the Savior.

GOING SOLO

In the summer of 1983, Steve, then twenty-seven, was an up-and-coming singer in a hurry. He and Marijean were part of the backup group for Bill and Gloria Gaither, but Steve's classically trained voice was attracting notice. Sparrow Records offered him a recording contract, and the buzz in Nashville circles was that Steve Green, solo act, was ready for orbit.

But Steve's spiritual life was stuck on the launch pad, where it had been ever since his college days. Steve, who had never spent much time in the U.S. until he attended Grand Canyon University in Phoenix, had discovered the *norteamericano* lifestyle to be very appealing. While his four brothers and sisters attended Bible colleges and pursued careers in ministry, Steve daydreamed about becoming a doctor or lawyer—moneymaking careers that could fuel his new-found aspirations.

"Although I grew up in a spiritual home," he says, "I had turned my back on the level of commitment to Christ that I had seen in my parents. I just wanted to be a 'regular Christian,' someone who wanted to know the Lord but also wanted freedom from the restraints that I felt inhibited me: rules, regulations, all the things that good Christians don't do. My desire to be free was really a license to sin. I disobeyed the Lord in a lot of areas. I rebelled against and grieved the heart of God."

Growing up, Steve wasn't allowed to go to the cinema. When he was on his own, Steve was attracted to lewd movies on cable TV, something new in the early eighties. Consequently, with his thought life running rampant, Steve's prayer life evaporated to nearly nothing. Yes, he still uttered a quick grace before meals, but his prayers didn't reflect any deep love for the Lord or a desire to be close to Him.

In early August 1983, Steve flew to Phoenix to attend his younger sister's wedding. For the first time in several years, Steve and his two brothers and two sisters were together, but it didn't take long for everyone to notice that Randy, Steve's older brother, had been through some sort of "revival" experience. For several days leading up to the wedding, Randy cornered each brother or sister and asked where he or she stood with the Lord. Were they all tracking with Him? Had they *really* given their hearts and lives over to Jesus Christ?

When Steve heard from other family members that he was next, he kept a wary distance from Randy. But one afternoon, the family jumped into a car to visit a hospitalized relative, and suddenly Randy had a captive audience.

"I couldn't get away," remembers Steve, "and he didn't care *who* heard him. He kept talking about the importance of holiness and the shortness of time, but I kept changing the subject. He kept changing it back. Finally, I became angry with him and told him, 'Just stop talking!'"

Randy, who was sitting in the front seat, began crying. He turned around and told Steve that he was not resisting him, but the Holy Spirit. He said God wanted to use Steve, but He couldn't because there was something bottled up inside of him.

"You're a liar!" Steve steamed. "God can look at me right now and see there's nothing wrong with my life!" But no sooner were the words out of his mouth than Steve thought he sounded hypocritical and empty.

That night sleep did not come easily. Steve tossed in bed, reliving his conversation with Randy. His older brother had peeled away a layer of his heart and exposed the hypocrisy that his life had become. *Wait a minute*, thought Steve. *I sing with famous people, and the audience cheers for me every night. They tell me that God is using me. No, I can't be that bad.*

But as Steve stared at the ceiling, he knew that he *was* bad. His brother's words haunted him, and worse yet, he had seen right through him. No one else had ever talked to him like that before. *Doesn't Randy know who he's talking to?*

Something powerful was tugging Steve's conscience, and after another hour of internal debate, he fell out of bed and dropped to his knees.

"Lord, I give up. I'm a hypocrite, and I've sinned against You. I've lived a dual life. I've made a mockery of You. I don't love You, and I hardly know You. And my brother is right. I've said no to You for so many years that I don't even know how to say yes, but if You will help me, I'll say yes. If You can do in me what You've done in my brother, please do it, because from now on, I'm Yours."

The next day, Steve called Marijean and asked her if she had spent any time with the Lord that day.

"No, I haven't," she replied. "Why do you ask? Has something happened to you?"

"God is doing something in me, but I'm not sure what it is. We'll talk about it more when I get home."

When he boarded a plane later that day, he started writing down his thoughts and prayers in a journal. "Is the cost of surrender too high?" he wrote. "Not if I'm sick of a bland relationship with no burning love and no power." Then Steve asked God to revive his first love for Him at any cost.

When he and Marijean were reunited, he confessed things to Marijean that she did not know about her husband of five years. Driven by a newfound passion for God and a clean conscience, Steve spent the next two weeks making restitution to those he had wronged. He was saying goodbye to an old life.

That *adios* prompted Steve to start a solo career. Several weeks later, he gave his first concert at Liberty University in Virginia. Steve had never really had much to say in public before. But that night at Liberty, he started talking about how his brother had lovingly confronted him at a time when he needed it most. As he neared the end of the story, he looked down at the front row, and he saw men and women dabbing their eyes with handkerchiefs. *Strange,* he thought. *That's never happened before.*

When Steve finished the concert, Marijean looked at him and started to cry.

"I'm looking at a different man tonight," she said. "When I saw you up there, it wasn't the same person I've known."

Marijean was right. Her man had changed.

TO THE PRESENT

Fast-forward more than fifteen years. These days Steve Green practices accountability. He and his brother David, who is his manager, meet once a year with a council of pastors to assess where they are heading. The pastors have full access to their financial records, and they also interview the Green brothers regarding their personal lives and goals for the upcoming year.

"It's a very meaningful time and a safeguard for us," says Steve. "Because David and I are brothers, we recognize the danger of doing whatever we think is right and deceiving ourselves. That's why we have a group of outside, unbiased individuals who give us counsel and advice. I even have the pastors review my lyrics to make sure the songs are biblically sound."

Except when he's performing in large stadium venues, Steve usually mingles with the audience following each concert. He patiently shakes hands, exchanges hugs, pats little heads, and *listens.*

"Even if I'm weary, it's still important to take the time to let people tell me things," says Steve. "I'm not just talking about flattery. Sometimes people have listened to my music, and they feel like they know me well enough to speak honestly and openly with me. I've been cautioned, sobered, encouraged, and exhorted. I've had men come to me, grasp my hand firmly, look me in the eye and say, 'Steve, you're in a dangerous position. I pray that God will keep you pure and keep you and Marijean in love with each other.'"

Fortunately, Steve doesn't have to deal with women throwing hotel room keys on the stage. But the temptations are there.

"I travel a lot, which means I have the danger of falling into impurity in hotel rooms with all the TV, and, I suppose, advances from women. Because Marijean has traveled with me or I've talked about her in front of so many people, I have a safeguard. In addition, I've made myself accountable to a few faithful friends. If I've seen something that has caused me to stumble in a certain area, I contact them about it and ask them to pray for me. I know my own need for accountability because I know myself better than anyone else knows me." These experiences inspired him to sing "Guard Your Heart."

Steve says it's very easy for people to see only the image packaged by the record company. "But I've tried for the past ten years to dispel what I call the 'mystique,'" he says. "It's something that is easy for artists to hide behind. We often live just out of reach of the public, and we often try to hold onto that mystique because it draws crowds. But that's something I've not wanted to do because it's not true. Marijean and I are, quite simply, regular people who have a specific function within the Body of Christ, and we are the most amazed that God chooses to use us.

"I know that I am one of the most unlikely candidates to be used by God, because of my eight-year period of running away from Him as a prodigal. I see my own frailties even now, even since God rescued me and turned my life around."

18

Miles McPherson:
NOW HE'S MILES AHEAD

AGE:
thirty-nine
OCCUPATION:
youth evangelist, author, and president and founder
of Miles Ahead Ministries
RESIDENCE:
San Diego, California
FAMILY SITUATION:
married to Debbie for fourteen years;
father of Kelly, thirteen; Kimmy, twelve; and Miles Jr., ten

When I speak at school assemblies and citywide youth rallies, I'm fond of telling this story:

There was a young person—let's call him Lorenzo—who grew up in a poor neighborhood. Lorenzo knew how to handle himself on the streets, and each day he walked by a small park. One time he saw an old man sitting on a bench. He wore a porkpie hat and pants that were too short, and he sported a wooden cane. The old man liked to come to the park and feed the pigeons.

One day Lorenzo spotted the old man and decided to check him out. They started a conversation, and Lorenzo was feeling very confident that day. He said, "Old man, my name is Lorenzo, and when I get out of school, I'm not going to go to college. I got so much intelligence that I'm just going to make money out on the street."

The old man looked up from his pigeons and said, "Lorenzo, Lorenzo, what would it profit you if you gained the whole world but lost your soul?"

"Oh, man, you're just jealous because you don't have any money."

The next day, Lorenzo saw the man sitting on the park bench. He strode over and began telling the old man about the great party at his house the previous night. "My parents were out of town, and man, did we blow the doors off. We had all these girls over and danced all night long. What did you do last night?"

The old man looked up from his pigeons and said, "Lorenzo, even when you're laughing and having a good time, I can tell your heart is aching and empty."

"Man, you're just jealous because you weren't invited," and he walked away.

Every day, however, Lorenzo couldn't stop himself from walking over to the old man in the park. Whenever Lorenzo tried to tell him something exciting about his life, the old man countered with a saying from the Bible. After several weeks, Lorenzo tired of the old man always quoting Scripture to him.

Another time Lorenzo spotted a small bird on the sidewalk, still alive and trying to get back up on its feet. Lorenzo decided he would show the old man who was the cleverest dude in the 'hood. He picked up the bird and cupped it in his right hand; then he put his arms behind his back and approached the old man.

"Hey, old man, you're so smart telling me these Proverbs, telling me I shouldn't do drugs, shouldn't mess with women, and that I should read the Bible. Let me ask you this question. If you know everything, tell me: Is this bird behind my back dead or alive?"

If he says the bird is dead, I'm going to show him that it's alive. If he says the bird is alive, I will crush it in my hands and kill it.

The old man didn't say anything.

"Listen, old man, I'm going to ask you again. Is this bird behind my back dead or alive?"

The old man didn't say anything again.

"Old man, I'm going to ask you one last time. If you don't answer my question, I'm going to smack you upside your bald head. Is this bird behind my back dead or alive?"

"Lorenzo, whether that bird is dead or alive or whether that bird will ever fly again is in your hands."

And that's how it is for all of us. Our destination or course, whether eternal life or eternal damnation, is in our hands. It took me a long time to realize that the life I held in my hands was being crushed by the Deceiver. When I grew up outside of New York City, I dreamed of playing in the National Football League. I started in Pop Warner and high school ball, and then I went to play at the University of New Haven, a Division III college with only twenty-five hundred students.

Before I arrived on the scene, New Haven had never won more than two games in a season. In my sophomore year, we went undefeated, and I became the first all-American player in the history of the school. These developments really went to my head: I started telling all the coaches that I was going to play in the NFL. They laughed behind my back, and I heard them whisper that I was too small, too short, too slow, and too weak.

I showed them how wrong they were. In 1982, I was drafted by the Los Angeles Rams. Flying out to California was a revelation to me. The freeways were landscaped with green plants and flowers, and the road had no potholes. Back east the expressways were riddled with dead dogs and burned-out cars.

Southern California was a whole new scene. I even enjoyed the earthquakes because I had never experienced them before. I went through training camp with the Rams, and all summer long, I survived each cut. Going into the final cut, there were nine defensive backs but only eight spots. I was the only rookie. On September 5, 1982, while awaiting my fate at training camp, I heard a knock on my door at the team hotel. Everyone knows what the knock means: I was going to get cut. I got all choked up. I took a deep breath and told myself that I was going to take it like a man. Then I opened the door, and it was the hotel maid.

Later I was summoned to the training facility, where I was the final player cut. Afterward, I went back to my room, lay on my bed, and cried. My life was over at age twenty-two. I had no college degree, since I had not finished engineering school, and I was three thousand miles from home.

I didn't know what else to do except to keep working out and hope I would get another chance. That chance came midway through the season when I was called up by the San Diego Chargers.

Now I was where I belonged, playing in the NFL, and once I secured my spot with the Chargers, I did what I wanted to do: I chased women. Ran from women. Got high. Went to parties. I thought I was The Man. I was in a nightclub one evening, and this girl walked by me. She was wearing a shirt with Chinese writing. Now, when you're in the NFL, you don't know that you're young and ignorant. You think the world revolves around you. So when this girl walked by me, I piped up, "Do you know what that shirt says?"

"No," she replied.

"Well, it means . . ." and I used some slang sexual terms that I can't repeat here.

"Oh, that's funny," she said before walking away.

Five minutes later, she was back. I knew she would be. *If this girl came back after what I said to her, she must be really stupid,* I thought. *That makes her stupid enough to go out with me.*

We picked up our conversation, and I was making some headway when she stopped me and said, "I'll be right back."

As I watched her parade away, a guy came over to me.

"You like her?" he asked.

"Oh, yes. She's fine," I replied, taking another swig from my beer bottle.

"Are you going to hook up with her?"

"I got her in the palm of my hand. No problem."

"Let me tell you something about her." He looked to the left, then looked to the right. Than he whispered into my ear, "That's a dude dressed up like a woman."

"Oh, I knew that, I knew that," I replied, trying to recover as gracefully as I could.

I spent my first two years in the NFL getting caught up in stupid stuff like that. But hey, I was young and single, and I liked to mingle. I was doing all those things because the devil told me they would make me happy. I started using cocaine and developed a full-blown drug habit.

STANDING IN THE WAY

Midway through my second season, the Chargers were flying back from an East Coast game with the New York Giants. Coast-to-coast flights were always long and boring, so I went to the lavatory, where I blew some cocaine up my nose. *That'll make the flight go better.*

As I walked up the aisle to my seat, a teammate named Sherman Smith was blocking my way. Sherman was our running back who stood six-feet-four-inches tall and came packed with 225 pounds of the most solid muscle you'd ever want to tackle. He had huge biceps, a nineteen-inch bull neck, and ab muscles that rippled like a washboard. This dude was a strong, bruising runner who plowed through defenses, which is why he was nicknamed "Sherman Tank" by the media.

Believe me, Sherman's body easily blocked the aisle. He stood with a giant Bible the size of the Ten Commandment tablets in one hand while leading a Bible study for several players.

"Can I get by?" I asked.

"What's up, little brother?" responded Sherman.

"Who are you calling 'little'?"

"You!"

"Okay, okay," I laughed. We both knew who the big boy was on the plane.

Before he let me pass, Sherman asked me out of the blue, "If you were to die today, what would happen to you?"

"I would go to heaven."

"How do you know?"

"Look, man, I went to Catholic school for eight years. I wore a green suit every day. I'm going to heaven for that."

"Nah, you ain't going to heaven for that."

"Look, man, we used to have nuns in our school who were five-foot-two, 260 pounds, and they used to smack us in the head. I'm going to heaven for that."

"Nah, you ain't going to heaven for that."

"Why not?" I asked.

"Let me tell you a little story, little brother." And Sherman proceeded to tell me the story about Nicodemus from the third chapter of John. Nicodemus was a Pharisee, well-educated in Jewish culture and the Old Testament. Nicodemus had been watching Jesus Christ heal lepers, raise a young girl from the dead, and restore the sight of a blind man.

Nicodemus asked Jesus, "Rabbi, we know you are a teacher who has come from God. For no one could perform the miraculous signs you are doing if God were not with him."

And Jesus said to him, "I tell you the truth, no one can see the kingdom of God unless he is born again."

"How can a man be born when he is old?" Nicodemus asked.

"Surely he cannot enter a second time into his mother's womb to be born!"

For a long time, I thought about what Sherman said to me. On April 12, 1984, I was lying on my couch. It was 5:00 A.M. I had been doing cocaine all night, but really, I had been doing drugs for eight years, ever since I started smoking marijuana at age sixteen. I thought that playing in the NFL, being on TV, and walking around like a star would make me happy, but after two years in the pros, I was empty inside.

I got on my knees. I said, "Jesus, I ask You to be my Savior today, and I will surrender my whole life to You. I don't want to live for myself anymore. I will do whatever You want me to do. I will be whatever You want me to be."

Christ became my Savior at that moment, and I stopped doing cocaine that day, stopped cursing that day, stopped smoking marijuana that day, and I got right with my girlfriend, Debbie, who is now my wife and mother of our three children.

THE CHANGES WE MAKE

Instantly, Sherman Smith and two other players started discipling me and helping me learn and memorize the Word of God. Then the Lord showed me why He gave me a big mouth. I started to teach the Word in prisons.

Prisons are the best place to do ministry. Do you know why? Because when you go to prison, you never have to convince anybody that he is a sinner. When you say, "All have sinned and fallen short of the glory of God," the prisoners respond with "Amen, brother. Amen. Get to the forgiveness part, okay? We're ready to repent."

I went to prisons, churches, and high schools to share my story. In fact, after sharing my testimony with one high school principal, he said, "You need to tell my school that."

So I started doing high school assemblies. Now I travel around the country talking about self-esteem and abstinence. Then I have "after-school parties," where I offer the students free pizza and free salvation, and we see about 20 percent of the school saved.

I became an ordained pastor and earned my Master of Divinity degree. Five years ago, I started "Miles Ahead Ministries." Probably the most exciting thing we do is hold youth crusades. At a crusade in the Los Angeles Sports Arena, more than seven thousand kids from nearby South Central L.A. came out, and twelve hundred received Christ.

God is showing me His plan for my life. Fifteen years ago, I was clueless about why He created me. I thought I was just going to play football, chase women, act wild, and have fun. The devil has probably told you something similar to that, but God has a plan, and its goodness is beyond your wildest imagination. Your eye has not seen, your mind cannot conceive, your ear has not heard what God has planned for you.

God wants you to come and follow Him because He has a plan for you. You don't know what that plan is. But God does, and only He knows how He's going to do it.

Think about how God used Sherman Smith to bring me to Christ. Before being traded to the Chargers, Sherman played for years with the Seattle Seahawks, and he was adored in the Pacific Northwest. Sherman couldn't cross a Seattle street without being stopped, patted on the back, or asked for an autograph.

In San Diego the story was different. He arrived in a city where nobody knew him and nobody cared. He wasn't with the Chargers for more than a month or two when he blew out his knee. While in rehab, he wondered, *Lord, why did You ship me to San Diego?*

I know why the Lord brought Sherman Smith to San Diego: to touch a lost soul like me.

19

The Thief on the Cross:
IN SIGHT OF THE SAVIOR

NAME:
unknown
AGE:
unknown
UNUSUAL FACT:
witnessed the crucifixion of Jesus Christ

I can't believe this is happening to me. It's all because I "liberated" a few knives and one sword from the Roman garrison. I never should have taken the job.

And now I've been tied to this cross to die. How did I ever find myself in this spot?

It's the Romans. I hate the Romans. I don't deserve to die for what they call a capital crime. I'll tell you what a capital crime is. A capital crime is when a foreign power rules God's chosen people, as Pharisee Simon Josephat said in the Temple just before the new moon. He said the holy Torah promises that God will send a Messiah who will overthrow the hated Romans and restore Israel to its rightful place of power. "How long will we wait, Lord?" he implored.

My friends and I have never been interested in politics like the chief priests and scribes at the Temple. Life is very short, and the Romans are too strong anyway. When a friend told me that someone was willing to pay handsomely for a set of Roman knives—the craftsmanship is the finest in the world, they said—I saw a chance to put a year's worth of shekels in my pouch. It was a calculated risk, but worth it.

The Romans did not take lightly to missing weapons, however, and they interrogated half of Jerusalem before I was turned in by someone trying to save his own skin. My accomplice and I stood before the Roman magistrate, and we were informed that we had committed a capital offense against the dominion of Rome, and there could be only one sentence: death by the cross. My knees buckled upon hearing the sentence, and then I began vomiting in terror. Crucifixion is a shameful way to die, tied up naked to a splintery cross and forced to die like a dog. The Romans borrowed crucifixion from the Carthaginians and adopted it as their own, but they added a terrible twist: all prisoners were scourged within a mite of their lives so that the actual crucifixion wouldn't take too long.

While languishing in my cell waiting for my death sentence to be carried out, the Romans arrested another prisoner.

"Who's he?" I asked my partner.

"Don't you know, stupid? He's Jesus, the carpenter from Nazareth. He created a scene last week when he rode into Jerusalem on a donkey. The people thought he was going to be the next king of the Jews and overthrow the Romans. I guess his reign didn't last too long, did it?" chuckled my cellmate.

"He doesn't look like the type who wants to be king," I commented. "Usually kings and chief priests boss everyone around. They can have you scourged for just looking at them sideways. He has no power."

Maybe this Jesus fellow didn't know the grave danger he was in;

he certainly didn't act like someone who knew he could be executed in a heartbeat by the Romans. His captors wanted to rough him up a bit before he saw Pontius Pilate, so they beat him with whips and poked him with sticks. They taunted him, and I felt sorry for this stranger. I saw one guard walk by my cell carrying a crown of thorns. "All hail, the king of the Jews," yelled the red-robed centurion, and everyone in his company broke out in deep laughter.

Me? I felt sick to my stomach. I watched two soldiers clear their throats and then spit on him; the heavy spittle ran down his face. They continued to mock him, saying he was what they expected of a Jewish king—without guts or power.

From my cell, I watched two centurions push the thorns into Jesus' skull, and that had to hurt. He stared straight ahead with a resolve that was disquieting. The pain had to be beyond human capacity, but he had a look of determination that was inspiring. Could this be the Messiah that everyone was talking about? *He could be.*

Then the Romans came to our cell and dragged us out to be scourged. The beating was horrible, but to take my mind off the pain, I kept thinking about Jesus and his example. When I was allowed to stagger to my feet, two centurions tied crosses to our backs and set the whip to our legs.

"Get a move on!" one screamed, as he snapped his whip against my right leg.

I shuffled out of the garrison and onto the city streets, where crowds were gathering. We trudged along, but we could hear people making noise behind us. Jesus had to be making his last walk, as well.

"I wonder if he'll die before he leaves the city," I commented to my accomplice.

"If he does, it will be the best thing that could happen to him," he said grimly.

Once we were just outside the city gates, near a main thorough-fare, a Roman soldier brusquely threw me to the ground. Before I captured my senses, a noose was wrapped around my neck, and I was hoisted into the air.

The crowd jeered, and all I could think about was taking my next breath of air. *I'm going to die today, and the end can't come soon enough. My biggest hope is that I die before they have to break my legs.*

I had heard horror stories from other prisoners about executions not going well, of prisoners hanging on a cross for two days before expiring, of botched attempts to "move things along." When the Romans thought the prisoner had suffered enough—whenever that was—they liked to take an iron rod and crack his legs. Then he couldn't use his legs to lift himself and keep his lungs breathing.

From my vantage point, I watched another spectacle unfold: the Romans grabbed Jesus' hands and nailed them to the cross; then they hammered a huge spike through his feet. Blood spattered everywhere, and I nearly fainted from the sight. The last nail was reserved for a sign on top of his cross: "This is the king of the Jews."

When the cross was upright, a centurion walked up to Jesus. He carried a lance with a sponge on the end soaked with sour wine. Before he raised the sponge, however, he mocked Jesus again. "If you are king of the Jews, then save yourself," he sneered.

My accomplice yelled out, "So you're the Messiah?" he scoffed. "Prove it by saving yourself—and us, too, while you're at it."

I had had enough. "Don't you even fear God when you're dying? We deserve to die for what we did, but this man has done nothing wrong."

Summoning what reserves I had left, I looked into Jesus' eyes. I wanted to believe. This man was truly the Messiah I had heard everyone talking about.

"Jesus, remember me when You come into Your kingdom," I pleaded.

Jesus looked into my eyes and smiled. "Today, you will be with Me in Paradise. This is a solemn promise."

It was a promise that the King of Kings kept.

20

Vicki Rose:
A SEARCHING HEART

AGE:
forty-five
OCCUPATION:
homemaker
RESIDENCE:
New York, New York
FAMILY SITUATION:
married to Bill for twenty-one years;
mother of Douglas, sixteen; and Courtney, thirteen

My ancestry is Jewish, and I can remember hearing the story of how my father, while visiting Germany in the twenties, was teased and belittled by other kids because he was a Jew. He is still haunted by the memory. I was born in New York City into a family of nonpracticing Jews. Then my father attended a Billy Graham Crusade in Ocean Grove, New Jersey, where he walked forward and received Christ. From that point forward, we experienced a cultural shift as we left behind all things Jewish and entered what I called our "Presbyterian period."

My father read the Bible to my sister and me at bedtime, but that was about it in terms of spiritual input. When we became older, Dad decided we should join Brick Presbyterian Church on Park Avenue and Ninety-First Street in Manhattan, where I attended Sunday school and was baptized and confirmed.

Dad's motives for joining the church were twofold: (1) he was seeking to go to church, and (2) he was seeking to be non-Jewish. I did not know where Mom was spiritually because she died of cancer one week before my high school graduation in 1971.

Mom's death scared me, but I also felt quite liberated. Armed with a short fuse and a critical nature, Mom had been very strict. After her death, we decided as a family that we would keep going. We would not grieve. We would stay busy. The summer passed in a whirlwind as friends of my father invited us to dinner parties and kept us entertained.

I started college that fall at Pine Manor Junior College outside of Boston. In my dorm, my roommate and I were chatting one night when she told me she had been dating someone named Bendheim.

"I know him!" I exclaimed. "He's a cousin of mine!"

"You must be Jewish then," stated my roommate.

"No, I'm Presbyterian," I replied, which must have really confused her. You see, I didn't think of myself as Jewish.

After graduating from Pine Manor, I transferred to Sarah Lawrence College, and when I graduated in 1975, I couldn't wait to start work in Manhattan. I entered the Saks Fifth Avenue Executive Training Program with the idea of becoming a corporate buyer with the prestigious department store chain.

INTO THE BIG LEAGUES

As I was launching my career, I met an energetic and impulsive guy named Bill Rose. He was a great baseball player until he wrecked his knee in high school, but Bill loved the game—and the Yankees. Bill became good friends with George Steinbrenner just after George purchased the Yankees in 1974. George would call Bill at midnight and say, "Hey, Billy, let's go eat. Can you meet me at P. J. Clark's?"

"Of course, George. Be right there, George."

The two would sit in George's favorite booth and talk baseball until the wee hours. Then George extended an invitation for Bill to buy into the Yankees. Bill didn't have that kind of money, so he talked his dad into buying a few "points" of Yankee stock, and they became limited partners with George Steinbrenner and the New York Yankees.

Bill and I married in 1977, but we both entered into marriage with no idea of what a marital union was all about. I thought my husband would bring me happiness, but deep inside, I knew we were wrong for each other. We had zero interests in common. I had never seen a baseball game in person, but in my first year of dating Bill, I attended seventy home games at Yankee Stadium and a few more on the road.

I was going along with the program, and if the program was hobnobbing with George Steinbrenner and his cronies in the owner's box, that's what I did. I was willing to forsake my interests for Bill if he would make me happy.

At my job I was promoted to buyer of evening wear for thirty Saks Fifth Avenue stores, but I quickly discovered that making million-dollar decisions didn't meet my emotional needs either.

I took stock: my marriage was empty and unfulfilling; my career wasn't as glamorous as you would think. I needed something else, and I found it in the back rooms of Studio 54, a nightclub where celebrities such as Bianca Jagger, Sly Stallone, and Vitas Gerulaitis held court, and cocaine was spooned to all takers. While Bee Gees disco music pulsated on the dance floor, my husband and I sat in the back rooms doing cocaine.

Did drugs make me happy? Not a chance. Bill and I separated for three months as we tried to get our lives together. We eventually reunited long enough to bring two children into the world: Douglas in 1982 and Courtney in 1984.

Then Bill, who was working with his dad in the textile business, decided overnight to open a sports bar and restaurant. Sports bars may seem to dot the landscape these days, but back in the early eighties, they were few and far between. Against conventional wisdom, Bill opened the Sporting Club in 1984 on the Lower West Side of Manhattan, within walking distance of Wall Street.

The restaurant, filled with sports memorabilia and a lively bar crowd, was an immediate hit. Feature stories praising the restaurant appeared in *USA Today*, *The New York Times*, and *New York* magazine. The glowing press reviews went to Bill's head, and more cocaine went into Bill's nose. The Sporting Club also attracted supermodels and beautiful babes, and Bill succumbed to the sexual temptations.

We were like two ships passing in the night anyway. His usual schedule was to fall into bed at 4:00 A.M. and sleep until 2:00 in the afternoon. Meanwhile, I had an infant and toddler to contend with. We had absolutely separate lives and little or no communication. At the same time, I tried to keep up outward appearances.

Bill tried to give up cocaine on several occasions, but his efforts at rehab were futile. I knew about the drugs; I didn't know about the women. By 1986, I couldn't live like virtual strangers anymore, so we separated again.

To help support the family, I went back to work, becoming a corporate buyer at Macy's. I felt better being back in the work force because I had no idea how to be a mom. I thought the kids would be better off with a Mary Poppins–type nanny. One of our nannies was Debbie Kirby, who had been a waitress at the Sporting Club. Eighteen months into my separation, Debbie handed me the following invitation:

Mrs. Arthur S. DeMoss cordially invites you to dinner at the Waldorf Astoria Hotel to meet and hear Secretary of the Interior Donald Hodel and his wife, Barbara. Mr. Hodel will be speaking about Christianity in the world today.

Having been separated for eighteen months and having no time or energy for a social life, I decided to go. When Don Hodel rose to speak, I was immediately captivated by his story. He told of his son's addiction to cocaine. *Cocaine? I have a husband who's hooked on coke.* Then the story turned tragic when his son committed suicide, causing the greatest pain in the Hodels' life.

"One thing I say to parents who come up to me with tears in their eyes is *you never get over it*," said Mr. Hodel. "The other perspective is that I wonder if Barbara and I would have come to a personal relationship with Jesus Christ if we hadn't been brought to our knees by such an event. It's sad, but it took something like that to make us realize that we were *not* in control."

Not in control. That was certainly my life to a T—totally out of control. I knew God was speaking to me, telling me *He* was the answer to all my problems. Jesus Christ could fill the terrible hole in my heart, the one that neither my husband nor money nor job could fill. For months I had been attending Al-Anon meetings (for families of alcoholics), and I had been going through the twelve-step program. The Al-Anon groups talked about the importance of having a Higher Power in your life. I was not willing to turn my life over without knowing who that Higher Power was.

Mr. Hodel outlined the steps to find that Higher Power, Jesus Christ. With Mr. Hodel leading the way, I gladly prayed to receive Christ into my damaged heart. The date was November 29, 1987.

VISIT EVERY OFFICE

When the event was over, Mrs. DeMoss invited everyone to attend a Bible study at the DeMoss House in Upper Manhattan. I eagerly started the following week, and I discovered the Bible answered every question I had. When I read my Bible, it seemed every word was directed toward me. For the first time, Christ was the center of my life.

I was so excited that I wanted to tell everyone about Jesus. I enrolled in a leadership training program at the DeMoss House in which I learned how to share the *Four Spiritual Laws*. At work I walked around the offices and said, "I'm taking a class on how to share my faith. Would you mind if I practiced on you?"

"No, go right ahead," they'd say, and they'd hear the gospel.

Something unexpected happened when I became a Christian: I had a sudden yearning to be with my children. I had always thought they were better off *without* me, but I now wanted to be home with them and teach them about the Lord.

My financial situation was not pretty, however. Bill and I had been separated for two years, but we had not made any moves to meet in divorce court. What our lawyers told us was that we would be better off not divorcing because a divorce meant we would have to sell the only thing we owned: the Sporting Club. Instead of finalizing a divorce, we just continued to live separately.

Bill saw the kids once a week at dinner. He would bring McDonald's over on an evening when I was not home. When we did converse, it was about money, and the conversation usually turned into an argument.

One morning at breakfast, I was reading a children's devotional book to the kids called *Leading Little Ones to God*. When we were finished, my six-year-old son, Doug, said, "We should pray for Dad."

In my heart I wanted nothing to do with my husband, but Doug was right. We started to pray for Bill. I asked my friends in Bible study to pray for him, and I cried out to the Lord for him because we could see how miserable he was.

On those intermittent times when we did see each other, Bill wasn't excited that I had become a Christian. When I explained the consequences of eternal separation from God, he told me that wasn't the kind of God he wanted to worship.

I persisted, even after the time he came to a DeMoss dinner at the Waldorf and got high in the bathroom and left before dinner was over. Then he agreed to come to a Baseball Chapel luncheon with former Yankee Bobby Richardson as the speaker.

"Are you sure Bobby Richardson is speaking?" asked Bill incredulously.

"Yes, I am. Why do you ask?"

"Growing up, Bobby Richardson was my hero. I wore number 1, just like he did, and I played second base, just like he did. It would be a thrill to hear him speak."

Bill was devastated that he never got his chance to see how far he could go in baseball. In his senior year of high school, Arizona State had offered him a full scholarship, and scouts from two major league teams were ready to sign him to a pro contract. Then he blew out his knee, which ended his hopes for a baseball career.

Bill was captivated by Bobby Richardson's testimony. When the former Yankee was finished, he approached Bill and asked to talk to him. The two found a booth and spent three hours chatting about the glory years of the Yankees and getting to know each other. Before he got up to leave, Bobby asked Bill if he could pray for him—not a prayer for salvation, but a prayer that Bill would open his heart to hear God's Word.

Bill was getting close, but it was hard for him to say goodbye to his old life. He was living with another woman, and he was still doing coke, so much so that he would wake up in the middle of the night and have to do drugs again to fall back to sleep.

Early one Sunday morning, Bill awoke and turned on the TV, settling on an evangelistic program. The message penetrated his heart, and Bill fell to his knees and sought God. This was no lightning-bolt experience for him, however. Bill finally asked Christ into his life at a DeMoss dinner in December 1990.

He got rid of the girlfriend and entered a week-long drug rehab program. When Bill was hit by the enormity of his wasted life of addiction, he fell to his knees again and wept bitter tears. The whole world seemed to stop, and a peace came over him. Bill *knew* the Lord had told him that from that day forward, he was healed from drugs. Bill got off the floor and found a counselor.

"I can go home now," he announced.

"Ah, I don't think so," said the wary counselor.

Bill completed the week, and since February 1991, drugs have been out of his life. Then we began repairing our relationship. We had been separated for more than five years, and we barely knew each other.

Bill's big problem had been a fear of commitment. He had no history of following through with that word. One afternoon we drove to a friend's house in Twilight Park in upstate New York near Lake Placid. Sheila Weber greeted us at her doorstep, and over coffee, she said, "Bill, that's great news that you've accepted Christ, but what are you going to do about your marriage? You're still married, you know. You're going to have to make a choice here."

"Excuse me?" replied my husband.

"A choice. You're going to have to decide whether you and Vicki are really going to get back together and have the marriage that God intended or if you are going to divorce. I think you need to go back home, but it's up to you."

Five months later, Bill did come home, and that's when the hard work really began. Through counseling, much prayer, and a lot of God's grace, we have become best friends. I love Billy more now than I ever did. He says the same about me, and now our children get to grow up with both their mom and their dad in the house. We thank God every day for His abundant mercy and for the privilege of this awesome miracle. As our daughter, Courtney, said, "If God could bring Daddy home, then God can do anything."

21

Michael Chang:
TENNIS'S BIG FISH

AGE:
twenty-seven
OCCUPATION:
professional tennis player
RESIDENCE:
Mercer Island, Washington
FAMILY SITUATION:
single

It's hard to believe that a decade has passed since Michael Chang stunned the tennis world by becoming the youngest-ever male player to win a Grand Slam event, the French Open.

Michael was just seventeen years old when he stormed Paris, but he wore his faith on the sleeve of his Reebok shirt, attributing his success to his newfound Christian faith. When he accepted the winner's trophy before millions of TV viewers, he said, "I thank the Lord Jesus Christ, because without Him I am nothing."

At first tennis journalists used the biblical metaphor of David versus Goliath to describe how a five-foot-eight-inch, 135-pound boy slew tennis giants Ivan Lendl and Stephan Edberg. *Los Angeles Times* columnist Jim Murray quipped that Michael had a variety of tennis instructors over the years, "but the four he relies on most are Matthew, Mark, Luke, and John."

As Michael continued to talk about Christ in his postmatch interviews, however, tennis correspondents stopped writing in their notepads or turned off their klieg lights. Michael noticed, but he stuck to his game plan. "Every time I brought up Jesus, everybody nodded and got sick of it, but it was the truth," he said.

One of the first things Michael did when he returned home to Los Angeles was attend a thanksgiving service at the Chinese Christian Church, where his grandfather was a founding member. The congregation cheered wildly when Michael rose to speak. He said his come-from-behind victories against Ivan Lendl and Stephan Edberg were not coincidences.

"That wasn't me playing out there," he said. "Jesus Christ is alive and well."

COURTING SUCCESS

The story of how Michael Chang asked Christ to be his doubles partner starts with his grandfather, Ken Wu Chang, who lived in China when the Communist regime of Mao Tse-tung outlawed religion in the late forties. Ken Wu had become a Christian when his wife experienced a miraculous recovery from terminal cancer.

The family fled to Taiwan in 1948, including Michael's father, Joe, who was four years old at the time. Joe was a keen student, and when he turned twenty-two, he arrived in Hoboken, New Jersey, for graduate studies in chemistry. He worked nights while attending Stevens Tech.

A friend arranged a blind date with a fellow chemistry student Betty, the daughter of Taiwanese parents. Her father was a Yale-educated career diplomat who immigrated to America in 1957. The rationale behind the blind date was at least Joe and Betty could talk in their mother tongues about inverse equations or molecular properties.

Joe and Betty married and moved to St. Paul, Minnesota, where Joe taught himself to play tennis. Two boys were born: Carl, in 1969, followed three years later by Michael. The Changs exposed their sons to tennis, thinking the game would be a fun sport to help them develop physically and mentally. Maybe they could get good enough to earn a college scholarship.

After putting in a full day as a research chemist, Joe would spend hours on the courts hitting balls with Carl and Michael. The boys showed an immediate aptitude for the game, and Joe read instruction books and studied coaching techniques to keep one step ahead of their growing skills. It wasn't long before they were ready for professional instruction.

"We didn't have enough money for both of us to take lessons," Michael recalls. "Carl would take the lessons, and I would sit on the sidelines and try to learn as much as I could. Later we alternated."

Carl became a very good junior player, but Michael became an extremely good player for his age. Although his Prince graphite racket was nearly as long as his legs, Michael won every tournament in the Minnesota area. If the Chang boys were going to be the best they could be, the family would have to move to a warm-weather climate. The family prayed about it and decided to move to southern California, where the boys could escape the icy climes of Minnesota and play outdoors year-round. To fund the lessons, tournaments, and travel, Joe took a job with Unocal, an oil company.

Age fifteen was monumental in Michael's life. He was the youngest-ever winner of the U.S. Junior National championship for players eighteen and under. With that victory, Michael qualified to play in the U.S. Open in New York City. There he became the youngest player ever to win a first-round match. Overnight, Michael—a high school sophomore—was ranked 163rd in the world.

Should he turn pro?

Actually the bigger question in Michael's mind at fifteen was, should he turn Christian? Michael had been raised in a loving, Christian home whose routine included attending church together on Sunday. But as he entered high school, a tinge of teen rebellion caused him to be restless about life. He also thought church was boring, just a bunch of adults sitting around talking.

"At fifteen years of age, I was doing a lot of searching," said Michael. "I was wondering about things like the meaning of life. I was really trying to find myself. I just had a lot of questions."

His grandparents, sensing the boy's need, gave him an *NIV Student Bible* and asked him to read it every day. "On one particular evening, I didn't have anything else to do, so I decided to take a good look at my Bible and see what it had to say. I looked at the index in the back and found that it covered all these different subjects, so I looked up areas like friendship and love. I found the Bible to be very true, very pure, in a way in which I wanted to live my life."

At their Chinese-American church, Michael heard a woman named Auntie Betty give her testimony, and afterward in a private moment between him and the Lord, Michael Chang accepted Him as Lord and Savior.

FISHER OF MEN

Michael did turn pro at fifteen and began his meteoric rise to number two in the world (in 1996), just behind Pete Sampras. He's made so many fifth-set comebacks that opponents wonder if he has a tennis-playing guardian angel perched on his shoulder. He plays often in the Far East, where he is known as the "Michael Jordan of Asia." Michael can't stroll the sidewalks of Hong Kong without bodyguards.

His older brother, Carl, who starred on the University of California at Berkeley tennis team, became Michael's coach in 1991. Together, they make a terrific team: not only does Carl know Michael's game best, but he knows Michael best. For instance, it was

Carl who suggested that Michael play with a Prince Longbody racket to beef up his serve.

Carl is part of the "Chang Gang" that sits in the players' box while Michael plays. Carl can usually be seen sitting with his wife, Diana, and sometimes Joe and Betty, who come to the Grand Slam tournaments.

"We work as a unit," said Betty. "Each one of us has his or her own role to play in this particular mission, just as each one of us has a role in God's kingdom. As a family, we know what helps Michael perform the best so he can go out there to glorify God's name and give Him his very best."

It was Joe who gave Michael a passion second to tennis: fishing. In Minnesota Joe used to take the boys fishing for some family bonding time at some of the state's ten thousand lakes. "Fishing was something fun that we could all enjoy together," said Michael, who fell for the sport.

Michael is crazy about fishing. His travels take him all over the world, and he can probably tell you the best fishing holes at every stop. His web site (www.mchang.com) devotes four pages to his favorite hobby.

Click on the right icon and you can view a picture of the forty-five-pound amberjack he snagged in Florida. Click on another to see the seventy-eight-pound marlin he reeled in at the tip of Baja California. Or click again and read about the ton of yellowfin tuna he and Carl caught during Carl's "bachelor party/fishing trip" off San Diego.

Michael also breeds fish in his huge aquarium at home. "I've found that raising fish is relaxing and peaceful and also very interesting," he said.

Michael's web site shows he is also a "fisher of men." He has placed his testimony and a step-by-step plan of salvation into cyberspace—in English and Chinese. This is not bait and switch; you have to click the Christianity icon to read how Jesus is Michael's first love, not tennis.

"If I'm able to draw people to the Lord, then they'll always have that joy and that love for Him," he said. "The fame and the money and the rankings can't compare to touching people's lives and encouraging them in the Lord, because that's something that lasts a lifetime and beyond."

Assisting in this chapter was Christin Ditchfield of Sarasota, Florida, who has written extensively about the Chang family and authored Sports Great Michael Chang (Enslow Publishers, 1999).

22

Bob Kiersznowski:
FINDING THE
LORD'S FREQUENCY

AGE:
thirty-nine
OCCUPATION:
president of Prism Development, a training development
company specializing in time management
RESIDENCE:
Atlanta, Georgia
FAMILY SITUATION:
married to Erin for six years; father of Courtney, three

I was born in Saudi Arabia, the son of a petroleum engineer for Aramco, the Arabian-American Oil Company. We were an American family living in Daharan, a company town during the fifties and sixties. In the oil business, if a person agreed to an overseas posting, the company took good care of him and his family. For instance, Aramco helped with the expenses of sending my older sisters to boarding schools in Rome, Italy, and Gainesville, Florida.

Fifteen years of Saudi desert were enough for my parents, however, so we moved back to the States. Dad took a job for the state of New York in the Environmental Conservation Department, while Mom stayed at home and reared the kids.

Dad made sure we went to church *every* Sunday, and religion was part of our weekly routine. I didn't want to go to college, so after high school I began working at a small radio station that my dad owned with his brother. The station, WLMP in Lewisburg, Pennsylvania, was strictly an investment for Dad. As an on-air DJ, I started "spinning the platters," as they say, playing Top 40 hits and easy listening music.

After a couple of years behind a console and microphone, I began to see that maybe college really wasn't such a bad idea after all. I enrolled in nearby Bloomsburg University and worked weekends at the radio station. I fell into a fairly typical lifestyle for college students: drinking and plenty of partying. I was more interested in blowing my meager paycheck on a good time than making sure I had enough cash to cover next quarter's tuition.

I ran out of money. I decided to work full-time and save my money, so I got another radio job in Williamsport, home of Little League baseball. I worked the "overnights" from midnight to 6:00 A.M., making barely more than ten thousand dollars a year.

I can't say I was a very happy person. In 1984, I came home from work one morning and flipped on the TV. It was 7:00 A.M., and my interest turned to a commercial from the Arthur S. DeMoss Foundation. "If you're missing something in your life, we invite you to ask for our free book, *Power for Living*," the on-air voice intoned.

Missing something in life? That was me. The book had chapters about Tom Landry and Roger Staubach of the Dallas Cowboys, and I was a huge fan of "America's Team."

I called the 800-number, and the book arrived in two days. I enjoyed the testimonies about my sports heroes, and *Power for Living* ended with a fill-in-the-blanks presentation of the plan of salvation. I learned I was a sinner. I learned that I needed a Savior. I learned that

God had provided a method to be reconciled to Him. I learned that God loved me, no matter how sinful I had been. I don't think I was saved that day, but I certainly came to an intellectual knowledge of what salvation was all about. I made a halfhearted commitment to learn more about who Christ was.

On the work front, I learned that in radio the money was in selling advertising. I stopped being a DJ and got into sales. I took a position in Baton Rouge, Louisiana, with WJKN, and by age twenty-five, I was knocking down sixty grand a year. This was the middle of the go-go eighties.

At the time, I identified with a Michelob Light beer commercial, scored with an Eric Clapton song, "After Midnight." The commercial's storyline was a couple of guys cruising the big city, tooling around in big cars, living large. That's what I was working toward. When I was promoted to sales manager at age twenty-six, I thought the world was my oyster. I could have whatever I wanted.

THE FAST LANE

I certainly indulged myself. I flew to Washington, D.C., for a friend's wedding and blew three thousand dollars in three days at the Ritz-Carlton Hotel. Tough to do, but I did it.

Two months later I attended a wedding in Beverly Hills. I tossed greenbacks around like they were Monopoly money. Coming home on the plane that weekend, I got very depressed. If I was living a real-life beer commercial, why did I feel so empty?

If you knew me at that time, you might have heard me say that I was a Christian. But I really wasn't. I thought that going to church on Sundays made me a Christian, but I didn't have any sort of relationship with Jesus Christ.

The one good thing about my spiritual life was that I was still reading the Bible. I learned about the attributes of a godly woman in Proverbs 31:10–31, and since I had turned the corner on thirty years of age, I prayed that God would bring me a beautiful wife with those godly attributes.

He didn't answer my prayer right away, so I took a new position with Katz Media in Atlanta, a media representative company. One day after work, I took my dog, Natasha, for a little walk around the park. She's a samoyed, a white furball that kids are naturally drawn to. As I sat on the park bench, an adorable four-year-old girl came over to pet my dog.

She stopped and looked around. "Hey, where's your wife?" she asked.

"Sweetie, I don't have a wife."

"Oh, that's sad. Didn't God make you one?"

"Yes, God made me a wife, but I haven't found her yet."

At that time I was introduced to a coworker, Erin Marie Donohue. From the time we shook hands, my heart pounded. She was beautiful. She had a wonderful spirit. I immediately checked her left ring finger. *Good, she's not married.*

A couple of days later, I saw Erin at church. *Hey, she's cute and she goes to my church.* I asked her out to lunch, where we talked about issues of faith and the meaning of life. Our conversations were intense. After a month of lunches, church, and dinner dates, I told her that God had brought us together to be married.

Erin dropped her fork. "You've lost your mind," she said.

"No, I haven't. We're going to get married."

NOT ON THE SAME WAVELENGTH

I guess I won over Erin's heart, because we were married on July 17, 1993, in a big, beautiful church. We wrote our wedding vows and told everyone we were Christians, but there was still this huge gap in our hearts.

Erin and I quickly moved to Baltimore, where I took a job running the sales department of several radio stations. The salary was excellent, enough to purchase a nice Cape Cod–style house, drive an Infiniti car, and eat at the right restaurants. After six months, it became apparent that my supervisor and I were not listening to the same frequency. Sure enough, I lost my job.

I wasn't overly concerned at the outset. My brother Dave and I had been talking about starting our own training and management company. We saw a niche in which we could help other companies in time management, values clarification, goal planning, and goal setting.

The timing wasn't right for a start-up company, so to keep the money rolling in, Erin and I moved to New Orleans. No one wanted to buy our house in Baltimore, which meant we had to dump it and lose equity. Those were the breaks.

We "church shopped" in New Orleans, but nothing seemed right, so we started reading the Bible more and more, and the Holy Spirit began filling the holes in our hearts. Salvation, we figured out, was not dependent on being good, helping old ladies cross the street, or even attending church. Salvation was a free gift from God to His people. When Erin and I came to that realization, we gave our lives to Christ.

POWER FOR LIVING

As baby Christians, we didn't know what the next step should be. What about that training company my brother and I had been talking about? Was God leading us to step out in faith?

One evening as Erin and I were praying, I said to the Lord, "Jesus, we're learning to walk by faith and not by sight. If You want us to start this company, You need to help our fear. You need to give us a huge, bright neon sign."

On a Wednesday in August 1995, I was reading my Bible late one evening. Sometimes I would pray for the Holy Spirit to lead me to a Scripture passage that He wanted me to read.

As I was thumbing through my Bible, I came to Matthew 16:24–25: "Then Jesus said to his disciples, 'If anyone would come after me, he must deny himself and take up his cross and follow me. For whoever wants to save his life will lose it, but whoever loses his life for me will find it.'"

Suddenly everything from the previous ten years made sense. What God was saying to me was that I had been living for myself and that I had *not* been living for Him.

Christ-centered versus self-centered. *Power for Living*. Everything about my life was self-centered. I had not been living for Christ one iota.

Erin, who was four months pregnant, had already gone to bed. It was 11:00 P.M., but I woke her up anyway.

"Yes, what is it, sweetie?" she asked.

"Let me read you these verses that the Lord showed me," and I proceeded to read Matthew 16:24–25.

"Is that all?"

"Honey, that's what I've been looking for the past ten years."

"That's great, honey. We'll talk about it in the morning."

She rolled over and went back to sleep.

The next morning, I woke up, made my coffee, turned on my computer, and checked my e-mail. My sister Terry had sent me an e-mail message. Actually, it was a verse of Scripture. Terry subscribed to an e-mail service that filled her in box with a daily Bible verse, which she often forwarded to me.

When it appeared on my computer screen, I printed the e-mail and took the piece of paper into the bedroom.

"What's that?" asked Erin, still groggy.

"It's the verse of the day from my sister," I replied. "Let me read it to you. It's from Mark 8:34–35, and it goes like this: 'Then he called the crowd to him along with his disciples and said: "If anyone would come after me, he must deny himself and take up his cross and follow me. For whoever wants to save his life will lose it, but whoever loses his life for me and for the gospel will save it."'"

When I finished, I sat on the bed, staring at my Bible.

"Are you okay?" asked Erin.

"Yes, but . . ."

"Isn't that the same verse you read to me in the middle of the night last night?"

"It wasn't the middle of the night, and that was from Matthew."

"But you said this was from Mark."

"Yes, I did, and it's the exact same words from Jesus."

"Wow! What a coincidence."

"Sure is."

I was a little unsettled myself. *Deny yourself. Pick up your cross and follow Me.* What was God saying?

The next day, a Friday, I was chitchatting with a friend, confiding my fears about starting a new company, and he said, "I think I have the right verse for you. Let me fax it over to you."

When it came out of the fax machine, the verse was from Luke 9:23–24: "Then he said to them all: 'If anyone would come after me, he must deny himself and take up his cross daily and follow me. For whoever wants to save his life will lose it, but whoever loses his life for me will save it.'"

I sat in my chair, too stunned to move. On three consecutive days from three consecutive Gospels, I had received the same Word from the Lord. I felt untethered, ungrounded, very unsure of myself. Actually, I was scared to death.

BUDGET TIME

Meanwhile, there was work to do before the start of the weekend. We were doing budgets at the radio station, and our divisional president was coming in Monday to look them over. On Friday afternoon, I finished my budget for the sales department and walked it into my boss, John Rockweiler.

"Here you go," I said, as I tossed the report onto his desk.

"Set it over there," he replied gruffly.

"Something wrong?"

"No, not with you, but some of the other departments aren't going to have their budgets done until late today, which means I have to come in tomorrow and finish them up."

"Do you want me to come in tomorrow and help?" I asked, trying to sound conciliatory, knowing that tomorrow was a Saturday. John and I had an adversarial relationship.

"No, that's okay. Have a nice weekend."

"Okay," I mumbled. *Just trying to help.*

I drove home that afternoon, still wondering what God was trying to say to me.

Early the next morning, I woke up feeling restless. I turned on WBSN, a Christian radio station, and heard an advertisement for a Promise Keepers Wake-Up Call to be held that morning at a nearby church.

Wake-up call, I thought. Erin and I had no plans, so on the spur of the moment, I drove over to the Promise Keepers event.

When I walked in, there were six hundred men with their hands in the air, praising God like I had never seen before. The hairs on my neck stood up; the presence of the Holy Spirit was that strong.

I felt very uncomfortable. I wasn't used to this.

I found a seat in the last row. I wasn't going to call attention to myself.

When everyone sang, "Lord, I Lift Your Name on High," the Holy Spirit got hold of me. Then a speaker said he would give us a different take on what it means to put on the full armor of God. "What God means is not putting on the full armor for protection, but if He provides you with time, treasure, or talent—*and burdens you with the understanding of His will*—then you must be obedient to His will, or you are sinning."

For the next ten minutes, I felt that the speaker's words were burning a hole through my chest.

"Men, listen to this: God doesn't call everyone to formal ministry

165

or to travel to the unreached peoples of the world. Instead, God knows what God needs, so He calls people to perform things that are part of His perfect plan. If God is calling you to something, you need to be obedient. If you feel that God is calling you to something today, I want you to come to the front, where we can lay hands on you and pray for you."

I had to walk forward. When I arrived in the front, two or three guys came over, placed their hands on my shoulders, and I just fell over and lost it—absolutely lost it. I had an outpouring of emotion that I had never experienced before. I felt an intense, pure joy, not sadness for anything I had done, but pure joy that the God of the universe had spoken directly to me.

Other guys were coming up and going back to their seats, but I remained up front, weeping inconsolably for fifteen minutes. I couldn't stand.

It was at that moment that I understood the cost of discipleship. If I was going to be a disciple of Jesus Christ, then it was going to come at tremendous personal cost. I had to be obedient. I had to give everything to what God was calling me to do.

As I stood up, I determined two things: From that point forward, I was going to live a Christ-centered life. The other thing I was going to do was drop by my office that day—where I knew John Rockweiler was working that morning—and resign my position.

I took my seat in the last row of the church. I must have looked like I had gone through an emotional wringer because several men asked if I was all right. Then I felt another hand on my shoulder. I turned to my right, and it was my boss, John Rockweiler!

"Wha . . what are you doing here?"

"I woke up at 4:00 A.M., too tired to go back to sleep. I knew I should be at the radio station working today, but the Lord told me to change my plans and come to this Promise Keepers event."

I looked him in the eyes. "John, I'm leaving the radio station."

"I know. That's why I'm here—to help you."

I lost it again, and the tears came out in buckets.

We hugged. Here was a guy with whom I had worked for over a year, and I never knew he was a Christian. Although we had an adversarial relationship, we knew that God had done a supernatural thing in waking him at 4 A.M. to help me carry through with what God wanted me to do.

When I came home, I was just drained. Erin walked in the door from a shopping trip, took one look at me, and asked, "Are you okay, Bob?"

"I'm all right," I allowed. "Ah, I saw John at the Wake-Up Call. I quit my job."

"I'm sorry," interjected Erin. "It sounded like you said that you quit your job."

"I did, honey."

Erin's peace about the decision was amazing, especially since she was four months pregnant.

We knelt and prayed about it, and then I phoned my brother.

"I have great news, Dave."

"What would that be?"

"We're in business!"

"We're in business?"

"Yes, I quit my job today."

"You did what?"

"Quit my job."

"What are you going to do?"

"Start that development company with you, and let God worry about the details."

THE GROUND FLOOR

We started Prism Development with very little money. In the first week, a business acquaintance Raymond Reggie called me from his downtown New Orleans office. He asked me how I was doing, so I laid out the whole story to him. "My brother and I only have enough money to incorporate the company, not rent office space or buy equipment," I said.

"Then I've got a deal for you," he said. "I'll give you an office, computers, fax machines, even some secretarial support. If you'll help me from time to time with some strategic stuff, you can move in."

I attended another Promise Keepers event and heard a talk by Chuck Stecker who was PK's South Central Regional Director. His talk was about how God was using Promise Keepers to provide the things that men need: organization, checklists, things like that.

I found Chuck after the event was over.

"Chuck, you don't know me, but God told me to start a training and development company, and maybe some of the things we are producing could be used by PK."

This began a round of discussions with Promise Keepers, and we were incredibly blessed to be selected in the summer of 1996 to manufacture the *Promise Keepers' Men's Planner Organizer.*

We made the deal knowing that it made no sense from a business perspective, but God had said to do it. Several people told us that we would be out of business in six months, but somehow we managed to produce the PK planner and make enough to keep the doors open.

Little stories kept our spirits up. I got a call from a gentleman who worked for a hardware company.

"How did you find out about us?" I inquired.

"There's a man in our Bible study. His name is Mike, and he's a truck mechanic who's always been somewhat disorganized. In recent months, Mike has gone from being pretty much nonparticipatory in our Bible study to being one of the most accountable and organized people."

"What do you mean?"

"I mean if someone asked for prayer concerning his wife's back, he'd mark it down in his planner, and then the following week he'd say, 'Hey, Tom, how's your wife's back?'"

Stories like that kept our spirits up, but our tiny company continued to struggle. We developed a business plan and looked for investors, but as we came closer and closer to folding the company, I wanted to get mad at God.

One Friday I called our two employees into my office.

"I'm afraid I can't pay you anymore," I said. "God doesn't want us to be in debt. You'd better start looking around for something else."

They kept returning to work.

"Listen, you need to figure out what you're going to do next," I said.

Neither Danny nor Vicki wanted to do that. Each time we prayed at the start of the business day that they wouldn't let me get mad at God.

In my own private prayer time, I said, "Father, I need to hear Your voice like I heard it in August 1995, when You told me to quit my job. If I'm that confused, forgive me for my lack of faith, but please move our investors to say yes or no. I need it to be that clear."

The following day I spoke on the telephone with some potential investors.

"Bob, I get the sense that you really feel called by God to start Prism Development," opened one fellow.

"Yes, that's right."

"I'd like to hear about it."

"I made a covenant with God that if anyone asked me to tell my story, then I would have to tell it from soup to nuts. It's sixty minutes long."

I thought he'd change the subject because he didn't have an hour to hear my story, the one I've recounted on the pages of this book.

"No, I want to hear it. Go ahead; I have the time," he said.

When I was done, he asked me, "How much money do you need?"

I gave him a figure.

"Put us down for that amount."

And just like that, the deal was done. Now I've heard dozens of people talk about God's perfect timing, but if God had done this any other way, I might have doubted that His hand was involved. Prism Development has been successfully capitalized to the extent that we can now go into the marketplace and try to be a light to a fallen world. The vision God has given us is to serve Him by being in service to others, and that is the mission of our company.

23

Amy Stephens:
A VOICE FOR THE LORD

AGE:
forty-two
OCCUPATION:
manager of Legislative and Cultural Affairs for
Focus on the Family's Public Policy Department
RESIDENCE:
Colorado Springs, Colorado
FAMILY SITUATION:
married to Ron for fifteen years; mother of Nicholas, seven

We landed at Hong Kong's Kaitak Airport on a cloudy day in the spring of 1966. Seven hundred miles to the southwest, President Johnson was pouring U.S. troops into the Vietnam conflict, and just over the border in Red China, as it was known back then, Mao Tse-tung's disciples were unleashing the Cultural Revolution in Tiananmen Square.

I was eight years old when our Lufthansa jet touched down. My family—I was the eldest of three daughters—was moving to Hong

Kong because my father, who worked for the FBI, was opening the Bureau's first Asian office. We were all proud of Dad because he was the youngest-ever director of an FBI field office.

Dad, who mastered Mandarin in Army Language School, was thirty years ahead of his time: he believed China was the wave of the future—economically and politically. He believed that China was a sleeping giant that would one day wake up and become a major player in global affairs; this was a view not held by many in the midsixties.

Meanwhile, Mom was a wonderful homemaker for Melissa, Laurie, and me, and I think it was because Mom's mother died suddenly when Mom was five years old. In spite of the insecurities she felt from losing her mother at a tender age, Mom vowed that she would be the best mother when it was her turn. She fulfilled that vow, and Mom was a great mother.

Mom, however, was holding a dark family secret within her soul: her mother had died from an illegal abortion. This was scandalous news in the thirties. At the time, she and her siblings were told that their mother had died from a ruptured appendix. Her father, to dull the pain and forget a shameful family matter, took solace in booze. He began drinking regularly and retreated emotionally from the family when he remarried. Mom's stepmom ruled the roost, and my mother did not like her new stepmother. That created much pain and anger in Mom.

In Hong Kong, Mom drove us to the American school by day and attended receptions by night at the U.S. Embassy, where the FBI offices were located. Mom and Dad spent four or five nights a week hobnobbing with various ambassadors and representatives of the British Crown Colony, and I accepted their frequent absences.

BACK IN THE USA

Our Hong Kong stint ended in 1971, and when we returned to the States and settled in the San Francisco Bay area, we feared how much the U.S. had changed in just five years. We had read about the political upheaval and antiwar protests. I felt like a junior-league Rip Van Winkle when I walked into my high school campus with knee socks, starched shirt, and a navy blue skirt, while my freshman classmates were attired in garish bell-bottoms and bobcat vests. I felt geeky, and our family had to settle into the culture—quickly.

The move from Hong Kong was hard on Mom, who expected life to resume in a fairy-tale land where nothing had changed. Well, a lot had changed. Boys no longer wore crew cuts but grew their hair down to their shoulders. Girls gingerly walked in tight miniskirts and skimpy halter tops. There was psychedelic music. Marijuana and LSD. Slogans like, "Don't trust anybody over thirty."

With my sisters and I becoming teenagers, we needed Mom less, and that development caused her to question her role. Mom began to flounder, which grew into depression and anxiety, and later into alcohol, just as her father did a generation before.

My father? He was busy looking for Weatherman bombers and, beginning in 1974, trying to solve the Patty Hearst kidnapping case from his FBI office in Berkeley. Life for him never missed a beat.

As I sailed through high school, I saw Mom becoming isolated and having a hard time making friends. I saw my parents arguing more. I saw more drinking. My parents were living out their dysfunctions, and the self-help "I'm okay; you're okay" movement hadn't arrived yet.

The nation was in an experimental mood, and women everywhere were declaring their freedom from the home. Dad, at times, sounded like the biggest feminist of all. "You have to have something to fall back on," he lectured us three girls. Maybe he did this because he saw men abandoning their wives and children for new honeys or foresaw millions of women entering the work force. In any event, Dad was adamant about our getting college degrees and pursuing careers.

Mom took a part-time job, but that wasn't her. I could tell she was struggling for her identity, but I didn't know what to do. Besides, I was the oldest and had to be "good." This was especially so since my middle sister was having trouble adjusting to junior high and was taking up much family time and energy.

I started dating in my freshman year and had my first serious boyfriend in my junior year when I was sixteen. *That's the guy*, I thought. He was my first love, and we knew it was a matter of time before we would have sex. Within a month or two of losing our virginity, however, I became pregnant. My boyfriend and I just looked at each other, absolutely petrified. My life appeared ruined, and things were so bad at home that talking to my parents was the last thing I felt I could do.

No, I will take care of this myself. No need to involve Mom or Dad.

I found a Planned Parenthood clinic, and the counselor listened to my story and said she had the answer to all my problems. She said a new Medicaid program was covering the cost of abortions, so it wouldn't cost me a red cent.

"What about my parents?" I asked.

"You are an emancipated minor capable of making this decision," the counselor replied smoothly. "No one has to know."

"Where do I sign?"

An abortion seemed like it would solve so many problems. It was 1974, the summer before my senior year at Ygnacio Valley High School in Concord, California. I had my whole life ahead of me. I was the school mascot, a member of senior choir, and an ace on the tennis team. Everything was going my way, and I wasn't about to let it all go.

The county hospital performing the abortion was in Martinez, a few miles from home. I had to go to the hospital the day before for a physical, and while there, I signed a lot of papers. Afterward, I asked a counselor what they were going to do. "Look, it's a quick and safe procedure," she said. "Everything's going to be just fine. You might feel a little cramping when you're done."

But I had seen an issue of *Life* magazine with a photo essay called "Window on the Womb," showing all these amazing color photos of tiny unborn babies inside their mothers' wombs. I couldn't reconcile what I saw on the glossy pages of *Life* and what the counselor was telling me, so I didn't try. *Better to not think about it.*

The following day the doctor offered anesthesia, but I was too scared to be knocked out because I was ready to get in and get out fast. I remember the procedure as being very painful, and then I saw the canister filled with what looked like a bloody mess. Something inside me said, *You just killed your baby.* But before I let that thought settle into my subconscious, I shut down emotionally. *Don't go there,* I told myself. *You've got to survive this.*

The attending nurse wheeled me into the recovery room and handed me a cup of orange juice and some crackers.

"How you feeling?" she asked.

"Oh, fine, just fine," I assured her, feeling more upbeat by the minute. "Hey, when do I get to go?"

I walked out in less than an hour, determined to leave that horrible event behind me. What began, however, was a pattern of denial. Over the next few months, I appeared fine. Looked healthy. Laughed at jokes. But inside I knew it was all a façade. I was experiencing post-abortal syndrome but didn't know it, and no one in the medical or counseling community in 1974 knew about postabortion syndrome (PAS).

My boyfriend and I broke up, but then we got back together—and I got pregnant *again*. This time I was referred to a doctor in private practice, and he performed the abortion. After finishing the procedure, he lectured me about the need for responsible sex and handed me a prescription for birth-control pills. I thanked him, left the office, and drove straight to an Ygnacio Valley High School basketball game, where my fellow cheerleaders were waiting for me. More denial. More smiling. More "everything's fine." Meanwhile, I went on the Pill.

I kept up appearances throughout my senior year. I continued to be a cheerleader, played on the tennis team, sang in *South Pacific,* and participated in Madrigals, a choir group. Still, on the inside, I felt out of control. I went on crying jags for no reason, and it became harder and harder to stuff everything. The only bright spot was when I won the prestigious Gladys Turk Scholarship for voice at UCLA. I could sing well, and people had noticed.

LIFE IN 90210

From the moment I stepped on the UCLA campus, I felt like the country bumpkin amongst a world of graduates from Beverly Hills High. I was overwhelmed by the size of the school. To compensate, I joined Young Americans, a group that sang and performed around the U.S. It was much like Up with People. Young Americans provided a safe haven. I could form friendships with forty singers instead of trying to find my way on a campus with thirty thousand students.

A musician from Young Americans became my next serious boyfriend. He was well-connected with the Hollywood lifestyle, having grown up in a Bel-Air mansion, complete with a pool house. For someone who had trouble finding a ten-dollar bill in her wallet, I found this pretty high living.

At his home, his parents weren't concerned in the slightest that we were sleeping together; they kept to their wing of the mansion. Besides, this was the seventies. Everyone was doing it.

At the end of my freshmen year, the Young Americans asked me to join them on a yearlong tour, performing stock theater. *Great, let's go.* One little problem: I was pregnant again, even with using the Pill! I did not take this news well. I became very angry and very methodical. By now, I knew the drill. I called Planned Parenthood and scheduled an appointment. My boyfriend was talking about keeping the baby, but in my mind, this was not an item for discussion.

"Sorry, this is the way it is," I announced. "I have to be on a plane to Michigan in two weeks for the Young Americans tour. See you later."

I walked into the abortion clinic in downtown L.A. with a hardened heart, and I walked out with a hardened heart.

This time, however, I didn't experience a rapid recovery. Instead, I felt nauseous. I ran a high-grade fever. I shook with chills under the covers. I knew something wasn't right, but I didn't want to find out what it was, so I toughed it out. I wish I hadn't because the abortion messed up my reproductive system.

When I recovered, going on the road with the Young Americans picked up my spirits. I liked seeing the country and performing in front of live audiences. While on the road, I received a letter from Dad. "Having a career in voice isn't going to land you much of a job, so why don't you think about going into radio, TV, or communications? This is a great field, especially for women."

UCLA had a brand-new communications program at the time, but Cal State Fullerton had a more mature one, so I enrolled at the Orange County school and landed a part-time job singing at dinner theaters on weekends.

Then I saw a newspaper advertisement for the Birth Control Institute, the Orange County equivalent of Planned Parenthood. They were looking for counselors to staff the 4:00–9:30 P.M. shift. They hired me in a heartbeat, and I began performing pregnancy tests, counseling women considering an abortion, helping with Pap smears, and handing out contraceptives.

It was very interesting sitting on the other side of the counselor's desk. Now I was the person delivering the bad news: "Yes, I'm afraid you're pregnant." I thought I was being very noble. After a few months, they asked me to quit school for a full-time job at the clinic. "You can move through the ranks here," I was told. "You're part of a movement that's taking women forward."

I wanted to learn more about the business and be able to better counsel women. Since abortions were performed during mornings and early afternoons, I asked to witness one. "I need to understand what the doctor is doing," I explained, "so women can understand the procedure."

Early one afternoon, I stepped into a small room, where a doctor and a young Hispanic woman, under general anesthesia, were waiting for me. What I saw was like an out-of-body experience. My pulse quickened, and I felt lightheaded, but I steadied myself. *Keep a stiff upper lip,* I told myself. I watched the doctor perform the curettage extraction, and then I left the room as fast as I could, sick to my stomach. I cried all the way to my apartment and cried the rest of the day.

Why was I feeling this way? Why was I crying for a woman I didn't know? I couldn't answer those questions because I was so grieved. But in the weeks to come, it became harder and harder to work at the clinic. I couldn't breathe when I walked in the front door. Finally, I begged off, telling my supervisor that my studies were getting intense and that I needed some time away.

The break didn't do much good. In January 1978, I began experiencing anxiety attacks at school. When I went to the student health center, they checked me over and pronounced me fine. Then they referred me to a counselor. When I explained my past abortions and what I was doing, the counselor never associated abortion-plus-anxiety as a form of postabortion syndrome. I was left to flounder on my own.

IN SEARCH OF SOMETHING ELSE

I graduated from Cal State Fullerton with a communications degree in my pocket, just as Dad wanted me to, but I drifted in and out of various singing jobs. I sang at Knott's Berry Farm and the Disneyland Hotel; the latter job started at 5:00 P.M. and ended at 2:00 A.M. In between, I picked up some studio work for commercials.

Basically I was bumming around, hanging out with bartenders, and working when the rest of the world was asleep. Not a great lifestyle. I had moved in with a new boyfriend in Long Beach. One night I got strep throat, and I called in sick to the Disneyland Hotel.

"Sorry, you have to sing," my boss told me.

"But I could damage my vocal cords," I replied.

"You'll be okay. There's no one to replace you."

I sang and promptly wrecked my voice; little nodules formed on my vocal cords.

Suddenly I was without a job. As I contemplated my world from a secondhand couch, I took stock. I was twenty-six years old. I was in a dead-end relationship with a rugby player who said he didn't want to marry me. I was a singer who couldn't sing and might never be able to sing again. *Where are you going with your life?*

First things first. I had to get out of my dead-end relationship, which was a big deal for me. My boyfriend didn't want to be tied down anyway, so he moved to Redondo Beach. But he still wanted to be "friends" and see me, so I agreed. I got a new roommate, a female, and at first, I thought she was a little daffy. Whenever she was home, she played Keith Green records.

"Who's he?" I asked.

"A Christian singer," she replied. "Don't you like him?"

I nodded. I hadn't been in a church in ages, except for a wedding or two. My parents had taken me to church growing up, but with the lifestyle I was in, I didn't know how to find redemption.

Indeed, I was spiritually illiterate. I remembered listening to street preachers at Cal State Fullerton and then talking one-on-one with one of them while they read *Have You Heard of the Four Spiritual Laws?* to me. I even prayed with them a couple of times, but I soon went on with my life. I was very lost.

A week later I was visiting my old boyfriend at his Redondo Beach pad. He told me that he had woken up in the middle of the night and had seen what he thought was a devil in his room.

I looked askance at him.

"No, really. It was as real as this bed you're sitting on."

"Cool," I replied. "You know, my roommate was telling me about this person called the Holy Spirit, and she told me that if we would just pray, the Holy Spirit would get rid of that devil for you."

So I prayed, not really knowing what I was doing. But inside my heart I had another prayer: *Lord, if You are real and there is a Holy Spirit, I am willing to give up this relationship with my boyfriend if You make Yourself real to me.*

One week later my boyfriend promptly broke up with me, which threw me for a loop. I retreated to my apartment and my secondhand couch to contemplate my next move. Brilliant idea! I could type for people. Don't students need papers typed? I could only hunt-and-peck on the keyboard, but that didn't matter.

I needed some typing paper. But I was out of it, so I walked over to Craig and Roger's apartment and knocked on the door. Craig and Roger were two single guys, and I knew they were Christians since I heard them play Christian music on their stereo.

"Oh, Amy, nice to see you," said Roger.

"I was wondering if I could borrow some typing paper."

"Sure, sure, but why don't you come in first?"

We made small talk while they found some paper, and then Craig said, "Amy, could we talk to you about Jesus?"

I felt trapped. "Sure, fine, go right ahead," I offered.

I took a seat at their kitchen table, and they literally walked me through the Four Spiritual Laws, taking their time explaining what happens when you get saved.

It all made sense. I needed Christ in a big, big way. But I also needed typing paper. They asked me if I wanted to pray to receive Him, and I said yes. I was trapped, and besides, I needed that typing paper.

Craig said, "We have this friend, a football player on the USC football team, and when he lays hands on people, they get healed. We'll bet you that you can get your voice healed."

Wait a minute. That's when I wanted to bolt for the door screaming.

They must have sensed my hesitancy. After some more explaining, I calmed down. "Sure, invite him over," I said.

Ten minutes later a huge guy named Tommy Sirotnak, weighing

290 pounds, nearly took the hinges off the door when he stepped into the living room. The first thing he said to me was, "After I got the call to come over here, I prayed for you, and God told me He was going to heal you."

Am I living in the twilight zone or what? I thought. *This is so bizarre.*

We all stood in a circle, and Tommy placed his Paul Bunyan–like hands on top of my head and began praying for me. I immediately felt heat from head to toe, and when he gently brought his hands around my throat, a burning sensation came upon me. I felt as if my throat was on fire.

"Lord, just heal her, let her know that You, the Great Healer, are all-powerful."

He removed his hands, and the heat left my throat. When I swallowed, my throat felt like new. Craig grabbed a guitar, strummed a few chords, and I started singing as clear as a bell. I realized then that I needed what these guys had, and that was Jesus.

Tommy asked if I wanted to pray to receive Christ, and I immediately said yes. Tommy explained that my old self would die and that I would become a new Amy. I knew deep down that these guys were for real and what they were offering was for real. It was as if I were stepping on a train that was traveling in the right direction.

After we prayed, Tommy asked if I wanted to be baptized. We all went back to my apartment, filled my bathtub, and Tommy dunked me in the water. When I came up, it was like the scales fell from my eyes. Where had I been? That's how clear everything looked. With the confusion lifted, peace took its place, and fear was replaced by joy. Something radical had happened to me—I had to get into the kingdom radically because I had been living so radically the other way. The date was January 21, 1983.

In the following weeks and months, the Bible came alive to me. I immersed myself in church, and I got involved in a campus ministry with Tommy and others on the USC and Long Beach State campuses.

I spoke with students about my abortions and told them there were other options. I described what I saw inside the abortion and birth control industries, and college students listened because my experiences were real. I urged them to consider abstinence, their sexual health, and to postpone sex until marriage.

I met my husband, Ron, through the campus ministry, and we were married on March 24, 1984. We wanted a family right away, but I learned that my last abortion had scarred my tubes, blocking them. After years of infertility, I was able to conceive through in vitro fertilization, giving birth to my miracle son, Nicholas, seven years ago.

As I began speaking out about abortion, abstinence, and what "safe sex" really is, I was recommended to and hired by Focus on the Family. I've been working for eight years in Focus's departments of Youth Culture and Public Policy, doing my best to present in the public arena God's view on sex and abortion.

You know, looking back at my life, it's easy to think I wasted many years. I once asked myself, *Why couldn't I have become a Christian when I was ten years old?*

Yes, God allowed me to experience great pain, but He did not waste those experiences. He's allowed me to use them to tell others not to travel down the same road I did. There are a lot of kids abstinent today because of my testimony, and I thank Jesus for every life He's touched through me.

24

Don Bartlette:
MACARONI AT MIDNIGHT

AGE:
fifty-nine
OCCUPATION:
speaker and author of *Macaroni at Midnight*
RESIDENCE:
North Canton, Ohio
FAMILY SITUATION:
married to Julie for thirty years;
father of seven daughters and one son

When I came into this world, I was met by my father, who was shocked when he held me up shortly after my birth. I had only half a nose hanging on the left side of my face. I had no upper lip. And there was a huge hole on the top of my mouth.

One look was all he needed. He knew I would never be the son he had hoped for, and his joy turned to anger.

Back then in 1939, when war clouds were circling Europe, people in North Dakota didn't know much about children born with a severe cleft palate. Even the local doctor gave up hope. When he walked into our log cabin and inspected me, he whispered to my father, "Send him away. He doesn't belong in your family or the community. He'll never learn like other children. He'll never think like other children. Do everyone a favor: send him away."

My father was a proud man, as you would expect for a man of Native American heritage. He had expectations of teaching me to fish and hunt, just as he did. But I had failed him, so he ran from his troubles by turning to the white man's curse—alcohol.

Down in the valley, people heard about the freak child born in the hills. I was taken from my parents and placed in a small hospital. Doctors didn't know what to do with me, so they pulled the left-hand part of my nose over to the right-hand side of my face, leaving me with a very flat nose. They tried to repair my upper lip, but the result wasn't much more than a crude attempt. Nothing was done about the hole in the roof of my mouth. Then they sent me back home. They couldn't do anything more.

Sticks and Stones Break My Bones

Growing up, my father never held me, never wrapped his arms around me, never looked at me with any pride in his eyes. He succumbed to a world of drink. My mother, however, was there emotionally for me.

I stayed inside my home most of the time because I couldn't speak. One day, when I was around nine years old, I wanted to see the world. I walked down the hill and found the town dump. I saw people throwing away household belongings, clothing, and perfectly good food. I was hungry all the time, so I took the food and pushed it down the hole in the top of my mouth. This is the way I had always eaten food. I never had to chew it; the food just dropped down into my stomach and gave me nutrition.

I liked the town dump. There was plenty of food to forage, and I never lacked for clothes. But the real reason I liked going there was because I met the first friends I ever knew: rats. I remember running and jumping and playing with the rats, pretending they were my friends. Actually, they were my friends. Rodents never laughed at me. They never pointed fingers at me. At night, however, they went into their holes, and once again I was left alone. I didn't like that. I was always wishing for someone or some animal to be my friend.

Not long after I befriended the rats, a school superintendent made the long trek to my parents' cabin. He said something about giving me some sort of education, although he was at a loss as to what the local school could do. My father was too ashamed to let me go, but Mom won the argument and pushed me out the door.

When I walked into the play yard, it was as if all the school kids had been waiting for me. At first, I received curious looks, but once someone called out, "Hey, Flatnose," it was open season on me. The taunts came in torrents:

"How come you can't talk?"

"Where's your nose? Don't you have one like everyone else?"

"You can't talk. You can't talk."

"Smelly Injun. You're a smelly Injun."

That hurt, but then one of the clever students came up with an inventive quip: "Donald Duck, say 'quack, quack.' Donald Duck, say 'quack, quack.'"

That night, I could not tell my parents what happened. As I tossed in bed, the taunts returned. . . .

Hey, smelly Injun.

Donald Duck, say "quack, quack." Donald Duck, say "quack, quack."

I never wanted to be a cartoon character. And I never wanted to go back to that school again, but Mom pushed me out the door again the following morning.

When I returned, the children were waiting for me in the schoolyard. Some were laughing. Others were mimicking a waddling duck. Then one child ran by, grabbed my hair, and threw me against a wall.

Another child kicked me. Another slugged me. The last ran up and—it took me thirty years before I could tell anyone this—spit all over my face.

I didn't know what to do, so I ran into my classroom and found a desk. I put my hands on it and hung on. I overheard one teacher say to another teacher, "Why my room? He can't learn. He can't talk. He's Indian."

They left me at my desk, but the teachers did nothing to protect me from my fellow classmates. They poked me with pencils, hit me with their knees, and right in front of me ripped my classwork papers in half. I was helpless because I could not speak. My mother had begun to help me read, and I could print quite well, but everyone believed I was the class dunce because I could not speak.

One day the teacher took me out of the classroom and put me in a little room down the hall. She closed the door, and I heard what sounded like a nail going into a hook outside the door. As I spent my school days in that little room, I began living in two different worlds. In one world, I wanted to be liked by my classmates; I wanted to learn how to speak; I wanted to learn. In my other world, I fantasized about bringing my father's knife or rifle to school and letting the children have it. That way, they would never laugh at me again. I can't tell you how many times I wanted to get rid of all the laughter around me.

I never went to second grade. The teacher wouldn't accept me. The first grade teacher wouldn't take me back, so I was placed in third grade, which only made things worse. I was not ready for third grade. I fell behind in my schoolwork and could not understand what was going on. The children laughed more and more. "Mental, mental," they sang; the words haunted me for years.

Walking home one day after school, a small group of children asked me to walk along with them.

Maybe they're going to like me, I thought.

When we reached the woods, they jumped me and tied my hands

behind my back. Then they took turns slugging me until blood ran down my shirt.

When I got home and my father saw I had a bloodied shirt, he beat me again. In my heart, I began hating the man who brought me into this despicable world. I vowed one day I would kill him. In my hate, I didn't care about anything or anyone. I became one of the worst troublemakers my little town had ever seen. Throughout my teen years, I kept getting into trouble until one night I was thrown in jail.

While I stewed in my cell, a man walked to the back door of City Hall, and I heard him say to the judge, "Don't send him away; that boy is my son."

I'd never heard that before. The judge released me into my father's custody, and I left the jail thinking, *Everything will change. My father called me his son.*

When we walked into our home, I quickly learned that I was wrong. He hurt me in such a way that I can't share the details with you. In my defiance, I took a rifle and aimed at my father. I thought, *You told them you'd help me, but you never did. You hurt me and hurt me, and I now hate you.*

Just before I pulled the trigger, my mother lunged and struck me on the face. I dropped the rifle, but I never dropped my intention to kill my father.

GIVEN A SIMPLE TASK

One day, my grandmother told me that a kind woman wanted to see me. *That's strange,* I thought. When I met this woman from down in the valley, I began moving warily away from her. I wasn't sure about her. She might laugh at me. Worse, she might hurt me.

"I know you can't speak, but I want you to do a simple task," she said. "Can you wash my car?"

I had never washed a car before, which she quickly surmised.

"Here, let me take your hand," she said. The woman grabbed my right hand and took me to a round knob on the outside of her house. Then she placed my hand on the spigot and turned it. For the first time in my life, I saw running water. I jumped out of the way, frightened.

Next, the woman demonstrated how to wash a car, and I mimicked her every movement. When I was done, she inspected my job. I had to wash it four times until she pronounced herself satisfied. Then she reached into her skirt pocket and pulled out a quarter.

A whole quarter! I had never earned any money before. I couldn't believe it. I wouldn't have to steal it. I didn't have to hide it under my tree. I couldn't be thrown in jail for having it. My father wouldn't be angry.

Then she did something else I had never experienced before: she asked me into her home.

"Please, come in," she offered.

She explained to me the meaning of a long word called "electricity." I walked from room to room, switching lights on and off.

I followed her into the kitchen, where a slice of bread was waiting for me on a plate. She watched me rip off a piece and push it down my hole.

"What are you doing?" she asked sympathetically.

I opened my mouth and showed her the hole in the roof of my mouth. She reached into my mouth and held my tongue. Then she took a fork with some bread on it, placed it between my teeth, and asked me to chew it, helping me make the right movements. I tried chomping on the soft bread, and then she gulped, asking me to do the same. I swallowed food for the first time!

In subsequent visits, she prepared a table with a long, white linen cover and set in front of me a plate of mashed potatoes and gravy with a T-bone steak. "We're going to learn about nutrition," she announced.

She began telling others, "He can learn, and he can read. He writes me notes. I know he can learn." They laughed at her. They couldn't believe her, but for years she continued to feed me, clothe me, and teach me until one day she said, "You have learned many things. Now you must learn to speak."

I didn't have her commitment or motivation. She put a little wooden box in front of me and pushed a knob. A picture came before my eyes. I couldn't believe it!

"This is a television," she said. One of the first programs I saw was a Donald Duck cartoon. Now I knew why all the school children flapped their arms and squawked "quack, quack."

"You must learn to speak, or they will laugh at you all the time," she said. She reached into my mouth and helped me guide my tongue to the right place. I struggled to make coherent sounds. One night I finally made a proper sound all on my own. It was almost midnight. I was so proud that I could hardly wait to run home to tell my parents.

My mother and father had just made some macaroni to eat when I came through the door. I was proud to show them all my progress. For the first time in front of my parents, I put the macaroni inside my teeth and began to chew. My parents realized for the first time how much this woman had taught me. They asked her if she could help even more.

That night a subtle but significant shift occurred in me and my parents: I was changing, and my parents were changing with me. Once my parents began believing in me, the whole community began to look at me in a different light.

But this woman was not finished yet. On a subsequent visit, she took down her Bible and opened it to Matthew 7:7. She read the verse—"Ask and it will be given to you; seek and you will find; knock and the door will be opened to you"—and began teaching me about three words: ask, seek, and knock.

When I motioned that I could not understand, she said that one day I would.

With her assistance, the community sent me away when I was seventeen to get some real help. In a fine hospital, I was given a new nose, and my cleft palate was fixed. A round steel plate was placed in the top of my mouth, and I received speech therapy for six long years.

When I returned to the community, I began speaking clearly. I re-enrolled in high school, and with the love and patience of that woman, who was white, I became the first handicapped Chippewa Indian to graduate at the top of his class.

I went to a university and became a social worker. Then I went to another university and studied education. But it seemed as though I was using education to run from my family and my bad memories.

Saved from a Dead End

One day I met a woman studying to become a special education teacher. We married, and like the woman of my childhood, she was a devout Christian. Julie loved me and tried to understand me, but I could never bring myself to a point where I could talk about my family and my past.

After several years, my wife invited me to a small church in Minnesota. As I walked into that church, I felt like the woman of my youth had multiplied into one hundred people. They greeted me, expressed interest in me, asked how I was doing, wondered where my family was, and just plain loved me. At an evening service, a man talked about Matthew 7:7, the same verse the woman from the valley told me about: "Ask and it will be given to you; seek and you will find; knock and the door will be opened to you."

That night I could not sleep. As I awoke and went driving down the highway, I turned off the road and came to a stop. I rolled down the window and looked up. I cried out, "God, if You're up there, then I want You to come into my heart."

At that moment, Jesus Christ came into my life. As I felt the hate leave me, I felt a great love take its place. I felt the arms of my heavenly Father come around me, and I finally felt a father's love.

Life changed from that point. I began learning how to love my wife and children. I began learning to love my father and start praying for him.

Looking back to some significant points in my life, I thank God for the woman of my childhood. Without her pure love that was based on Christ's love for us, I was probably destined for a dead-end existence on earth and in eternity.

I make my living speaking these days, and when I stand before audiences, I challenge them to reach out and touch every child. "Look for the child who has special needs, and remember the woman who touched me. Through her patience and love, she helped me to learn the most important lesson of all: Jesus loved me, died for me, forgave my sins, and taught me to love all men."

25

Terri Blackstock:
WRITING HER OWN ROMANCE
STORY WITH THE SAVIOR

AGE:
forty-one
OCCUPATION:
novelist
RESIDENCE:
Clinton, Mississippi
FAMILY SITUATION:
married to Ken for seven years;
mother of Lindsey Blackstock, nineteen;
Michelle Herrington, seventeen; and Marie Herrington, eleven

There was a time, when I was a little girl, that I was sure I would be an actress when I grew up. I was gifted with a vivid imagination, which was cultivated by my solitude for the first part of my life. I was born to a couple of married teenagers—my mother was fifteen and my father eighteen. My father became a fighter pilot in the Air Force, and our young family moved every few months.

Because I was never able to forge lasting friendships, I turned to my imagination to entertain me. Even as a preschooler, I would make up plays in my head and get neighborhood kids to perform them with me. I was always the writer, the director, and, of course, the star.

My mother, who'd been raised Southern Baptist, was diligent to keep us in church wherever we lived. My father, on the other hand, was an agnostic who rarely attended with us. When I was ten, my Sunday school teacher told us we needed to ask Jesus into our hearts. It sounded like the right thing to do. Not long after, I was baptized.

When my father was sent to Vietnam, I prayed for him often. It was a tense time for families back home, and in an effort to deal with my conflicting emotions, I began writing poetry. My father survived the war, but unfortunately, my parents' marriage did not. Within a year of his returning home, my parents were divorced. My mother moved us back to her home state of Mississippi. After that, we only saw my father once a year, after Christmas. He would call on our birthdays, but that was the extent of our relationship with him.

It was a combination of my sense of loss over the divorce and my bottled-up fears during my father's time in Vietnam that prompted me to write what would be my first published work. At the age of twelve, I wrote a short story in poetry form, about a little girl whose older brother was killed in Vietnam. It was a tearjerker but very therapeutic for me.

My mother, dutifully impressed, mailed it to the local newspaper, the *Clarion-Ledger* in Jackson, Mississippi. I was so excited by the idea of seeing my own work in print that I decided right then that I was going to be a writer when I grew up.

The concept of mortality became more real to me two years later when a boy at my school was killed in a car accident. As always happens when a teenager dies, the whole school turned out for the funeral. His parents, devout Christians, chose to use this tragic time as an opportunity to witness to all of his heartbroken friends.

Just weeks before he died, Ricky Bogan had preached the sermon on youth night at his church, and his parents decided to print that sermon and distribute it to the world. In the sermon, Ricky was very clear that if he died, he had perfect peace that he would go to heaven. That caused me to think deeply about spiritual matters for the first time. I took my broken heart to Christ and gave it to Him, along with my life. It was the first time I had felt intimately connected with my Lord and Savior and the first time I understood exactly what He was saving me from.

THE ART OF THE COMPROMISE

I walked closely with the Lord for the next couple of years, but then my youth group fell apart, and I found myself without the close fellowship I needed. I drifted into friendships with several unbelievers, and, in my senior year, I wound up dating one of them.

Although my father was supposed to have provided my college education, my parents couldn't agree on how much or when it was to be paid. I attended a community college for my freshman year, but quickly became frustrated at the ongoing fight between my parents over the money. In my second semester, I switched my major from journalism to secretarial science because I had decided that college was not worth the fight. After my freshman year, I went to work full-time as a secretary. At the age of eighteen, I rented an apartment and moved away from home. At the age of twenty, I got married to my unbelieving, unchurched boyfriend.

We moved to Monroe, Louisiana, and soon we decided to work our way through Northeast Louisiana University. With the help of student loans, neither of us had to depend on our parents for college money, but working my way through college created a fierce intensity in me. I didn't want to waste a dime of my hard-earned money, so I took my studies very seriously. I wound up majoring in English and studying the masters of literature so that I might become a better writer.

As soon as I graduated, I began trying to find a way to break into the publishing world. I heard of a group of romance writers who met monthly in Shreveport. Because I so desperately wanted to be around other writers, I joined the group. I had no interest in writing romance, because in college we had all turned our noses up at genre fiction. I had dreams of writing the Great American Novel.

But as I got to know these women and began to read their work, I realized that some of them were very skilled writers. The books were not sappy melodramas as I had believed, and I found that I enjoyed reading about relationships of all kinds. I decided to try to write a romance novel.

However, I knew that most romance novels contained explicit sex. My Christian beliefs would not allow me to write that, so I told myself that I was only going to write what was called "sweet romance." Those were romance novels without sex or profanity. When Silhouette accepted my first novel, *Blue Fire*, I was ecstatic. Finally I was a published author. I had arrived!

But the second sale didn't come as easily as the first, and as I collected rejection slips, I wrote my second, third, and fourth novels. Meanwhile, the friends in my writer's group were making lots of money and experiencing various degrees of fame. I began to feel competitive and ambitious, but I realized that my market was much more limited than theirs because I refused to include sex scenes.

So I decided to make some compromises. I began including a little more sensuality than I had before, and suddenly I sold a book to Harlequin. I was still trying to market my two other books, so I added a little sex to one, justifying to myself that it was between a husband and wife. That book sold to Silhouette. Feeling quite successful and telling myself that the Lord would not allow these to sell if He didn't want them to, I included even more sex in the next book, and these characters were not married. That book sold to Dell. There I was, with three publishers interested in more novels from me. I felt very successful.

But success didn't bring me happiness, because I was a Christian and the Holy Spirit I was grieving was making me miserable. Thinking more money and more published books would make me happier, I began working twelve hours a day at my computer. Writing consumed me, and I was turning out four books a year. In 1986, I had six books out under my own name, Terri Herrington, and my pen name, Tracy Hughes. But still, happiness didn't come.

I finally decided that the stigma of writing romance novels was keeping me from reaching true happiness, so I began working on a mainstream novel. I sold *Her Father's Daughter,* a modern-day *King Lear* story, to HarperCollins, and it did very well. I had now hit the big leagues of publishing. But I still had no happiness because the books contained worldly plots and illicit sex and even a good bit of profanity. I sold several more books to Harper and continued writing for Harlequin and Silhouette. I was very busy, and the royalty checks were pouring in.

COMPARTMENTALIZATION

Although I was so consumed with my career, I was an active member of our church. As my daughters came along, I made sure that they never missed a service on Sunday or Wednesday nights. I even began teaching a Sunday school class for three-year-olds. I compartmentalized my career, as if writing romance had nothing to do with my spiritual life. Sometimes I would sit in church and get convicted that what I was doing was wrong. It would make me very uncomfortable, but then I'd walk out into the light of day and shake that conviction from my mind.

I told myself constantly that I wouldn't be that successful if God wasn't opening these doors for me. I told myself that I wasn't hurting anyone and that these books were just harmless entertainment. I told myself that I couldn't help how my characters behaved—it wasn't reflective of who I was. I repeated those thoughts to myself like some kind of mantra. They replaced prayer in my life.

Eventually I realized that I never prayed—unless I was facing a crisis. I kept my Bible in the car so it would be handy on Sunday mornings when I needed it for church. I never read it, however. I did not hunger or thirst for righteousness. Instead, I hungered and thirsted for more money and more recognition. If I had been hauled into court and accused of being a Christian, I could never have been convicted.

Outside of church, I was giving interviews and talking about my writing career as a romance novelist. Reporters, I discovered, always wanted to talk about two things—sex and money. When my local paper, the *Monroe News Star*, decided to do an article on me, I found that this reporter was no different.

His questions, as expected, followed the sex-and-money trail. I tried to steer the conversation to other parts of my life that I was more proud of. I told him of my church work and the children I taught in Sunday school, figuring he'd "balance" the story of the demure woman who writes erotic romance with the Church Lady who is the pillar of the community.

No such luck. The article came out in the newspaper one Sunday morning as I was getting ready for church. My husband brought the paper in and read me the first line: "Terri Herrington has no trouble weaving tales of sex and romance in her novels, but she never sweats in church."

I was just mortified, too mortified to go to church that morning. "How could he have written that?" I asked my husband. But the answer was clear. He could write it because that's basically what I had said in the interview, and it was true.

Again I came under conviction that what I was doing was wrong. Between Sunday and Wednesday night, when I had to go back to church to teach my class, I began playing scenarios over and over in my mind. Would a committee meet me at the door and declare me too brazen to teach their children? Would I be one of the first Southern Baptists to be excommunicated? Would my pastor call me into his office for a heart-to-heart talk?

None of the above happened. Instead, the associate pastor met me in the hall, hugged me, and told me that he was proud of me.

Proud of me? I wanted to ask. *Didn't you read the story?* But I accepted his praise with relief and pushed my fears aside. No one at the church seemed upset by the article, and I received many more congratulations that night.

Deep in my heart, however, I knew that the Lord wasn't congratulating me, but I didn't have the faith or the sensitivity to the Holy Spirit to give up my writing.

I still wasn't rich because of some less-than-scrupulous policies at the publishing houses, but I was making more than most jobs I was qualified to do. I told myself that my family depended on the income I produced. When my husband hit thirty and became restless, we sold his small business and moved to Safety Harbor, Florida. That put more pressure on me to sustain us because for much of the time after that, he was unemployed. I didn't feel I had the option of quitting.

My efforts to work harder to produce more income created tension in our marriage, but I had no choice since my husband's jobs weren't working out. My high income during those years had created a prison for me.

Then a thunderbolt struck me in a scene that could have come from one of my books. My husband left me for another woman, leaving me to raise two daughters who were eight and three years old. If I had been walking with Christ at that time, maybe He would have shown me how to save my marriage. But I wasn't. Instead of turning to God first, I turned to a psychic for direction. She told me my marriage was over and I'd better do what I could to take care of myself.

STARTING OVER

I packed up my children and moved back to Mississippi where my mother still lived. My girls and I rented an apartment, and I worried about making a living while I was mired in depression.

The year was 1990, and I was thirty-three years old. The Lord gave me several very sweet signs that He had not forsaken me, even though I had forsaken Him. He gave me a Christian neighbor who was also divorced with two children, and she helped me nurse my wounds and pointed me back to God.

When I took my eight-year-old, Michelle, to a family counselor to help her with her anger, the Christian counselor took one look at me and said I was the one who needed counseling. He was right. Then one night Michelle heard on the radio about a Divorce Recovery Seminar being offered at a local Baptist church.

Even at eight years old, she knew Mom needed some serious recovery, so she encouraged me to go. I'll never forget the night we walked up to the sign-up table. I had brought my children because a nursery was provided, and Michelle announced in a very loud voice, "I'm the one who told my mom about this. She took me to counseling, you see, but the counselor said that she was really the one who needed help!" I was very embarrassed, but those dear people, who were later to become very close friends, just laughed and told me that they were going through the same thing.

When the Divorce Recovery Seminar was over, some of us moved into a divorce support group, where I was able to begin healing. When I felt I was on my feet again, I quit attending, but by then I was firmly entrenched in this church home.

In spite of everything, I kept writing romance. While I tried to clean up my act a little by writing less-explicit love scenes, the sex was still there. I hated what I did, and I began coming under intense conviction that I needed to quit. Once again, however, I sought the counsel of men rather than the Lord. My family counselor suggested that I didn't need any more major changes in my life for a while, and I certainly didn't need the stress of uncertainty about how I was going to support my kids. Others suggested that I shouldn't quit because I had such a huge readership. "Think how many people are touched by your writing," they said.

So I started trying to balance out the sex with some sort of faith message. But it was watered down and had little impact. I guess the small effort salved my conscience for a while, though, because I once again ignored the conviction and kept writing.

About a year and a half after my divorce, I went back to that divorce support group because a friend of mine was suffering through a divorce, and she didn't want to go alone. This time, I met a man named Ken Blackstock, who seemed like a godly Christian man. He was a Sunday school department leader, and no one had to drag him to church. People liked him and looked up to him, so I assumed that he was everything he seemed. We had a whirlwind courtship and were married within six months.

We had a rocky first year of marriage, and I discovered that Ken wasn't a strong Christian guy, after all. If he had been, he wouldn't have married me because he would have seen that my career contradicted the faith I claimed to have. We fought about tiny things and huge things, and often those fights ended in one of us saying, "This just isn't working."

One year into our marriage in 1993, Ken, who drives around eight hundred miles a week checking on accounts all over the state of Mississippi, happened to tune into a Christian radio station. Ken was a rock 'n' roll buff, so he was the last guy in the world who would listen to Christian radio. But for some reason, he kept tuning back to that station.

Every day for several days he heard Dr. Adrian Rogers, senior pastor of the Bellevue Baptist Church in Memphis, Tennessee. Every day he was moved and disturbed, but finally one morning, he was so overcome with conviction that he had to pull to the side of the road. He lowered his head against the steering wheel and wept; then he repented for the life he had led.

When he came home that afternoon, I could tell something was different about him. "I need to talk to you," he said. "Today, something happened to me. I met the Lord for the first time."

I was shocked. "Wait a minute," I said. "You told me that you had accepted Christ when you were a little boy."

He shook his head, and tears came to his eyes again. "I've known about Christ all my life, but I didn't really meet Him until today." He told me about pulling over to the side of the road. I didn't know whether to be happy or angry that I'd been duped, but I finally realized that this was a good thing no matter how I looked at it.

I saw changes in my husband immediately. He suddenly wanted to tell everyone about Christ, and he became involved in an Evangelism Explosion program at church. When I saw my husband wanting to pray with me and become a spiritual leader in our home, I hungered to become closer to God myself. I remembered how far I had fallen. In the beginning of my Christian journey, I, too, had been that zealous for the Lord. But my zeal had faded, and I realized now that it wasn't supposed to. I had come a long way from where God had wanted me.

People were praying for me, even then, and I didn't know it. But all at once people started coming up to me and telling me that they were praying that I'd turn my writing talents to the Lord. I was almost offended by that because I wasn't ready to make a commitment. Friends offered to pray that I would do God's will. My mother-in-law interceded daily about this. Even complete strangers who had seen articles in the paper about me were praying for me. Years later I would learn of them.

The conviction became so strong that I couldn't deny it anymore. One day, I finally got on my knees and told the Lord that I never wanted to write another word that didn't glorify Him. I confessed my fear, and I told the Lord that if He never let me write again, that would be fine. I would trust Him.

Unfortunately, I still had some problems. Just because I'd made the decision didn't mean that my contractual ties would dissolve. I was contracted for several more books, and I didn't know how to get out of those contracts. Also, I had been working with a New York agent for many years. I thought of her as a friend and dreaded telling her of my plans to quit writing romance. It would end our relationship, I felt, because she didn't have the knowledge to represent me in the Christian market, if that was where the Lord was leading me.

One day, out of the blue, she called to tell me that she was leaving the business after fifteen years. After a moment of stunned silence, I started laughing. I told her of my plans, and she was amazed that we had come to this decision at the same time. I wasn't, because I knew the Lord was simply answering my prayers.

Then I felt that the only way to get out of my contracts with my publishers was to confront them directly and just tell them what I wanted to do. One of my editors set me up on a conference call, and they proceeded to tell me that I was just suffering from burnout or some mid-life crisis. I told them that wasn't true, this was a spiritual decision, and I really felt this was something God wanted me to do.

In the end, they agreed to let me out of all but one of my contracts, if I paid back the advance. I agreed and then began to pray about where I would get the money, since I had been living on it for the past year. When an accounting was done, it turned out that my previous books had sold well enough that Harlequin owed *me* more money than I owed *them*. Again, the Lord had answered my prayer.

The one book I still had contracted for was part of a series I had agreed to write with two very close friends. Because I didn't think my decision needed to impact them financially, I told them that I would go ahead and write that book, but it had to glorify God, and it would not have any sex or profanity whatsoever. They agreed, and Harlequin published it that way.

CHECKING OUT CHRISTIAN FICTION

Meanwhile, I didn't know if I could write Christian fiction because I knew that my background might make me poison to any of the Christian publishers. When I started researching Christian fiction to see where I might fit, I found that mostly all that was available was historical fiction, westerns, and prairie romances. I had mostly been a contemporary author, and I wasn't good at writing anything from another period.

About that time the chemical company Ken worked for sent us on a cruise. While we steamed from port to port in the Caribbean, I sat by the pool and noticed something interesting: almost everyone on board was reading a John Grisham novel, including me. I realized that my reading tastes now leaned toward suspense along the lines of Grisham or Mary Higgins Clark.

I knew that some of those readers must be Christians, and I started talking to the Lord about the idea of giving them a Christian counterpart to those authors. Was it possible to write page-turning suspense with a spiritual message that could impact lives? The moment we got home I began working on some ideas that were forming in my mind.

But before I could submit those ideas to a publisher, I had to find another agent who knew the Christian market. I wanted someone who loved the Lord and who would set the ministry of my writing as a higher priority than money. I talked to one agent who agreed to represent me, and the day his agency contract was to come, I felt very uneasy about it. When I told Ken of my anxiety about this, he sat down with me and prayed. He asked the Lord to let me know if I was not supposed to sign that contract and asked Him to send us the right agent so I could get on with what I felt called to do.

Two hours later Ken was driving in his car, listening to Christian radio again. He heard Greg Johnson talking about a book he had co-authored called *Faithful Parents, Faithful Kids*. I was also driving in my car, listening to the interview, but I didn't hear all of it. Ken heard Greg say that he was a Christian literary agent. Remembering our prayer of that morning, he pulled over to a pay phone and tracked down Greg in Colorado Springs. He told him about me, and Greg expressed interest in talking to me.

When I got home, Ken called and told me about Greg, and I was a little worried. I didn't know anything about him and thought Ken might have acted in haste. But to appease him, I called the phone number he gave me. The moment we began talking, I knew that this was the agent whom God had sent to answer our prayers. Peace fell over me, and I could see that he was excited about my books.

He didn't agree to represent me right away, however. He asked me to send him some of my published work, as well as some proposals for new Christian suspense novels. At the same time, he sent me a prospectus about his agency, Alive Communications, and I was blown away by the caliber of authors they represented: Gary Smalley, John Trent, Jerry Jenkins, Tim LaHaye, Brock and Bodie Thoene . . . a list as long as my arm. I realized the Lord had not just sent me *any* agent— He'd sent me the best. Greg liked my work and agreed to represent me, and very quickly he was able to sell my four-book suspense series to Zondervan Publishing House.

Then we had another decision to make. Should I call myself Terri Herrington, which was my name before I married Ken and the name my readers were used to, or should I use my real name, Terri Blackstock?

We chose Terri Blackstock and decided to forget about having readers "follow" me into Christian fiction. I was worried that, if I wrote under my former name, they would read one of my Christian novels, then go back and find an earlier steamy romance, and get confused. I didn't want anyone thinking I was writing both things at the same time.

My first Christian suspense novel, *Evidence of Mercy,* was well received. The first book in the SunCoast Chronicles series was the story of a lukewarm Christian whose life gets entangled with an atheist as they both encounter a deadly string of events.

Since then, I've had several more books published with Zondervan in three separate series. Now that I'm writing for God's glory, I've received many letters from readers who tell me how the Holy Spirit has used my books to impact their lives. That's more rewarding than any award or bestseller list.

I wish my story were different. I wish I could say that the Lord told me as a young girl that I was supposed to be a writer and that I'd used my gift for Him from the beginning. There's no telling what He might have done with me. But what I can say is that the Lord took what I gave Him when I gave it to Him and made all the ugliness beautiful. He's turned all of my past sins into a testimony for Him.

There was a time, through all of this, when my best hope was that I'd stop grieving God. I didn't think He would ever be able to use me again.

And God said, *Watch Me.*

26

Ken Blackstock:
THE REST OF THE STORY

AGE:
forty-five
OCCUPATION:
industrial water treatment specialist
for Anderson Chemicals
RESIDENCE:
Clinton, Mississippi
FAMILY SITUATION:
married to Terri for seven years;
father of Lindsey Blackstock, nineteen;
Michelle Herrington, seventeen; and Marie Herrington, eleven

You read in the previous chapter of my intense conversion experience, but part of my story is missing. That missing part deals with a subject that is often swept under the rug by society and the church: pornography.

Before I deal with that subject, however, let me tell you a little bit about myself. I grew up in the church. We were Southern Baptists;

Dad was always a deacon, and Mom was a faithful, active member. I was one of those kids in church every time the doors were open.

Like my wife, Terri, I was baptized at ten years old, but looking back, the only thing it did was make me a wet fourth-grader.

Growing up mainly in Mississippi, I was a pretty good kid who didn't create much trouble. In my teen years, I decided I was smarter than God, and when I got out of the house and started attending Mississippi State University, I stopped going to church altogether.

I married my first wife, Jane, at a young age, and to keep up the appearance that she had hooked up with a fine Christian man, we went to church regularly. Although I knew all the jargon and used all the little phrases, I became uncomfortable in church because I was sure everyone could see right into my heart. Besides, Christianity was much like a jacket for me. I would slip it on at the appropriate time—like Sunday morning—but then put it back in the closet for the rest of the week.

Jane gave birth to a little girl, Kelly, but she was a sickly baby with lots of coughing, congestion, and bouts of pneumonia. We took her to the doctor, who diagnosed her with cystic fibrosis. We began skipping church since we didn't want Kelly picking up stray germs in the nursery. Her illness didn't deter us from taking her anywhere else we wanted to go.

We dealt with Kelly's hospitalizations, and three years later, my son, Lindsey, was born, but he was not affected by cystic fibrosis. As the years passed, our lives became very busy, and our marital relationship grew apart, especially in the area of intimacy. I decided something was needed to add some spice to our physical relationship. That something was pornography.

SCARY STUFF

I had no idea what effect porn would have on our marriage. I tell people the really scary thing about pornography is the more you're exposed to it, the more certain you are that the things you see and read are absolutely normal—and the way things should be in your marriage.

That's a lie from Satan, and he used that lie to keep my mind away from God. The more involved I became with porn, the more convinced I was that it was okay. My involvement reached the point where I crossed over the line and introduced sexual sin into our marriage. What do I mean by that? I'm too ashamed to say, but take my word for it, it was horrible. I took the covenant relationship I had entered into with my wife and with God and completely shattered it.

My wife had enough. The only way she saw to end this personal hell for her was to file for divorce.

For me, a nine-month stretch between the end of 1990 and the summer of 1991 became my personal hell: in December Kelly, at the age of thirteen, died of cystic fibrosis; in July our divorce became final; and in August I lost my job.

A few months later, I managed to find employment in Jackson, Mississippi, 150 miles away from my hometown, leaving behind my ten-year-old son with his mom.

My life became a monotonous routine of working and returning home to an empty apartment. After three months of counting ceiling tiles, I concluded that I had to get out of the apartment or go crazy. I had heard about a divorce recovery program at First Baptist Church in Jackson and decided I would go there and see if I could get help. That's where I met a beautiful red-headed lady named Terri. We hit it off, started to date, and shortly thereafter, I asked her to marry me.

Terri, I learned, was a redhead to the bone—fiery and tempestuous. I came to find out that I was a redhead by nature, although my hair was black. The clash of these two temperaments resulted in much conflict, but we only fought about the "important" things of life: whether you can refreeze meat after you have thawed it, who turned off the light switch, and the merits of phonics in education. These conflicts about trivial issues would blow up into high-volume shouting matches, after which divorce began to look like an attractive option.

After one squall, I remember Terri uttering a phrase that both of us started using: "This is just not working out."

The problem was the same problem that plagued my first marriage: I was still the god of my life. My second marriage was headed for divorce court as well.

But an odd thing happened in our Sunday school class (remember, Terri thought she was marrying a Christian, so I had to keep up appearances). We were studying the Gospel of John, chapter 15, in which Jesus speaks of Himself as the vine and His followers as the branches, and He challenges them to look at the fruit of their lives.

Well, I did that for the very first time, and the sight was not pretty. As I took stock of the fruit that had been borne in my life, I realized that the majority of it was rotten. I carried that thought while God continued to work on me. He led me to tune in to American Family Radio WQST, 92.5 FM, as I made my rounds throughout Mississippi. That's when it seemed like God told Adrian Rogers, "There's a guy out there named Ken, and I want you to make him miserable." In his program *Love Worth Finding,* Dr. Rogers convinced me that my life didn't reflect Jesus Christ and that knowing *about* Jesus was not the same as *knowing* Jesus.

No, I hadn't been a Christian, in spite of my baptism at ten years of age. When Dr. Rogers's message penetrated my heart, I pulled my Ford Ranger truck to the side of the road and asked God if He could forgive me for the pitiful fruit of my life and all the horrible things I had done against Him. I asked Him to be Lord of my life.

I came home that afternoon and told Terri about the decision I had made. You can imagine her shock, but as I explained it to her, she totally understood.

As the Lord began to change me, I knew there was something else I had to do. Even though pornography cost me my first marriage, I still kept a stash of three or four XXX-rated videos hidden from Terri. I was terrified that she might find them.

The next day when no one was around, I found those videos and dropped them on our driveway. Then I took a hammer and pulverized them to pieces. I tossed the pile of plastic and videotape into the trash.

Was I finished with pornography? The answer was yes, but the problem with porn is that once you've seen it, it's in your head. This causes a new problem: controlling your thoughts. The battle for our thoughts is one that many men struggle with on a daily, even hourly, basis. Too often we deliberately lose the battle in order to wallow in harmful images, forgetting how desperately we hurt the heart of God.

I've found that when these thoughts first occur the answer is to cry out to God for help. He is the only one strong enough to defeat this enemy. Philippians 4:8 is a verse that has been a constant source of strength for me: "Finally, brothers, whatever is true, whatever is noble, whatever is right, whatever is pure, whatever is lovely, whatever is admirable—if anything is excellent or praiseworthy—think about such things."

I am constantly amazed at God's long-suffering and willingness to forgive what seems to man to be unforgivable. As He revealed to me the false god of my life—my own pleasure—He delivered me from the weakness that Satan had used to keep me from God. He is truly the Lord of deliverance, the Lord of forgiveness.

27

Larry Wright:
A LUCKY MAN

AGE:
sixty-six
OCCUPATION:
founder of Abundant Life, Inc.
RESIDENCE:
Glendale, Arizona
FAMILY SITUATION:
married to Sue for forty-four years;
father of three married daughters: Laurie, Luanne, and Linda;
grandfather of nine grandchildren

Boy, did I have the world by the tail.

In the turbulent sixties when rock 'n' roll was at its peak, when Top 40 radio was king and DJs like "Wolfman Jack" and "The Real" Don Steele were its crown princes, I ruled the Arizona airwaves.

I was known as "Lucky Lawrence," my on-air name when I was hired by Phoenix's KRUX-AM in the spring of 1956, the year Elvis and his blue suede shoes shook up America. I was a chart-climber,

211

too, and by the time the Beatles and the Rolling Stones swept the country in the sixties, I was spinning the hits with a chatter that catapulted me to number one . . . in the ratings, that is. I was the Valley of the Sun's top jock in the all-important morning drive-time slot from 6:00–9:00 A.M.

Perched in my control booth surrounded by platters of 45 rpm records, I was sitting right where I wanted to be in life. Although I had grown up with a Christian mother, I tossed my faith aside like an old Fabian record.

On the home front, I treated my marriage to Sue just as shabbily. She was a Phoenix girl whom I had met on a blind date, and we married three months later. Three years into the marriage I wondered why, for we had nothing in common. For instance, Sue came from a wonderful, warm, loving, huggy-kissy family. But my father died when I was a toddler, and Mom was never around because she had to work all the time to support the family. I had no concept of what love was all about.

Sue's family was big on picnics in the desert and getting together on George Washington's birthday to tell each other the truth. Arbor Day was worse. Can you imagine a family outing to plant little trees and using it as an excuse to get touchy-feely with each other? I wondered what kind of mushy family I had married into.

That stuff wasn't for me. I didn't know how to love, and besides, I was far too interested in moving up the radio station ladder. As long as I worked my tail off and delivered an audience, the station bosses loved me. The radio business was driven by ratings, and everyone lived and died with the twice-a-year rating reports. I felt the pressure to produce, but I also felt insecure because I had seen too many jive-talking jocks handed their pink slips when their ratings nosedived. You either get the listeners, or you look for another line of work. I preferred to stay in mine.

Besides, I liked my larger-than-life persona as "Lucky Lawrence," rock 'n' roll disc jockey. I liked having the nice home, closets full of hip clothes, and two shiny cars in the driveway.

MY NEW FRIEND

That kind of pressure to stay ahead of the pack led to a search for some way to relax, to blow off steam. I found a place about a mile south of the station that served this marvelous, relaxing liquid that I began to partake of quite heavily. In fact, it got so bad that I'd get off the air at 9:00 A.M., and at 9:02, the barkeep would pour three or four fingers of Smirnoff vodka into a double-shot glass and set it in front of my favorite stool, knowing that my arrival was moments away.

My work day ended at 9:00 A.M., so what better way to "relax"? The trouble is that I would spend the rest of the day relaxing in the bar and go home so relaxed that I could barely move. When I was in a celebratory mood, I sometimes didn't come home all weekend.

This development created, shall we say, some problems in my marriage. Most wives don't welcome their husbands with open arms when they come home smelling like a Russian distillery, and neither did Sue. Nor did she like it when I flopped myself on the couch and watched TV for the rest of the evening.

She tried everything she could to change me, including withholding that famous love her family was known for. She could ream me forwards and backwards, coming and going. Our feelings for each other evaporated like an August thundershower, and when we did communicate, all we did was argue, fight, and bicker.

The more Sue tried to fix things and change me, the more I retreated into my shell. I came to a point where I couldn't care less for my wife and our three daughters, thanks to the alcoholic haze I lived in. It got so bad that I stopped caring about my job or myself. I just wondered why I was here on earth. I had set goals in the radio business, met them with flying colors, and once I reached the summit, the view of the horizon left me unfulfilled.

Family life certainly didn't fulfill me, either. The girls, I noticed as they grew older, were no longer asking, "How high, Daddy?" when I said, "Jump." Instead, their actions were telling me, *Now wait a minute. I don't know if jumping is what I want to do.* This frosted me, and I lashed out in anger. If they dared to disobey me, they paid the price.

One time my middle daughter sat on the bed, looking at me with her jaw clenched. "I hate your guts!" she screamed. When I heard that, I really let her have it.

"If you're going to hate me, then I'm going to give you a good reason!" I screamed back. Then I laid into her again.

My mind stewed as my family life disintegrated before my eyes. One afternoon while coming home from the bar in a boozed-up stupor, I was driving on the freeway. I contemplated how poorly life was going. With tears running down my face, I asked myself, *How could you do that to those three little girls? How could you treat your wife like that?* I felt like the number one jerk in the country.

I apologized to Sue and the kids that night, promising they would see a new father and a new daddy. Unfortunately, words are cheap, especially in the radio business, and after a couple of weeks, I was back to being the old Lucky Lawrence. They kept a barstool reserved for me at Kim's Lounge.

JUST A QUESTION OF WHEN

Sue, meanwhile, was wondering what her next move should be. Divorce was not a matter of whether; it was just a matter of when. One day Mrs. Ballentine, a petite gray-haired lady who baby-sat the children, noticed the turmoil. When she asked Sue if she was saved, Sue took the question as a personal affront.

"Well, what do you mean by 'saved'?"

"When did you become a Christian?" Mrs. Ballentine reiterated.

"Oh, I've been a Christian all my life," Sue replied, thinking that regular church attendance qualified her to call herself a Christian.

That discussion caused Sue to stop and take stock. As a wife in a dead-end marriage and a mother in her early thirties, she thought she hadn't prayed enough or gone to church enough. She felt like a failure as a wife and a mother. Then her fifty-eight-year-old mother killed herself with an overdose of pills. It didn't help matters when her father married another woman two weeks after the suicide and skipped town. Feeling as if the moorings of her life were slowly sinking in quicksand, Sue wondered if she, too, should take the ultimate step and kill herself. Life certainly was not worth living.

I was oblivious, for the most part, to Sue's feelings. I could see that she needed a little pick-me-up, not a shot of vodka, but something nice—like a new car. I shopped around and found a used '57 Thunderbird. I didn't spare any expense to have the convertible redone from the hubcaps up. The T-bird was repainted a cherry-red and white, the chrome bumpers refinished, the seats reupholstered, and the engine rebuilt. I spared no expense because I thought I could solve Sue's problem by throwing money at it.

The big day arrived. I drove the shiny T-bird home, parked it under the carport, and found Sue inside the house. "Honey, there's something I want to show you."

"What's that, Larry?"

"It's a surprise. Come take a look."

Sue walked outside and stared at the red-and-white Thunderbird. She didn't say anything. Then she stared at it again.

"What did you do that for?" she finally asked.

"What do you mean, 'What did you do that for?' That's a gift that cost me a lot of time and money. I thought you needed something after the events of the last few months. Don't you appreciate it?"

She stared at the reconditioned car one last time, and then she turned and walked back into the house.

Mrs. Ballentine, a sweet woman, continued to reach out to Sue and discuss what it meant to have a relationship with Christ. "Why don't you go to a church that teaches the Bible?" she suggested.

That was a novel thought. We had been going off and on to a more "social" church, one that didn't make many demands. We decided to try a new Bible-teaching church—for the sake of the kids, of course. I tagged along, but I slept in the pew during the sermon. I certainly wasn't engaged.

Sue was listening, however. When she heard that Jesus loved her, right where she and her miserable life were, she surrendered her life to Christ during an altar call.

When Sue accepted Christ, the blinders came off. What the Lord showed her was that her constant nagging and unrelenting criticism of me were not what I needed. She asked the Lord for wisdom, and she said this is what He showed her: *What is coming out of your mouth is far worse than what is going into Larry's mouth every day.*

She stopped asking me how many I had had that day. She stopped trying to smell my breath. Instead, Sue began to love me. I didn't deserve it, but she was reflecting the love of Christ. Her love was no longer conditional on my not drinking or my coming home on time.

"I realize that you grew up without love as a child," Sue told me one evening. "Now I know why God has given you to me: it's so that I might give you the love you missed all your life."

When I saw that Christ was alive and real in Sue, I couldn't resist this new woman. Before, I knew how she was going to react when I came home drunk, and I knew how to manipulate her emotions like a yo-yo. Now I wasn't able to do that any longer. She had a peace amidst all the chaos and turmoil that I was creating at home. That peace came from Jesus Christ.

My heart was softening. A man I respected, a "man's man," invited me to a weekly Bible study, where I read a verse that made a lasting impression on me: John 17:3, in which Jesus was praying with His disciples and said, "This is eternal life: that they may know you, the only true God, and Jesus Christ, whom you have sent."

The verse grabbed me by the lapels, and I yearned to know more about Christ. I began investigating this Jesus, reading the Bible, going to church with Sue, attending a Bible study. In the summer of 1968, I opened my life and asked Christ to come in and do in me what He had done in my wife.

Like many who give their lives to Christ, changes did not happen overnight. No, I was a long-term project. I remained in rock 'n' roll radio, still as popular as ever, but when I encouraged the girls not to listen to rock music, it did strike me as rather inconsistent.

The hypocrisy of it all convinced me that I had to make a change, but to what? Christian radio was just a blip on the AM dial. Other Phoenix stations didn't want to take me on since "Lucky Lawrence" and KRUX were nearly a brand name.

No matter. I resigned my high-paying gig and found a job playing "elevator" music to far fewer folks. Meanwhile, I continued to ask God what His plan was for my life. I started leading Bible studies in my home and sharing my testimony as much as I could in the greater Phoenix area. I did this for several years. I felt the Lord was preparing me for something, but I wasn't sure what that would be.

Then the Lord compelled me to quit radio, although I had no idea what I was supposed to do. What happened next was from the sovereign hand of God. Over a one-month period, four men—who didn't know each other—asked to speak with me. They all had the same message: "If you decide to go into full-time ministry as a Bible teacher to reach the unchurched, then we want to be part of your support."

The four men and I formed a nonprofit ministry called Abundant Life, Inc., in which Sue and I do considerable counseling and marriage enrichment seminars in Phoenix and across the country. We also do Bible teaching in "nonthreatening" places, such as country clubs, women's clubs, and corporate lunchrooms—places where people turned off by the organized church can seek the Lord in a more comfortable setting.

Looking back, I'm amazed at what God has done in the last thirty years. He took me, "Lucky Lawrence," the most selfish guy who ever walked the face of the earth, and touched me in an incredible way, and I've shared that story to bring others closer to Him.

28

Russ Lee:
SINGING A NEWSONG

AGE:
thirty-eight
OCCUPATION:
lead vocalist for NewSong,
a contemporary Christian music group
RESIDENCE:
Atlanta, Georgia
FAMILY SITUATION:
married to Mary for fifteen years;
father of Casey, eight; and Addy, two

I was born the oldest of four children to parents who scratched out a meager living. We were so poor that we drank out of Mason jars long before Cracker Barrel opened. Our family lived in Tennessee's No Pone Valley, down by the Hiwassee River in the southeast corner of the state. I grew up so far out in the country that the guys with white, short-sleeved shirts and black ties never dropped by and knocked on our door. Basically, you could call it "the sticks."

Dad was a country boy who worked the swing shift at the paper mill. Mom suffered from bipolar disorder—a debilitating and little-understood disease that caused her to act crazy at times. She wasn't institutionalized until later when her illness worsened.

When Mom wasn't struggling with her bipolar disorder, she worked to keep food on the table. She would drop off my siblings and me at Aunt Betty's, who would look after us during the summer months. Her husband, Uncle Albert, pastored a country church called the House of Prayer, an old-time Pentecostal church filled with lots of praise and worship and fire-and-brimstone preaching.

Each day Aunt Betty would take us down to the church to play with the toys. As a young kid, I loved all the toys since I didn't have many at home. I also loved attending Vacation Bible School, memorizing Scripture verses, and playing Bible games. I had things all around that reminded me of Jesus' love. It was such a peaceful place.

I told Mom and Dad how much fun church was, and I begged them to take me on Sundays. Finally they relented, and for several years, we all went to church as a family. Every time Uncle Albert said he was doing a "baptism," I stood in line for my turn. I think I was baptized two hundred times, making me the wettest third-grader in Bradley County.

Dad wasn't happy with that church. All the "prophesying" made him uncomfortable, so one day he decided that we wouldn't go to that church again, or anywhere else for that matter.

By the time I hit my teen years, I saw nothing but family dysfunction and a dissolving marriage between my parents. We were always one small step ahead of the creditors. Between bankruptcy and having to move several times, it was hard to find a place to call home.

We remained in No Pone Valley because that's all we knew, and Dad had his steady job at the paper mill. We lived in a "dry county," which meant that the only legal liquor was beer—no wine or hard liquor. That didn't stop Dad from drinking more and more. With chaos all around me, I was left to fend for myself, whether it was finding something to eat in the house or deciding how late I wanted to stay out drinking with my buddies.

By the time I hit ninth grade, I was drinking all the time. I saw nothing wrong with it. Neither did the crowd I hung out with, and it was a small step to start smoking dope. I couldn't afford to get high all the time, so while I was in high school I started selling drugs from the back of my car.

Playing for Drinks

I was mad at the world—a world in which other kids had parents who clothed and fed their children, parents who took their kids on memory-making vacations.

I taught myself to play the guitar, and at the age of seventeen, I started playing with a bar band at the Rocky Top, a honky-tonk joint. I was paid in drinks. I continued to play there on weekends during my senior year at Bradley High School, working odd jobs, including McDonald's, so I could earn enough money to keep my car in working order. I had a '68 orange-and-white Camaro SuperSport, but I burned out the engine by drag racing with my friends. I used up all my money to purchase a Chrysler Cordova with an eight-track tape player.

The following summer I graduated with the class of 1980. I got a job working with Dad at the paper mill, and that, combined with flipping burgers and making money selling drugs, left me with plenty of cash in my pocket.

I hated my life, however. I took speed all the time, which meant I never got any sleep. There was no rest in my life, no place to land. I tried my best to stay busy and stay airborne to ignore reality. My life was one loud noise, and it had to stay noisy lest I hear the roar of my misery.

Late one Thursday night, I was driving home from the Rocky Top after another night of playing for drinks. I was listening to the Rolling

Stones's "Satisfaction" on my eight-track, wondering if I would have enough money to enroll in Cleveland State Community College in the fall.

I can't get no . . . sat-is-faction, I sang with Mick Jagger.

I turned off the music, and on that dark country road, I began to think about my life. I realized that there was nothing in my life that was making me happy: not my girlfriend, not my drugs, not my guitar playing, and certainly not my jobs.

My thoughts turned to a happier time—really, the happiest days of my life. I transported my mind back to the carefree days when Aunt Betty took me to church to play with the toys, my mornings in the Sunday school, and the times I stood in line to get dunked in the baptistery by Uncle Albert.

Why were you so happy then? I asked myself.

I wasn't sure, but in my gut, I thought it had something to do with Jesus.

I looked out into the dark, starry night, alone in my thoughts.

"Dear God," I began saying out loud, "if You are up there, if You can see me and You can hear me, then You know all about my life. God, I am miserable. If You can show me what's missing, then I will listen to You. God, if You are up there, if You really are God, if You will show me what You want me to do, then I will do it."

I was broken, but I didn't know what to do next. When I got home and slumped into bed, I cried myself to sleep. The next day, I woke up and punched in at the paper mill. That had to be the emptiest, most difficult work shift of my life. I felt as if I was carrying a thousand pounds of lead on my shoulders because I was living without hope. When the whistle blew, I dragged myself home, showered, and drove to the Rocky Top to play for drinks again. I didn't know what else to do.

At the same time I couldn't shake a gnawing feeling of restlessness. Something inside of me was crying out. Two days later I worked Saturday at the paper mill to pick up some overtime. I couldn't shake my emptiness, so after my shift, I stopped at a convenience store on the way home—a store where I knew they would sell me a six-pack of beer even though I was underage. I finished all six cans in the half-hour drive home. After I pulled into our dirt driveway, I flopped on the floor of the living room, feeling miserable and pretty drunk.

A knock on the door snapped me out of my stupor. I stepped out on the porch, and standing there was David Vassey, my off-and-on buddy from grade school through high school. Next to him stood an earnest-looking Donny Osmond look-alike in his midtwenties.

"Hey, Russ, how are you?" David asked, thrusting out his hand to shake mine.

"What the @#&$% are you doing at my house?" I asked, wondering why David and his friend had come over to see me. David ignored my profanity, but I expected that. You see, David came from a *good* family. I went over to his house. He didn't come over to mine, and we both knew why.

Growing up, I always compared myself to David and his all-American family. He and his family sat down and ate a home-cooked meal together each night; I searched the cupboards for a box of Hamburger Helper. David returned to school each fall recounting adventures from his family vacations; I stayed silent and wondered when we would ever take a holiday. David had a cute girlfriend from the "right" family; most of my dates were not what you would call marrying material. When the *Smokey and the Bandit* movie was released in the midseventies, David's parents bought him the coolest red Trans-Am in the county; my Cordova was definitely not cool. David was an awesome drummer; I was stuck playing guitar with a bar band.

I wish I had been born into the Vassey family, I thought. *I'm just a stray.*

"Russ, there's someone I would like you to meet," said David, interrupting my thoughts. "This is Gary Miller. He's the music and youth pastor at Hopewell Baptist Church."

"Pleased to meet you," I said, my face red with embarrassment from using profanity.

"Russ, I want to tell you what happened to me on Thursday night," David said.

"Thursday night? You mean two days ago?" I was still shaking off the effects of the beer.

"Yes, Thursday night," David repeated. "I was in my car. I had just dropped off my girlfriend, and I was thinking about life. I thought about my wonderful family. I thought there should be no reason why I shouldn't be happy. I knew I didn't want for anything, and I had everything I needed. But I really felt something was missing in my life, and I needed to do something I had never done before."

"What did you do?" I asked.

"I prayed a prayer to God."

"You did? On Thursday night?"

Something inside told me something special was happening.

"I just told God, 'I don't know if You are up there, but if You are and You can hear me now, then You know everything that is happening in my life. If You really are God, please show me the truth and I'll believe it.'"

His prayer was almost word-for-word what I had prayed on Thursday night. This was really a bizarre moment for me.

I looked over at Gary. He was smiling.

David continued with the story. "The weird thing is that when I prayed this little prayer, I thought of that time in first grade when you told me how much fun you had at VBS and all that stuff they taught you there about Jesus. Do you remember that?"

"Yes, I do," I said.

As my mind drifted back to the peace and joy on Aunt Betty's face, I realized that I hadn't thought about those days in a long time.

"Well, after I prayed," said David, "up in the distance, I saw this church, Hopewell Baptist. Although it was a little late, I stopped by and talked to Reverend Bill Walker. When I told him what happened, he shared Christ with me and asked me to accept His free gift of eternal salvation. I prayed with him, and afterward, it felt like a thousand pounds were lifted off my shoulders. It was the greatest feeling."

"That's great, David. I'm happy for you."

"I came over to tell you what happened and ask you a favor. I was wondering if you would come to church tomorrow and watch me get baptized."

I was touched. "Why, sure, that would be fine," I said, as I watched David and Gary leave.

The next morning, I borrowed a dress shirt from my grandpa and drove over to Hopewell Baptist. David was really excited to see me, along with a couple of hundred people in the congregation. All the people seemed friendly and looked like they were enjoying themselves.

David wanted us to sit close to the front. During the preacher's sermon, he talked about sin and forgiveness. This time those verses I learned in VBS held new meaning, and I listened with my heart. At first, I thought David had set me up, but everything the pastor said from the pulpit connected with me.

"In a minute, I'm going to ask you to come forward," said the preacher. "If you're ready for a change in your life, to accept God's free and eternal gift of salvation, then you will have your chance."

I sat in the pew, my heart beating so fast that I thought my chest was going to explode. I couldn't take it any longer. Before the preacher could finish his sentence, I stood up and walked to the front.

He stopped his sermon and looked at me. No one had ever come forward *before* the invitation.

I continued to stand before him. The preacher stepped out from behind the pulpit and came down to me.

With a gentle smile, he asked, "Son, what are you doing up here?" He wasn't upset or anything. The concern in his voice was evident and put me at ease. He just wanted to know.

"Sir, you just described my life, and I need to be a Christian. My life is messed up, and I need Jesus."

"Well, amen! Praise the Lord!" the preacher exclaimed. "Will you pray with me?"

And the preacher led me to the Lord.

After the service, I walked back out to my car. In the trunk was a garbage bag filled with drugs I had been selling. *I won't be needing those again,* I thought, and I was right: I threw the bag away. From that day forward, God literally transformed my life from the inside out. I became a new creation, a new song for the Lord.

CLEAR DIRECTION

I began being discipled by Gary Miller, who asked me to join the choir. He must have liked my voice because he asked me to sing with him and his wife, Cathy, in churches and other venues in the area. Gary taught me to read choral music and sing with a new passion.

That Christmas I sang a solo. In the audience was Gary's college roommate, Brian Harden, who was the vocal director for the Spurlows, a gospel group popular in the late seventies and early eighties.

After the service, Brian asked me to join the Spurlows. I soon began singing with the group on a full-time basis, but more importantly, I really began to grow as a Christian.

My journey in Christian music had begun. Today, as a lead vocalist with NewSong, I can look back and see how God took a country kid from east Tennessee and gave him some incredible opportunities. The Lord has allowed me to travel all over the world, sing in more than fifty countries, and share my story before hundreds of thousands of people.

My relationship with Jesus Christ continues to be amazing, fulfilling, and the most important thing in my life. His goodness makes it hard to sing about anything else.

Editor's note: In the summer of 1999, Russ Lee left NewSong to pursue a solo recording career.

29

Clebe and Deanna McClary:
A Commitment to Christ

AGE:
fifty-seven and fifty-one, respectively
OCCUPATION:
speakers and authors
RESIDENCE:
Pawleys Island, South Carolina
FAMILY SITUATION:
married for thirty-two years;
parents of Tara, thirty; and Christa, twenty-eight

D<small>EANNA</small>: Daddy says he named me Carol Deanna after the singer Deanna Durbin. But I know the truth: I was named after my mother and father—Caroline and Dean. I was the oldest of four children growing up in Florence, South Carolina.

My grandparents owned a farm not too far from our home. Pa-Pa and Ma-Ma were friends of Jesus. Their quiet, almost casual references to the Lord made a deep impression on me. Although I didn't know what salvation was, I believed Jesus was active in my life long before I really understood what it meant to be a Christian.

My father was a nice man, but when he drank, he became mean and unpredictable. I know I am not the first child of an alcoholic parent, but he could make me feel worthless with his verbal salvos.

When relatives and friends at church told me I was pretty, I couldn't understand why. I didn't know it then, but my self-image was wrapped up in what I believed my father thought of me. Since I was insecure about my father's love, I didn't relate very well to God the Father.

In high school, I modeled and competed in beauty contests, but I was never satisfied with myself. I was a popular cheerleader, but I had picky things to say about almost every guy I dated in high school. I lay awake at night praying for a boy who would be the opposite of what I saw in my father. I desperately wanted someone who didn't drink and smoke, someone strong, smart, athletic, kind, and gentle. I never considered an older man until the day my younger sister, Annette, asked me to drive her to the new Florence Mall.

CLEBE: I was a teacher and track coach at Annette's junior high school. I was twenty-four years old, not too young to be a teacher, but young enough. When Annette introduced me to Deanna, I found her easy to talk to. Deanna blushed like a schoolgirl, but I just kept grinning. She was a beautiful young woman, and I took a powerful liking to her.

I called Deanna a few days later, which must have surprised her.

DEANNA: Surprised? I was so excited. That was the start of a wonderful courtship, and we were married two years later on March 26, 1967, an Easter Sunday. My heart pounded as I walked down the aisle. I looked for Clebe because, in keeping with tradition, I hadn't seen him all day. Since we had become engaged, Clebe had enlisted in the U.S. Marine Corps, and he looked more debonair than ever in his marine dress blue uniform, standing at parade rest with his hands behind him.

CLEBE: After we exchanged vows and the minister pronounced us husband and wife, he said I could kiss the bride. When the audience chuckled, I got cold feet.

There were six hundred people there. The church was packed, and the lights were on. When the minister said to kiss the bride, I said, "I'm not kissing her in front of all these folks. Momma and Daddy are sitting out there."

I threw the veil back, smiled at Deanna, and said, "Let's go." With that, we turned and walked down the aisle to the surprise of our friends. Outside the church, I could see my convertible with the top down.

My lovely wife turned to me and said, "Clebe, I'll lose my veil if you don't put the top up."

It was a beautiful, sunny day, and I couldn't see any reason not to enjoy it. "I'm not putting the top up, Deanna. Let's go!"

But the brand-new Mrs. McClary said, "I am not riding to the reception in that convertible with the top down, Clebe. I'll just ride with Daddy."

I thought about that for a minute. "You ride with your daddy," I said, "and you can just go home with your daddy."

DEANNA: We hadn't been married more than two minutes when we had our first argument. I decided to ride with Clebe and just hang on to my veil—*and* my husband.

On my honeymoon night, I disappeared into the bathroom to slip on my negligee. I discovered that Aunt Gee-Gee, to whom I had entrusted my suitcase to protect it from pranksters, had sewn up my negligee! I had to sit in the bathroom and painstakingly remove hundreds of stitches.

CLEBE: Our honeymoon lasted only a few days because I was on short leave from Marine Corps training. I had just passed Officer Candidate School at Quantico, Virginia, becoming a second lieutenant at twenty-six years of age. I knew that marine second lieutenants were being shipped directly into action in Vietnam as quickly as we could be trained and processed. I also knew that second lieutenants led platoons into battle and were usually the first to die in combat.

I wanted to be where the action was. I was a patriot, born and bred. I was sickened by antiwar protesters burning the American flag and refusing to support our country during the war. I couldn't do much to stop the protesters, but I could step forward and serve my country.

DEANNA: Clebe said he was thinking about volunteering for reconnaissance duty. That sounded like some kind of suicide mission to me. A friend had told me that recon teams led the way, scouting areas behind enemy lines in advance of the troops. I made Clebe promise me he wouldn't ask for recon duty, although we both knew he would be good at it.

The first letter I got from Clebe had this return address: Lt. Clebe McClary, First Recon Battalion, Alpha Company. I could not believe it. I wrote and told him how upset I was, but in his next letter, he said, "I feel more secure in this position. This is the place for me."

CLEBE: If you slept at night while on patrol, you got your throat cut, so I napped only during the day. Besides, 98 percent of the fighting in Vietnam took place at night.

A fight was usually quick. It didn't take a man long to fire four hundred rounds and throw four grenades. My men were disciplined, well-trained, and prepared to fight hand-to-hand, if necessary. Our recon motto was "Swift, Silent, Deadly"—and usually surrounded! Yet marines refused to leave an injured or dying man behind.

On my last patrol in Vietnam, we went into an area where few men had been. Our recon crew of thirteen men landed at Hill 146 near a small tea plantation in Quan Duc Valley. Once on the ground,

I cleared the stakes out of a punji pit and climbed in. I had my radioman and corpsman in the foxhole to my left and three men in a foxhole on my right.

We had been sent out ahead to report enemy activity, but then the operation was canceled. The weather turned bad, and choppers couldn't get in to lift us out. For two days we were on the hill, knowing full well that the enemy was out there, watching and waiting.

The third night, March 3, 1968, was Deanna's birthday, but it was not a time of celebration for me. The night was totally quiet. I could hear my heart beat. At midnight I thought I heard enemy movement. I grabbed my shotgun, but before I could alert my men, a grenade soared into the pit, with shrapnel hitting me in the face, neck, and shoulder.

"Call for air support!" I yelled to the radioman.

To my horror, I saw about a dozen of the enemy running up the hill. They were "sappers"—North Vietnamese strapped with explosives. They were on a suicide mission, having been told to die for Ho Chi Minh that night. Their goal was to jump into our foxholes with their satchel charges, exploding and killing us all.

Suddenly a sapper jumped into the air in front of me. I swung my shotgun around and fired, but I must have shot him low because he still kept coming. He fell into my punji pit and exploded. Blinded by blood and choking on bits of my own teeth, I realized my left arm was gone.

I got up and started running to another foxhole, but a hand grenade knocked my legs out from under me. As I lay in the dirt, pretending to be dead, I heard an NVA soldier walk up to me. He pointed his AK-47 at me and tried to shoot me in the head. The bullet passed through my neck, however. Then he stuck an enemy flag right next to me.

Someone once said, "Courage is a strong desire to live, taking the form of a readiness to die." I was willing to die for my country and my freedom, but two powerful desires drove me that night: to get my men off that hill and to see my beautiful Deanna one more time.

A few minutes passed. I felt a buddy start dragging me. A chopper had come in, and he got me in halfway when it lifted off. Five more minutes and probably no one would have gotten off that hill alive.

DEANNA: When I saw a marine officer and a physician at my front porch, I was sure that Clebe was dead.

The officer, Major Burleson, caught me by the shoulders. "He's alive, Mrs. McClary! He's alive!"

I felt numb as Major Burleson read the official telegram: "Mrs. McClary, your husband, Lieutenant Clebe McClary, has suffered a traumatic amputation of his left arm and shrapnel wounds to all extremities. His prognosis is poor. His outlook is very dim."

CLEBE: The nurses wouldn't let anything shiny in front of my eyes. They didn't want me to see what I looked like. They thought I'd give up hope if I looked into a mirror.

As I lay there, I actually thought it would be better if I died. Deanna and I didn't have any children, and I figured she would be better off without a mangled husband to care for.

DEANNA: It took almost two months before Clebe was in good enough shape to be flown to Bethesda Naval Medical Hospital in Maryland. The staff tried to prepare me for what he was going to look like.

I walked down a corridor and thought I heard Clebe's voice. I peeked around a door and saw two men. One had two arms dangling, so he couldn't be Clebe. The other had his head bandaged, one eye, and *no* arms! I stared at the huge red-and-pink scars, the jagged stitches, the broken teeth, and lips so swollen that they were turned inside out.

I'm in the wrong room, I thought. Just as I turned, I heard a voice. "Dea, honey, it's me. I know I'm not too pretty to look at, but I thank God I'm alive to be with you."

CLEBE: Deanna hadn't recognized me because my right arm was in a cast and bound against my body. After hearing my voice, she rushed to my side and told me how much she loved me. Lying in that hospital bed, I was all too aware of the many wives who turned around and kept on walking, never looking back. But Deanna sat down next to me and promised we would always be together.

DEANNA: As I worked with him every day in rehabilitation, I saw his strength and determination, and I fell more and more in love with him. Although he was just scabs and scars and stitches, with metal sticking out of his body, he was still the most handsome man in the world to me.

CLEBE: We settled back in Florence while I continued to rehab. One afternoon I read in the newspaper that there was going to be a crusade in town. An evangelist named Billy Zeoli was going to speak.

"I believe I'd like to go," I said to Deanna.

"No way, not the way I look," she replied. "That's just what the locals would love to see, me comin' back in all my glory with greasy, flopped hair, looking haggard. Forget it."

So I called Deanna's mother, and she said she would be happy to drive me to the crusade. Deanna stayed in her room pouting, but at the last minute, she jumped in the car with us.

DEANNA: The high school football stadium was packed when we arrived, so we had to find seats at the very top of the grandstands. Clebe could barely set one foot in front of another; I felt like all eyes were on us as we slowly trudged up the steep bleachers. I couldn't understand why we were there anyway. I believed in God. Clebe and I read the Bible every night and prayed before every meal. I tried to impress him, and he tried to impress me. I guess God wasn't too impressed!

When Billy Zeoli spoke, however, I was captivated. He told stories, dramatized them, and was funny, convincing, and dynamic. When Billy spoke of Joshua's battle plan to lead his men around the walls of Jericho thirteen times in seven days, Billy said Joshua was surely ridiculed as a fool.

"Joshua heard the voice of God, and he was victorious. He was a fool for God. There are only two kinds of fools in this world: a fool for Christ and a fool for others. Whose fool are you?"

I knew one thing: I wasn't a fool for Christ. Billy kept preaching.

"There are only three things you can say to Jesus Christ: yes, no, or maybe. If you say yes, you can know right now where you're going to spend eternity, even if you died tonight."

CLEBE: Billy Zeoli's speaking of death hit close to home. I had been very, very close to dying. Deep down, I had never settled the question of Jesus as my Savior; I had never honestly dealt with where I would spend eternity.

Billy explained that saying no would bring its own results—that a person who said no would be Satan's fool, guaranteed of an eternity in hell without God. That wasn't an option for me. I could never say no to God.

DEANNA: Neither could I, although I thought I might say maybe.

Billy Zeoli was reading my mind. "The maybe category is a very dangerous place," he said. "When you die, your maybe becomes an automatic no in the eyes of God if you've never said yes to the Lord Jesus."

My heart was pounding. I *was* a maybe.

"All over this place, I want you to bow your heads and close your eyes," said Billy. "If you mean business with the Lord tonight, if you want to receive Him as your Savior, I want you to raise your hand. No one is looking. This is just between you and God."

I wanted to raise my hand. I wanted to say yes. A battle raged in my mind. *I'm human. Who is perfect? Why do I have to raise my hand anyway? I don't even want to be here. I can't do this.*

CLEBE: I heard Billy say, "Whose fool are you? A fool for Christ? A fool for others? Your own fool? The biggest fool in this place is the person who will sit here right now and hear God's simple plan of salvation and then walk away saying no or maybe."

I needed to say yes to Jesus and make Him Lord of my life.

DEANNA: I wanted to say yes, too. But first, I opened my eyes and peeked around. I didn't want anyone to see what I was about to do. The other people seemed to have their heads bowed and eyes closed. I closed mine again and raised my left hand. My bangle bracelets made an embarrassing racket! But my little sister told me that hearing my bracelets bang around gave her the courage to raise her hand as well.

Billy then challenged those of us who had raised our hands to get up out of our seats, walk forward, and acknowledge the Lord publicly in front of our friends and families.

This was too much. I was way up in the bleachers, closer to heaven than nearly everyone there. The Lord had seen my hand. He knew my heart. I couldn't walk forward. The battle continued to rage.

But I knew it was time to make a decision *for* Christ. I decided to take that first step. My legs never weighed so much. I was oblivious to Clebe, other family members, or anyone else as I walked down the steep aisle. What a sense of relief, knowing I was doing the right thing.

I glanced behind me, and who was coming toward me but Clebe! How sweet of him! He was coming down to support me in my decision, one step at a time. Besides, I wanted what Clebe had.

CLEBE: When Deanna saw me, she thanked me for coming down with her.

"Honey," I said, "I'm not coming down for you. I'm coming down for me!"

DEANNA: If I had false teeth, they would have hit the ground. If there was one person in the world who I thought already knew the Lord personally, it was my husband. When we arrived in the infield,

Clebe pulled aside Sam Anderson, a pastor, and Clebe asked him to pray with us for salvation. How wonderful to receive God's free gift of eternal life with him on the same evening—July 26, 1968!

That event happened more than three decades ago, and it was the best thing that's ever happened to us. We made a commitment to Christ that evening, and when Clebe completed his rehabilitation, we started our own speaking ministry. Little did we know that we would be able to tell our story to millions of people and urge untold tens of thousands to say yes to Jesus, not no or maybe.

30

Luis Palau:
DON'T CRY FOR HIM,
ARGENTINA

AGE:
sixty-five
OCCUPATION:
evangelist, fluent in English and Spanish
RESIDENCE:
Portland, Oregon
FAMILY SITUATION:
married to Pat for thirty-eight years;
father of four adult sons: Kevin, Keith, Andrew, and Stephen;
grandfather of eight grandchildren

You can call me a Russian salad in many ways. I was born and raised in Argentina, the first grandson of immigrants who sailed from Spain on my father's side and from Scotland and France on my mother's side. While I'm from Latin America, I'm just as much from Europe, as are nearly 97 percent of Argentina's sons and daughters.

My grandparents had little time for religion, except for my maternal grandmother, who was devoted to the French Roman Catholic

Church and then made a personal commitment to Jesus Christ later in life. I had a great-grandfather who was officially raised in the Church of Scotland, which he referred to as "Scotch Presbyterian." Although he wasn't a heavy drinker, he definitely preferred Scotch to Presbyterianism.

My parents, Luis and Matilde Palau, were like most Argentinians: they belonged to the state church, which did not mean a whole lot to them. Through the witness of a British executive with the Shell Oil Company, my mother—and then my father—trusted Jesus Christ for their salvation.

Overnight, my father, a well-to-do businessman who ran his own construction company, became a bold member of the evangelical community, which was a despised minority in Argentina. Only later, as a boy accompanying my father on evangelistic forays in the countryside, did I begin to realize how much grief he endured preaching the Good News. That news was often greeted with insults, derision, stones, and worse.

My father was my hero. After hearing him preach so often, I began imitating his gestures, his voice, and even his words. Actually, I got quite good at playing "church" with my younger sisters. According to my mother, I was three or four years old when I knelt beside her and heard her say, "Lord, I pray that Luisito will truly come to know You."

I looked at her and said, "But, Mommy, I do know the Lord Jesus," and I did, in my own way. But I did not know Him in a personal way until later.

IN HIS FOOTSTEPS

My dad was the same person at home as he was at church. He rose early on cold winter mornings to start a wood fire in the stove. I should have been sleeping, but often I sneaked out of bed just to watch him putter around the house.

I can remember watching him go into his study and kneel down, wrapping himself in a poncho to ward off the cold. Then he would read the Bible and pray before going to work. One day he told me that he read a chapter from Proverbs every day since it had thirty-one chapters and there were thirty-one days in most months. His example stuck with me.

When I entered first grade at the local government school, I had not actually trusted Jesus Christ as my Savior. I was proud, however, that my dad and mom were committed Christians. When we rode on benches in the back of my dad's truck and passed out evangelistic tracts in various neighborhoods, I reacted to the taunts and insults with resolve. I saw the religious parades, common on the many holidays in Latin America, and I determined that one day biblical Christians would do the same thing, but with an emphasis on salvation through Jesus Christ.

At school, I was the only child of evangelical Christian parents, which meant I was subjected to name calling in the schoolyard and petty punishments by the teachers, such as kneeling on corn kernels in a corner. That news prompted my father to send me to Quilmes Preparatory School, a private British boarding school near Buenos Aires. My father, who wanted the best possible education for me, dreamed of sending me to study at Cambridge University in England. He also knew it would be to my advantage to become completely bilingual, equally fluent in English and Spanish.

Naturally, I missed my parents and family a great deal, but I enjoyed my classes, sports, and other school activities. Discipline was rigorous, as you would expect for a British school, and they had rules and regulations for everything.

When I was ten years old, I received a call from my grandmother, who didn't live far from Quilmes Prep. "Luis," she said, sparing any amenities, "your dad is very sick. Your mom wants you to go home immediately."

I had a terrible feeling that my father was dead or dying, and the three-hour train trip seemed interminable. Father had contracted bronchial pneumonia, but December 1944 was not a good time to need penicillin. The drug was earmarked for the war effort in Europe and the Pacific.

When the train finally reached our town, I bounded down the steps and ran home. Any shred of hope was quickly dispelled when I heard the traditional wailing. Relatives tried to intercept me as I ran through the gates and up to the house; I brushed past them and burst into my father's bedroom. The sight unnerved me: my dead father was yellow, bloated, and still secreting fluids. His body had dehydrated. I hugged him and kissed his cracked lips, but he was already gone.

Mother escorted me outside, where she tried to stifle my sobs. "When the doctors realized they couldn't do anything more for him, we gathered around his bed, praying and comforting him. He was struggling to breathe, but suddenly he sat up and began to sing."

I looked up at my mother, hardly believing what she was telling me.

"Papito began to sing, 'Bright crowns up there, bright crowns for you and me. Then the palm of victory, the palm of victory.' He sang it three times, then he fell back on his pillow and said, 'I'm going to be with Jesus, which is far better.' A short time later, he went to be with the Lord."

Still, my grief devastated me, and I was angry at everything and everyone. It wasn't fair. Why couldn't my father die in old age like everyone else?

A SUMMER CAMP EXPERIENCE

Three months after my father's death, I transferred to St. Alban's, a tough, all-boys, Anglican school. A couple of years after my father's death, Charles Cohen, one of my teachers, talked to me about going to his two-week camp in the mountains with several dozen other boys. Camping sounded like fun, but I didn't want to go because I knew the camp would be overly evangelistic. I was sure someone would put the pressure on me to receive Jesus Christ. Oh, I could stand up and quote many Bible verses, sing songs, and even say a prayer if you put me on the spot, but in my heart, I knew I wasn't a real Christian.

When I put off Mr. Cohen, he smiled and let me paint myself into a corner. As soon as I mentioned "my family's tight financial situation," he offered to pay my way. So it was off to camp I went in February 1947—summer in South America. I was twelve years old.

Just before my departure, I was helping deliver a load of cement bags with a twenty-year-old worker who drove a truck in the family business. I enjoyed jumping in the cab and feeling like a man. One day he pulled over to the side of the road and pulled out a magazine from his pocket. At first, I couldn't tell what it was.

"Luisito," he said, "since you are becoming a young man now and have no father, you need someone to talk to you about the facts of life."

My heart began to pound. My mother had made one halfhearted attempt to talk to me about sex, but she had put me off, saying she would tell me more when I was thirteen. Sitting in the truck, I was excited that I might get some straight answers from someone who really knew the score. "I want to make a man of you," he said, but instead of telling me anything, he simply opened his magazine and turned the pages while I stared in disbelief. I was shocked and disgusted, but at the same time, I couldn't take my eyes off the pages. I had never seen anything that revealing. I knew it was all wrong, dirty, and not pure, yet I was curious. I found the pictures appalling and appealing at the same time.

For days and weeks, I couldn't put those images out of my mind. I felt horrible, degraded, sinful. I was certain my mother and family could read the guilt all over my face.

Not knowing that I was hardly unique among boys my age who'd had their first shocking encounter with pornography, I could not reconcile it in my mind. Seeing that magazine was wrong, and yet it held fascination. I was in such a state that I was actually glad I was going to camp!

Trekking off into a hilly, mountainous area called Azul in southern Argentina carried a special sense of excitement for me. I tried to forget what I saw because I got a dreadful feeling in the pit of my stomach whenever I thought about those images.

At the Christian camp, I recognized most of the boys from St. Alban's. We used Argentine army tents and brought our own foldable cots. We dug trenches around the tents, policed the area, and generally learned how to "rough it." The counselors were all Britishers or Americans concerned for the spiritual welfare of the campers. We had Bible lessons, memorization, and singing every day, along with the usual fun and games.

One morning an American spoke about purity in that ambiguous, roundabout way many people do when dealing with the subject of sex. His talk didn't give the detailed instruction I needed, but it was helpful for one reason: this man knew what he was talking about, and even as refined as he was discussing the subject, I was impressed that he was a pure man in an impure world.

I assumed most people were as coarse as they boasted they were, and I still felt badly about my own confused thoughts on the subject. But this Bible teacher impressed me and gave me hope that there were indeed pure Christian men—men I could model myself after. Though I was attracted by the dirty images in my mind, somehow I knew what was right, and this godly teacher affirmed that.

APPOINTMENT IN THE NIGHT

Each counselor had about ten boys in his tent, and each night one boy was taken for a walk and given the opportunity to say yes or no to Christ's claims upon his life. After the second night everyone knew his turn was coming because the first two kids were telling everyone what had happened.

If you really didn't want to receive Christ, the counselors didn't force you. This was a making-sure exercise. Finally, my appointment with destiny arrived. When my counselor, Frank Chandler, came into my tent on the last night of camp, I knew why. I wanted to run and hide because I was embarrassed that I had not received Christ yet; still, I couldn't lie and say that I had.

I pretended to be asleep when Frank stepped into the tent. He shook me, but I continued to act sound asleep. Frank knew I was faking, so he picked up the cot and dumped me onto the ground.

"Come on, Luis," said Frank. "Get up."

We went outside and sat down on a fallen tree. The evening was cool, and a light rain was beginning to fall. A thunderstorm was coming our way, so Frank knew he had to hurry. He pulled out his flashlight and opened his New Testament.

"Luis, are you a born-again Christian?"

"I don't think so."

"If you died tonight, would you go to heaven or hell?"

I sat quietly for a moment, a bit taken aback. "I'm going to hell," I said.

"Is that where you want to go?"

"No."

"Then why are you going there?"

"I don't know."

Frank turned to Paul's letter to the Romans and read: "If you confess with your lips, [Luis], that Jesus is Lord and believe in your heart, [Luis], that God raised him from the dead, you, [Luis], will be saved. For man believes with his heart and so is justified, and he confesses with his lips and so is saved" (10:9–10, RSV).

"Luis, do you believe in your heart that God raised Jesus from the dead?"

"Yes, I do."

"Then what do you have to do to be saved?"

I hesitated as it began raining harder. Frank handed me the Bible and had me read Romans 10:9–10 once more.

"Luis, are you ready to confess Him as your Lord right now?"

"Yes."

"All right, let's pray."

Frank put his arm around me and led me in a prayer. I opened my heart to Christ in the wilderness, sitting out in the rain on a log, but I made my decision. I prayed, "Lord Jesus, I believe You were raised from the dead. I confess You with my lips. Give me eternal life. I want to be Yours. Save me from hell. Amen."

When we finished praying, I was crying. Frank put his arm around my shoulders, and we ran back to the tent. I crawled under my blanket with my flashlight and wrote in my Bible: February 12, 1947, I received Jesus Christ.

I could hardly sleep, I was so excited about committing my life to Christ. After all, it is the most important decision anyone can make. Compared to eternal life, other decisions aren't that important when you think about it. C. S. Lewis, the famous English author and Oxford professor, said it well: "No one is ready to live life on earth until he is ready for life in heaven."

Editor's note: Luis Palau is one of the most gifted evangelists of the twentieth century, preaching before millions around the globe and leading hundreds of thousands to Jesus Christ.

Epilogue:
HE AIN'T HEAVY;
HE'S MY BROTHER

In closing, I would like to relate a story about my brother, Pry, who received his unusual nickname from his initials: Peter Richard Yorkey. Pry was just sixteen months younger than me, and as only siblings, we enjoyed a close, but competitive, relationship.

We grew up as California beach boys in the seaside town of La Jolla, just north of San Diego. We lived about one hundred yards from a beach called Sea Lane. From the end of school until Labor Day, we were in the Pacific every day, riding well-formed waves on our belly boards or body-surfing the pounding shorebreak.

Pry grew to become a strapping six-foot-two-inch fellow with remarkably blue eyes and dirty blond hair that lightened with the summer sun. After high school, Pry drifted through college before learning the carpenter trade from my dad, who was a general contractor specializing in remodeling. The construction business had its ups and downs, so when the surf was up, Pry was down at the beach. He became a pretty good surfer and was living a nomadic life when he dropped by my aunt and uncle's house one evening. There was a birthday in the family, and we all came. After enjoying the usual cake and ice cream, I left with my wife, Nicole, and the kids. Pry lingered for a second helping of ice cream. Out of the blue, his body began trembling involuntarily. His mind tried to comprehend, but his legs and arms shook, and his eyes bulged as convulsions racked his frame.

Pry, just twenty-nine years old, had suffered a grand mal seizure. When paramedics arrived, they hustled him to nearby Scripps Hospital to stabilize him. Then the battery of tests began. A CAT scan determined that a large tissue mass had formed on the right side of his brain. The decision was made to delicately slice off the tumor.

The operation was a success. When the neurosurgeon left the operating room to greet my anxious parents, he had a smile on his face. "I think we got it all," he said. That was good news, because two weeks later, tests revealed the tumor to be cancerous.

Meanwhile, Pry recovered quickly and picked up where he had left off with life. While raised in a Christian home, Pry didn't have much time for "religion," and he was more interested in finding what surf spot was breaking than in breaking open a Bible.

Every six months he went in for a CAT scan, and he always walked out of the doctor's office with a smile on his face. "The doctor says I still have a hole in my head," he quipped. Pry appeared to be one of the lucky ones.

Several years passed, and just when Pry appeared to have beaten back the cancer, a seizure struck again. He was rushed to Scripps Hospital for more tests, and the same neurosurgeon elected to perform brain surgery. The tumor had returned, bigger than ever.

When he greeted my parents this time, however, the smile was gone from his weary face. "We'll have to wait until the tests come back" was all he would say to my parents.

I now understand why doctors do that—make you wait—when they already know. They want the patient and the family to get used to the idea of dying. When Pry walked into the neurosurgeon's office two weeks later, he heard this point-blank statement: "Pry, you have two to six months. There's not much we can do."

Pry took the news like a man. Then he had a few questions. "What will it be like when I die?" he asked. "Will it hurt?"

"Really, you'll feel nothing at all," replied the neurosurgeon. "In your last week or last few days, you'll be sleeping a lot, and one time you just won't wake up."

Naturally, I was devastated by the news, but my first thoughts were heavenward. I wanted eternal life for my brother. Pry knew *about* the Lord, but he had never accepted Christ into his heart, never had a personal relationship with Him. Pry hadn't darkened a church door in ages.

Nicole and I were living in the Los Angeles area at the time, and nearly every weekend we drove to San Diego to be with Pry. During his good periods, we golfed at Torrey Pines. During his bad periods, he sat on a couch and listlessly played a computer backgammon game all day.

Nicole and I were looking for ways to present Christ to Pry. I brought him books that I thought he would enjoy, like Pete Maravich's *Heir to a Dream,* thinking sports-minded Pry could identify with Pistol Pete. Another time, I asked him to watch a Focus on the Family evangelistic video. When I popped it into the VCR one afternoon, I counseled Pry to watch closely. The speaker clearly presented the gospel.

But Pry didn't seem to be paying attention, preferring to play the hand-held backgammon game. I was watching Pry more than the video, and I resisted the urge to reach over and slap the video game out of his hand and say, "Pry, listen to what that tape is saying! You're facing eternity, guy, and you've got no time to lose." But I didn't. I sensed the Lord telling me to wait, so I did.

Throughout the fall Nicole and I tried to talk to Pry over the phone. One time I said I wanted to be sure I'd see him again in heaven.

"Oh, that's a ways off," said Pry. That was his way of not dealing with his cancer.

Meanwhile, Pry weakened badly, and the cancer spread to his spine. He was checked into a convalescent home after Thanksgiving, but he was so weak he couldn't even decorate a foot-high Christmas tree our mom had brought to his room.

His time was getting close. When we visited him two weeks before Christmas, Pry could barely summon the strength to sit up in bed. After five minutes of talking, we'd notice that Pry was snoring. Then we'd leave the room and return several hours later, only to have him fall asleep once more.

I had been praying for an opportunity to talk to Pry directly, for one last shot, but he could never stay awake!

On Sunday afternoon, December 11, we were making our last visit of the weekend. We had to get on the road to return home. Pry had just finished lunch and looked alert. We chatted for a few minutes, but then he fell asleep again. "Drats," I muttered under my breath. We gathered our things to go.

"Goodbye, Pry," Nicole said, and he opened his eyes. I rushed to his bedside and asked my parents to take our children for a walk.

Nicole walked to the other side of his bed, and we each took a hand.

"Pry, would you mind if Nicole and I pray for you?" I asked.

"No, go ahead," he replied.

We lowered our heads and closed our eyes. My emotionally charged prayer asked the Lord to be with Pry during his last few days on Earth, to walk with him every step of the way, to comfort him and be a strength for him.

When we opened our eyes, Pry looked at me with a soft gaze. He didn't say a thing, but his blue eyes told me: *Go ahead, big brother. Do what you are supposed to do.*

"Pry," I said, "would you like to ask Jesus Christ into your heart and repent of your sins?"

"Yes, I would."

"Then please close your eyes and repeat this prayer after me."

Dear Jesus, I come to You right now . . . and admit that I am a sinner. I repent of my sins against You. I believe that You died on the cross for my sins . . . and that You rose again three days later. I ask that You forgive me . . . and that You come into my life. Amen.

That was it. We opened our eyes. For the first time in months, I could relax. I began telling Pry things I had kept bottled up inside.

"Pry, I'm really sorry you got sick like this. You are my only brother, and I love you. I'm sorry this has happened, but now I know that you will be waiting in heaven for me."

I hugged Pry's decaying body and wept. The warm tears were a welcome release. Pry didn't say much, but he looked happy.

After saying goodbye, Nicole and I walked outside and past his room. Through the miniblinds, he looked at us one more time. He raised his right arm and waved weakly, and I waved back. I knew it was goodbye until the next time.

A few days later, Pry slipped into a coma. When I came down the following weekend, he was incoherent. I could smell death in the room. He died early Sunday morning, one week after he had asked Christ into his heart.

Although the event happened at the eleventh hour, God's timing was perfect. Looking back, I can see how Pry had something to come back to. My parents had raised him in a faith in Christ. Pry had learned that Jesus Christ was his Savior, that Jesus had come and died for his sins. When it came time to walk into the Lord's vineyard as a prodigal son, Pry didn't have that far to walk.

That's how you want it to be for your family and friends. You can introduce Christ to them, even lead them to the Lord, but only they can reach out and take His hand. Your duty, then, is to present Christ to them. He will do the rest. Then, one day, you'll hear Jesus say the best words you can ever hear: "Well done, my good and faithful servant."

Appendix:
NAMES AND ADDRESSES

\\\||//

Some of the people in *Touched by the Savior* may be contacted at the following addresses (in order of their appearance in this book):

John Trent
Encouraging Words
12629 N. Tatum Blvd., Suite 420
Phoenix, AZ 85032
(602) 922-8640
(602) 922-8639 fax

Mickey Mantle
If you would like a sample copy of Mickey Mantle's gospel tract, contact the American Tract Society at (800) 54-TRACT, or write the American Tract Society, P.O. Box 462008, Garland, TX 75046-2008. The web site is www.gospelcom.net/ATS

Dr. James Dobson
Focus on the Family
Colorado Springs, CO 80995
(719) 531-3400

Appendix

Steve Largent
U.S. House of Representatives
426 Cannon House Office Building
Washington, D.C. 20515-3601
(202) 225-2211
(202) 225-9187 fax

Rebecca St. James
P.O. Box 1741
Brentwood, TN 37024
Web site: www.rsjames.com

Jackie Kendall
Power to Grow
P.O. Box 210042
Royal Palm Beach, FL 33421-0042
(561) 795-4792

John Croyle
Big Oak Ranch
250 Jake Mintz Rd.
Gadsden, AL 35905
(256) 892-0773

Chuck Colson
Prison Fellowship Ministries
P.O. Box 17500
Washington, D.C. 20041-0500
(703) 478-0100

Bill Bright
Campus Crusade for Christ
100 Sunport Lane
Orlando, FL 32809-7875
(407) 826-2000

Zig Ziglar
Ziglar Training Systems
3330 Barhart, Suite 204
Carrollton, TX 75240
(800) 527-0306 or (972) 233-9191
(972) 991-1853 fax

David Berkowitz
#78-A-1976
Sullivan Correctional Facility
P.O. Box AG
Fallsburg, NY 12733-0116

Appendix

Steve Green
Steve Green Ministries
P.O. Box 210707
Nashville, TN 37221-0707
Web site: www.stevegreenministries.org

Miles McPherson
Miles Ahead Ministries
9888 Carroll Center Road, Suite 122
San Diego, CA 92126
(619) 271-0700
(619) 566-0804 fax
Web site: www.milesahead.com

Bob Kiersznowski
Prism Development
P.O. Box 422385
Atlanta, GA 30342
(800) 218-4205
E-mail: bobk@prism-development.com

Dr. Don Bartlette
2602 Ocelot St. NE
North Canton, OH 44721
(330) 497-1822
(330) 499-0745 fax

Larry and Sue Wright
Abundant Life, Inc.
12654 N. 28th Dr., Suite L
Phoenix, AZ 85029
(602) 547-3800
(602) 547-9747 fax

Clebe and Deanna McClary
P.O. Box 535
Pawleys Island, SC 29585
(843) 237-2582

Luis Palau
Luis Palau Evangelistic Association
P.O. Box 1173
Portland, OR 97207
(503) 614-1500